Ex...

THE WAR.

ANOTHER DIVISION TO AID RUNDLE.

ATTACK NEAR BLOEMFONTEIN.

MISHAP TO THE WORCESTERS.

ROBERTS'S NEXT MOVE.

CLEARING THE FREE STATE.

THE SHELVING OF WARREN.

We are doubtless on the eve of stirring events in South Africa, and, although they still tarry by the way, the storm may burst at any moment with decisive results. The whole aspect of affairs is in our favour, as will best be realised by a survey of the situation. In the centre at Bloemfontein Lord Roberts holds a great army, 60,000 strong, effective at all points, and rapidly becoming perfectly mobile, perfect in all arms, with an abundance of transport and stores. It may be confidently expected, when he resumes the offensive, to strike with overwhelming force. His line of advance will be by his right, to the eastward—that is to say, so that he may lend a hand to Buller, clear the Drakensberg passes, and open up the railway from Harrismith by Ladysmith to Durban and the sea. This will be the crucial operation of the war, for it will help and simplify the final advance by supplying a shorter line of communication.

Lord Roberts despatched the 11th Division, under Pole-Carew, to reinforce Rundle on the 22nd inst. (Sunday), and they made their way to Kareefontein, thirteen miles from Bloemfontein, without much opposition; but the fact that they were opposed at all shows that the eastern flank is closely infested by the enemy, and the fighting was not without some losses. Yesterday (23rd) Pole-Carew's mounted infantry seized the Leeuwkop Hill, three miles in advance, and the Boers retired precipitately, abandoning their rifles and ammunition. Leeuwkop is a short twenty miles from Dewetsdorp, so that another division is now close up in support of Rundle. The force at Dewetsdorp is evidently in the presence of an active enemy, as a patrol ...

... infantry and Mounted Infantry, and our guns drove the enemy away.

We are greatly extending our position. —Reuter's Special.

WAKKERSTROOM, April 22.

Our camp has now been extended to include the top of a hill just two miles south-east of De Wet's Dorp.

Our lines have been extended for a considerable distance to the south of the town.

The Boers are clearly visible, and are in great force.

All to-day there has been rifle firing between the outposts on each side from cover.—Central News.

FROM THE BOER CAMP.

REPORTS OF BRITISH LOSS ABOUT WEPENER.

THABA N'CHU (undated, probably per express rider to Brandfort, April 22), via

Lourenco Marques, April 23.

Fighting continues day and night at Jammersburg Drift.

Robertson's lower mill is reported to have been taken yesterday afternoon.

The Cape Mounted Rifles lost 120 men out of 500, including Major Sprenger, Capt. Goldsworthy, badly wounded; Major Waring, slightly wounded; and Lieut. Bouscy, seriously wounded.

Lieut. Joe Taplin was among the killed, as were also Sergeant-Majors Court and Ledham.

The following prisoners are now on their way to Pretoria: Capt. J. H. Little, Lieut. H. J. Steele, Sergt. Evans, Troopers Morton, Geddie, Fletcher, Cameron, Smith, and West, also Julius Weil's manager, Holbery, and Reuter's correspondent, Mr. Milne.

PATROL COMES TO GRIEF.

BRANDFORT, April 21.
(Via Pretoria, April 22.)

A British patrol, consisting of ten men, ventured near Brandfort to-day.

The Federals caused them to retire, killing one man and capturing two, including a Free-stater, who was leading the party.—Reuter's Special.

FACING METHUEN.

HIS COMMUNICATIONS SAFE.

"EXPRESS" CORRESPONDENT.

...

The Boers, who ...aggered six miles f... ...orce.

The communication... Kimberley are open...

The Northumberla... St. George's Day wit... Methuen.

CAPE COLON...

TREASON PUNISHED.

BUSHMEN EMBARK.

SPIRITED ADDRESS BY N.S.W. GOVERNOR.

GRAND PATRIOTIC DISPLAY

"EXPRESS" CORRESPONDENT.

SYDNEY, April 23.

St. George's Day was celebrated in a manner worthy of the Great Empire of which this colony is a part.

The Imperial Bushmen embarked to-day and were given a magnificent send-off.

The people turned out in extraordinary numbers, exhibiting the most fervent patriotism. The ships in Circular Quay and the various craft in Man-of-War Bay were arrayed in bunting, while pleasure boats filled with enthusiastic sightseers flitted over the magnificent harbour.

As the Bushmen, who were addressed by both the Governor and the Premier, went on board, they were cheered to the echo.

SYDNEY, April 23.

The New South Wales portion of the Imperial Bushmen, consisting of 750 officers and men, with 800 horses, embarked in the Armenian this afternoon. There was the same display of patriotic enthusiasm as on the occasion of the despatch of the former contingents.

Earl Beauchamp, the Governor, travelled from his country seat at Mossvale, and paid a special visit to the Bushmen at Rookwood immediately before their departure.

His Excellency, addressing the men, said that the colony was proud of them because of the sacrifices which they were making in order to uphold the honour of Australia. An affectionate admiration was felt for them throughout the British Empire, from her Majesty the Queen down to the humblest boy in the streets of London. The sympathies of all would go with them in the hardships they would be called upon to undergo.

He thought that the people scarcely realised how great a day that was in the history of Australia. For the first time Australians were leaving their native shores as soldiers in the pay of the Imperial Government. He hoped that on their return they would form the nucleus of a force which would be more permanent in its character than now appeared possible. He believed they would return, having added fresh lustre to New South Wales, to all Australia, and to our common race.

... a safe return ... ...Admiral ...bishop ...gratula... ...South ...had the ...tion as ...behave ...would ...tage of ...giving ...behalf

... of the Government and people he wished them every success. All the country asked was that they should go to the front and add lustre to Australian arms.

Daily Express

MONDAY, SEPTEMBER 4, 1939

PHOTONEWS

ELEVEN O'CLOCK SEPT. 3 1939

"This morning the British Ambassador handed the German Government a final Note stating that unless we heard from them by eleven o'clock that they were prepared at once to withdraw their troops from Poland, a state of war would exist between us," said the Prime Minister. And zero hour arrived with one British soldier typifying all his kind—waiting and ready.

"TAKE COVER!"

London policemen gave the air raid warning in various ways, but there was no mistaking what they meant—

—and the crowds who were waiting outside Parliament for the arrival of Ministers and the fateful decision heard instead the sirens. As they hurried to shelter there was no trace of panic.

In a park they all went down to their public shelter with cheery confidence.

New Chief of Staff enjoys a cigar

General Sir Edmund Ironside, new Chief of Imperial General Staff, walks past the German Embassy (Duke of York's Steps), a few hours after the declaration of war.

German Envoy says goodbye

Herr Kordt, German Charge d'Affaires, shakes hands with his English chauffeur, Mr. A. Barker, outside the German Embassy in Carlton House-terrace while his wife enters the car. Just before this—it was 2.28 p.m.—he had shaken hands with the policeman in the background with a "Good-bye; I thank you."

VOICE OF BRITAIN
THE INSIDE STORY OF THE
DAILY EXPRESS

R. ALLEN
with co-operation from
JOHN FROST

Foreword by LORD MATTHEWS

 Patrick Stephens, Cambridge

Front endpaper *April 1900 and a new newspaper hits the streets of Britain. Putting news on the front page was considered revolutionary, although the layout and type size were unadventurous. In his first editorial Pearson stated: 'Our policy is patriotic; our party is the British Empire'.*

First published in 1983

British Library Cataloguing in Publication Data

Allen, Robert
    Voice of Britain: the inside story of the Daily
    Express.
    1. Daily Express—History
    I. Title   II. Daily Express
    072'.1   PN5129.L7D/

    ISBN 0-85059-569-X

Photoset in 11 on 12 pt Baskerville
by Manuset Limited, Baldock, Herts.
Printed in Great Britain on 115 gsm Fineblade coated
cartridge, and bound, by The Garden City Press,
Letchworth, Herts, for the publishers,
Patrick Stephens Limited, Bar Hill, Cambridge,
CB3 8EL, England.

Contents

Er

Page
Page 6
Page 7
Sec
Page
from fo
effect
of Fle
Matth
Mor
(nine
of £2.9ͅ
on March
from ordina

Foreword

You are either for the *Daily Express* or against. The *Daily Express* is either a great newspaper or a 'bloody awful' one. It has never been a newspaper of half measures. I hope it never will be, for when the *Daily Express* loses its heart, so it will lose its hold on its huge body of loyal readers.

This book, by Robert Allen, traces the history of the *Daily Express* from its faltering beginnings, through the Great War, the 1926 General Strike and the depression of the '30s. Then comes the Second World War and the part the *Daily Express* played, a very controversial one.

Lord Beaverbrook, his great editor Arthur Christiansen . . . these legendary figures of Fleet Street are examined, as are the links between newspaper proprietor and those walking the corridors of power. The days of the wealthy individual proprietor began to come to an end after the war. Now they are gone forever.

But as Chairman of the Company which now owns the *Daily Express*, I feel I have a responsibility to keep up the traditions of the past and to lead a great newspaper into the future. Times have never been more difficult. But my task is a labour of love as well as a challenge. Those who read this book will understand why.

The Lord Matthews of Southgate.

Introduction

The *Express* has occupied a unique position in the history of British journalism. For many years it was the country's top-selling newspaper and, as the instrument of Lord Beaverbrook's political ambitions, it became well known for its strongly held pro-Empire views. Beaverbrook regarded the paper—and, indeed, all his papers—as nothing more than instruments of propaganda by which he could advocate his favourite causes, vilify his enemies and attack political views with which he disagreed. However, if the paper had been no more than a propaganda sheet it would have failed completely long ago. Its proprietor was not only a rich and powerful man with limitless ambitions to dominate the public life of his times—he was also a skilled and imaginative journalist and businessman who breathed new life into a paper which, when he bought it during the First World War, was on its last legs.

Yet, for all his formidable energy, Beaverbrook would not have succeeded alone. He was aided by a host of talented journalists whose abilities, combined with his own, made a rare and unbeatable combination. Chief of these must be numbered Arthur Christiansen, a man often accused of having played Trilby to Beaverbrook's Svengali, but who, in truth, was a supreme newspaperman. Whereas Beaverbrook understood politics and business, Christiansen knew about people. He knew what interested them, what were their hopes, fears, aspirations and frustrations. Throughout his time with the *Express* he kept before him the image of 'the man on the Rhyl promenade', the average man who, if he was wooed successfully, would turn an ordinary newspaper into a mass-circulation journal.

Of all the many Press Barons who have inhabited Fleet Street, Beaverbrook was, without any doubt whatsoever, the most controversial. In closing his mammoth biography of him A.J.P. Taylor said simply, 'Max Aitken Lord Beaverbrook was quite a Somebody'. Lord Reith described him as 'shit'. Arthur Christiansen idolised him. Donald Edgar, a former employee of his, called him 'the unacceptable face of human nature'. This forceful, dynamic and highly successful Canadian adventurer brought to British journalism a spark of life which had previously been missing. His intense curiosity about people and events was reflected in his newspapers in a vivid way which would appeal to the average reader. What is more, the Beaverbrook philosophy was not merely concerned with the presentation of news. He believed strongly that everyone should have the opportunity to make it to the top by his own efforts. This was a revolutionary idea in the class-bound Britain of the inter-war years. It was far from conventional Toryism but just as far from Socialism—Beaverbrook was the supreme advocate of an all out catch-as-catch-can capitalism which, he intended, would open the flood gates of opportunity to the mass of the people.

His other obsession was the British Empire. His love affair with the ideal of Britain and its Empire sitting safely in splendid isolation was one which he pursued relentlessly throughout his life. At the root of it was a deeply held admiration for the British people, whom he described as 'the greatest race on Earth'. In a world which was rapidly becoming more complex and internationalist, the ideal of a self-sufficient Empire was doomed to remain unrealised, but it says much about Beaverbrook that he never abandoned this idea even when it must have been quite clear that its time was long past.

The proprietor's personal whims were an integral part of the *Express*. Impartiality was unknown. This did not apply merely to causes; people who offended the Beaver—and there were many—promptly became 'unpersons' who could never even be mentioned in his columns. Yet, he was also capable of the most loyal friendships. Throughout their long association he never permitted Churchill to be criticised in any of his papers. The two men had political views which could not have been much further apart but, as far as Beaverbrook was concerned, Churchill was inviolate.

As an employer he could be just as idiosyncratic. He liked to 'make' people, to take some bright young man and give him the scope to develop his potential to the full. He believed in high wages as a sure means of getting the best from his staff and he paid out enormous sums to ensure that his people and his papers were the best. Yet, perversely, he also took a strange delight in breaking what he had created. The most dramatic example of this must have been that of Arthur Christiansen who, after more than 30 years of loyal service, was cast off rather in the manner of a worn out shoe.

Although in any history of the *Express* Lord Beaverbrook will inevitably hog much of the limelight, his involvement with the paper is not the whole story by any means. After his death the paper plunged into troubled times. His heirs were not made in the Beaverbrook mould. He had been a supreme dictator, rather in the manner of a Cromwell, and the flair for that sort of leadership is not something which is automatically passed down from father to son. Sir Max Aitken, son of Lord Beaverbrook, had been a flying ace in the Second World War and had made a successful career in the *Express* organisation. However, his father had always tried to ensure that he would never be *too* successful.

Eventually the family lost control of the organisation to the Trafalgar House group, run by Lord Matthews. The story of the *Express*, far from ending, was just about to start a new chapter. Under Matthews there was an initial and prolonged period of uncertainty about the paper's modern role. The old Beaverbrook formula no longer worked, it had been made obsolete by changing economic and social conditions. New editors were tried in an attempt to give the paper a renewed identity, but that essential rapport with the readers was not as strong as it had been in the past. The paper had become a tabloid, it went down-market, it came back up-market—and all the time it was searching for a way to re-discover the mass readership it had enjoyed in earlier times. Where was the man on the Rhyl promenade? What the hell was he thinking in the last gasp of the 20th century?

Over this period in the paper's history there presided two men. One was Matthews himself, a tough and resilient self-made tycoon whose financial interests covered a great variety of fields from shipping and hotels to newspapers. He is a fundamentally different character from Beaverbrook. For Matthews sees Express Newspapers not as a means of making political propaganda but rather as a potentially profitable enterprise. In these days, when newspapers make a profit only with extreme difficulty, if at all, it takes a man of some considerable determination to buy one purely as a business investment. Especially when the man concerned is not primarily a newspaperman.

The other figure who was bound up with *Express* story for many years is Jocelyn Stevens. If Beaverbrook had character and a powerful personality, then Stevens, who joined the organisation in the days when it was still owned by the Aitkens, was out of the same stable. Being a wealthy man in his own right, he had bought himself *Queen* magazine as a 25th birthday present. Very soon he had established a dual reputation. On the one hand he was the able businessman and journalist, a man with a very bright future in the world of publishing. On the other hand he quickly became surrounded by his own legend. He was known for his violent outbursts of temper and was widely rumoured to be fond of throwing furniture when the mood took him. In journalism this sort of myth-making is all part of the game. Many of the stories are not even remotely true, but journalists become victims of their own profession and the need to dramatise life until it fits the banner headlines becomes paramount.

However, Stevens at the *Express* was no mere eccentric. He was a competent organiser and he had the added advantage that he managed to establish an all too rare understanding with Fleet Street's giant unions. Yet he was not able to do all that was necessary to bring Express Newspapers back to the prominence which they needed. As this book was being researched, Jocelyn Stevens was sacked from his position as deputy chairman and managing director. It was something of a revolution in Fleet Street coming, as it did, shortly after the appointment of yet another new editor for the *Express*. Now the paper is at the beginning of yet another phase in its development. As this book goes to press it is still not clear whether the plans for revitalising the paper will succeed. The new editor is full of hope and feels that he can succeed where others have failed. But then, what new editor does not feel that way?

It is an exciting and dangerous period in British journalism. The competition is tough and steadily becoming tougher. Newspapers are faced with rising costs, an inefficient system of manning which they are apparently powerless to reform, and intense competition from TV and radio. The strain has certainly begun to tell. For instead of competing to try to provide their customers with better and more entertaining papers, a number of the major dailies have become locked in the insanity of the bingo war. In the '30s a very similar thing happened and, because of a great outbreak of free gift campaigns among the leading newspapers, a large section of the industry came near to financial ruin. Fifty years later the same thing may be happening again.

Yet, in spite of the dangers, there are also signs of hope. The *Express* is ready to make a new attempt to regain the high ground. It used to be the paper of the young and hopeful, of those who believed that by hard work and diligence they could attain great heights. It was a paper renowned for its extreme, even excessive, optimism. Yet it slowly declined to be a paper for the middle-aged and defeated. 'Things are not what they were' was the gist of much of the writing which filled its columns. An air of faded grandeur hung over the paper like a cloud. That cloud is now due to be dispersed. The *Express* is once more intending to be a bright, interesting, lively and hopeful paper which will reflect the aspirations of its readers, instead of harping upon their fears.

No paper has had a more eventful history than the *Daily Express*. It was born with this century and has aged with it, sharing its triumphs and disasters for more than 80 years. Nobody could summarise the whole of that story in a few thousand words. Just one edition contains as many words as a novel. During the course of its history it has reported not just on the great political, social and economic matters of the day, but also on a bewildering variety of stories covering every subject it is possible for the human mind to conceive. To summarise all that would not be possible in any book, it would take a library.

However, the more modest aim of the present volume is to give both readers of the *Express* and those interested in the history of journalism, a précis of the paper's past. For older readers, many of whom have contributed to this book by writing to the publishers with their reminiscences, there will be a strong element of nostalgia in looking back at the early days of a journal they have enjoyed for so long. For the younger generation it is hoped that it will be interesting and informative to see the way in which the newspaper they have started to read only recently has evolved.

Acknowledgements

The author should like to acknowledge the help of numerous people who have made this book possible. Firstly, my thanks to Lord Matthews for writing the Foreword. Then I must mention the very considerable help given to me by the management of Express Newspapers Ltd in the persons of Mike Murphy and Jocelyn Stevens. They not only put research facilities at my disposal but also most generously allowed me to reproduce copyright material from past issues of the *Daily Express*. A number of journalists and cartoonists agreed to give up valuable time to be interviewed, these were: Victor Blackman, Michael Cummings, George Gale, Jak, Sir Osbert Lancaster, Jean Rook, Peter Tory, Roy Ullyett and Christopher Ward. Carl Giles not only agreed to a long interview but was kind enough to produce the cover illustration.

My research at the *Express* was organised and aided continuously by Struan Coupar and his super-efficient secretary, Jan Kreiger. I should also like to thank Morris Benett who, as well as being interviewed, was inflicted with the task of reading the manuscript on behalf of the *Express* organisation.

Special thanks must go to my friend and colleague, John Frost, whose enormous newspaper collection was put at my disposal. For others engaged in similar research John's address is: 8 Monks Avenue, New Barnet, Herts (Tel 01-440 3159).

Any book such as this must owe a considerable dept of gratitude to those who have gone before. I should particularly like to mention Arthur Christiansen's *Headlines All My Life* (Heinemann, 1961), which has been quoted by permission of David Highams. I have also drawn much information on the recent history of the *Express* from *The Fall of the House of Beaverbrook* by Lewis Chester and Jonathan Fenby; this work is quoted by permission of Andre Deutsch. Material from *Express '56* by Donald Edgar is quoted by permission of John Clare Books. Other works referrred to are: *The Life of Sir Arthur Pearson Bt GBE* by Sidney Dark (Hodder and Stoughton); *Beaverbrook—A study in power and frustration* by Tom Driberg (Weidenfeld & Nicolson, 1956); *Don't Trust to Luck* by Lord Beaverbrook; *Publish and be Damned* by Hugh Cudlipp (Dakers, 1956); *The House of Northcliffe* by Paul Ferris (Weidenfeld & Nicholson, 1971); *Ruling Passions* by Tom Driberg (Jonathan Cape, 1977); *Dangerous Estate* by Francis Williams (Longman, Green); *The British Press and Germany 1936-1939* by Franklin Reid Gannon (OUP, 1971). Finally, no book could adequately cover this subject area without reference to A.J.P. Taylor's excellent *Beaverbrook* (Hamish Hamilton, 1972).

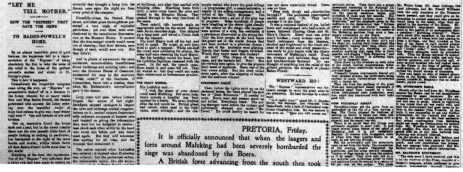

Above *A hint of sensationalism as Mafeking is relieved. Although a banner headline was used there were no illustrations on the front and only a couple of poor quality line drawings inside. Even this timid effort was regarded by some as the worst kind of sensation seeking.*

Below *At last an attempt to break up the acres of close-packed type. This sort of presentation was tried from time to time, but it was years before it was used regularly.*

Chapter 1

The greatest hustler

Ask a cross-section of the population who founded the *Daily Express* and most people would name Lord Beaverbrook. From the days of the First World War, right up to the early '60s, it was he who so suffused the paper with his personality that, whether they liked it or not—and plenty of people came into the latter category—everybody knew that Beaverbrook and the *Express* were one.

However, the paper's founder was not the Canadian magnate but Arthur Pearson, a man who—although prominent enough in his own time—has now been relegated to the footnotes of history. Pearson was born in early 1866 at Wookey, near Wells. His father was a curate and the only claim the family could make to literary fame was that the grandfather had written *Abide With Me*.

Although by no means wealthy, Pearson's father came from the class which was expected to put sons through public school and so, at the age of ten, young Arthur was sent to Eagle House School at Wimbledon and then, after four years, to Winchester where he joined Culver House in January 1880. Arthur's school career was not marked by any especial brilliance, in fact he seems to have been a rather average student, but he possessed an energy, enthusiasm and zest for living which made him popular in spite of his lack of other gifts. However, one disadvantage which was to mark his entire life soon became apparent—his sight was chronically poor.

His nervous, excited movements and habit of peering short-sightedly at things soon earned him the nickname 'Pigeon'. In an environment where a boy's popularity and worth were almost entirely gauged by his prowess at games, Arthur should have had problems. However, he actually enjoyed games, though he could seldom see any of the action, and he put in such enthusiasm that he became popular in spite of his lack of success. In fact, his only sporting achievement was a spectacular catch he once made on the cricket field. Unfortunately he afterwards discovered that the ball he had caught had come from an entirely different game being conducted on an adjacent pitch.

His family's financial situation did not get any healthier and Arthur took to writing pieces for *Tit-Bits* in order to earn pocket money. By the time he was 16 his father had to withdraw him from the school because he could no longer meet the fees. Arthur was probably not too unhappy at the parting. In later life he often berated the public school system for its emphasis on dead languages and its arrogant dismissal of modern subjects which would fit its pupils for the outside world.

He returned home to be taught by his father and, in his spare time, he took up the fashionable hobby of riding a bicycle. As luck would have it, his reading of *Tit-Bits* and his cycling were to play a great part in starting him on his future career.

Sir George Newnes had first published *Tit-Bits* in 1881. As the name implied it was composed of a great selection of morsels, some funny, some informative, some literary and so on. In an age when copyright legislation held no terrors for a publisher, Newnes was able to lift pieces out of weightier journals and edit them down for use in his own. The formula was highly popular. The Victorians were great believers in self-improvement and there was a prosperous middle class eager to acquire education and achieve success.

One feature of many newspapers and magazines from the earliest years has been the competition. Even today it is still one of the most effective ways to secure the interest of the readers. Newnes decided to run a competition which was quite different from the rest. It would consist of a really difficult task of research involving numerous general knowledge questions. The plan was initially a great success but then Newnes had the idea of introducing a novel prize. The announcement of the tenth competition, made on May 31 1884, was as follows: 'It is stated throughout the country that there are at the present moment over one hundred thousand clerks out of employment, the large majority of them, though constantly endeavouring to obtain work, are unable to make a living. We there-fore propose to put a SITUATION up to PUBLIC COMPETITION; and we offer as the FIRST PRIZE in the tenth inquiry column competition A SITUATION in the offices of *Tit-Bits* at a salary of £100 per annum'.

The test was to be a hard one to pass. Each week for 13 weeks there would be a list of ten questions in every issue of *Tit-Bits*. The winner would be the person who achieved the highest number of correct answers out of the possible 130. The questions were extremely varied and many called for quite a lengthy answer— 'What is a "patent" theatre?', 'What were the eight sorrows of Ireland?', 'Who was "Stella" of literary fame?' and so on.

Arthur was determined to win the prize. Not only did he badly need a job but this was exactly the sort of task he was good at. He had a great liking for 'odd' bits of information and collected facts and interesting anecdotes compulsively. What is more, the answers did not have to be given straight off the top of one's head, they could be researched beforehand. Arthur set to work in his father's library but, though it was particularly well stocked, it was not up to providing the vast variety of reference material which was needed. However, now his love of cycling came to the rescue. In Bedford, some 30 miles from where he lived, the Free Library had a reference section which was capable of providing the necessary information. Three times a week Arthur would make the trip there and come back armed with what he hoped were the right answers.

As the competition progressed the magazine printed the correct answers to the previous week's questions. Frequently Arthur saw his own work reproduced word for word and was thus encouraged to carry on and finish the mammoth test. By

September the competition was finished and it was announced that Arthur was the winner with 86 correct answers.

At the age of 18 he came to London, took lodgings in Wimbledon and started a career in journalism which was to bring him fame and wealth whilst he was still a young man. For, by the spring of 1885, he was to be found working as George Newnes' right-hand man with the title of 'manager'. It had taken a fair bit of persuasion on Arthur's part to get Newnes to let him fill the manager's job when it became vacant but he was pushy, good at his job and worked extraordinarily hard.

Working in the heart of the world of publishing, Pearson soon began to meet many personalities who were familiar on the literary scene of the time. An unknown among these was the young Alfred Harmsworth—later to become Lord Northcliffe, owner of the *Daily Mail, Daily Mirror* and *The Times*. However, when he first met Arthur he was an aspiring author trying to sell an article for publication in *Tit-Bits*. His effort, written none too legibly on lined exercise book paper, was entitled 'Some Curious Butterflies'. Arthur also records that Harmsworth was the author of a handbook entitled *A Thousand Ways to Earn a Living* which was accepted by Newnes and was a very good seller. This early acquaintanceship was not to blossom into friendship. For though Pearson and Harmsworth had much in common they were both aiming for the heights of their profession and, in later years, they were to become deadly rivals.

Arthur married in December 1887, when he was nearly 22, and lived over a tailor's shop in Wimbledon. By the time he was 24 he had two daughters and his finances were rather strained. However, he had never given up the habit of writing and he sent a continuous stream of articles to a huge array of newspapers and journals. His records show that in the first half of 1889 he earned £100 in this way—a very useful sum of money. His writing retained the practical tone which suited him best and he produced articles entitled 'Dust', 'Duelling', 'Perfumes' and 'Some American Song Birds'. While this is not the stuff of which modern journalism is made it was right for the time and gave information, instruction and amusement, the formula which appealed strongly to his readership.

Newnes had for some time been thinking of producing a British equivalent to the illustrated American magazines such as *Harper's* and *Scribner's* and in 1889 he discussed the idea with W.T. Stead, a noted journalist and editor of the *Pall Mall Gazette*. By coincidence, Stead had already been contemplating some such venture and had plans for a 6d monthly magazine. Between them they produced the idea of a *Review of Reviews*. This was to contain a summary of the events of the month which would be followed by a digest of information contained in some of the more weighty publications. Newnes proposed that Stead should be the editor and Pearson should be business manager. Pearson was also given the job of going to America to launch the magazine there. He stayed a few weeks and then, whilst returning, became seriously ill with congestion of the lungs.

It had not escaped Arthur's attention that, whilst he had been slaving away building up Newnes' organisation, his salary had not increased. He was now earning £350 per annum and it was just not enough. He approached Newnes to

An early use of photographs to illustrate the dramatic story of the Siege of Sidney Street. However, compared with other papers of the era, such as the Daily Mirror, *this treatment of the story lacked impact.*

ask for a rise but was met with a blank refusal. It was time to put into operation his plan to start up his own business.

Together with Peter Keary and Ernest Kessell, colleagues at *Tit-Bits*, he left to form Pearson's Limited. The capital was put up by Stephen Mills, someone Arthur had met whilst playing tennis. Mills put £3,000 into the venture and Arthur took offices in Temple Chambers. From here he launched *Pearson's Weekly*, using the motto 'To Interest, to Elevate, to Amuse'. He stated his aims more fully to his readers: 'There is always room at the top, and *Pearson's Weekly* will, it is hoped, prove to be conducted with such ability as to ensure a position at the very head of the numerous periodicals which aim to supply a want not met by weekly newspapers. It has been planned with a view of giving the best pennyworth of sound literature, presented in attractive form, that can possibly be produced . . . *Pearson's Weekly* will be of equal interest to men, women and elder children of every class, creed and profession. It will appeal to master and servant, rich and poor, to parent and child'.

No one could ever have accused Arthur of lack of ambition. Much of the magazine was given up to competitions, each more bizarre than the last. One was designed to find the person with the longest name. The winner? Miss Marie George Ethel Victoria Eve Eugenie Beatrice Cleopatra Cordelia Warren. But Arthur saw his journal as an organ of serious comment and even coined the slogan, 'If you see it in *Pearson's Weekly* it is so'. However, the public did not share his confidence and eventually the venture began to founder. The partnership with

Mills was dissolved and Arthur agreed to pay him 5 per cent on his £3,000 until the loan was completely repaid.

Financial doom seemed unavoidable until Sir William Ingram, the proprietor of the *Illustrated London News*, was persuaded through an intermediary to meet Arthur. At first Ingram was very unwilling to meet with a young man whom he knew was in deep financial trouble and who would almost certainly try to ask him for a loan. However, the meeting eventually took place and, much to Arthur's delight, it turned out that Sir William was a Wykehamist. Old school ties were flourished and *Pearson's Weekly* was, after some slight haggling over terms, bailed out.

It was just after his reprieve that Arthur hit on the idea of the 'missing word' competition. The first contest appeared in December 1891 and consisted quite simply of a verse of poetry from which one word had been omitted. All the contestant had to do was to make a guess at the missing word and send in his entry, together with a one shilling entrance fee. The entry fees were then divided between all those who named the correct word. Although this competition started slowly it gradually gained momentum and, by the time competition No 53 took place, there were 473,574 entries. The idea for these contests was soon taken up by the rest of the Press until, unexpectedly, the authorities brought a prosecution against another journal on the grounds that it was running a lottery. The boom ended as suddenly as it began—missing word contests were outlawed almost overnight.

Arthur Pearson went to court to hear the verdict which would have a great effect on his own business. With him was a young American called R.D. Blumenfeld, at that time the London representative of the *New York Herald* but destined to become one of the greatest editors of the *Daily Express.*

Arthur's venture became a success in spite of the occasional setback and, as well as his journalistic interests, he invested with success in a wide range of other businesses. He also started several new magazines such as *Royal Magazine, Novel Magazine* and *Smallholder.*

By 1897, when Arthur was 31, he found himself rich. Although his eyesight continued to give him problems, he was now so successful that he could afford to live in semi-retirement. For some time he devoted his time to relaxation, good works and the many pleasurable activities open to a young man with both money and time on his hands.

However, before long this idleness began to pall. His rival, Alfred Harmsworth, had entered the newspaper business and now owned the *Daily Mail* and the *Evening News.* Pearson could not tolerate being out-manoeuvred by a competitor and so he decided to enter the unknown territory of daily journalism.

Even before the birth of the *Daily Mail* he had toyed with the idea of running a newspaper. His idea had been to launch one which would concentrate on American news and would contain extracts from the major American papers. He took offices in London and sent a representative to America to investigate the possibilities but, when the costs were analysed, it became obvious that the venture would be a financial failure.

He abandoned his novel idea in favour of a conventional daily and, on April 24 1900, the *Daily Express* was born. The paper consisted of eight pages, cost a ha'penny and, unusually for the time, it had news on the outside page. The paper was what is known as a 'broadsheet', that is, it was roughly the same size as today's *Daily Telegraph* or *Guardian*. Each of the large pages was divided into seven columns of minute type so that a large amount of information could be included without an excessive use of paper. Reading such a journal must have been hard on the eyes of even a healthy man but Pearson, whose sight was becoming steadily worse year by year, somehow managed to read acres of this tiny print himself.

The policy of the paper was announced in the first issue and, like all journals it was, of course, going to be entirely impartial: 'It will be the organ of no political party nor the instrument of any social clique . . . Its editorial policy will be that of an honest cabinet minister . . . Our policy is patriotic; our policy is the British Empire'.

It was the last phrase which was to be truly prophetic for, long after the death of Pearson when the *Express* had passed into Beaverbrook's hands, the emphasis on the Empire remained the paper's political trade-mark. Even today, when the Empire is just a memory, the patriotic tone of the *Express* is scarcely muted.

There could have been few better times at which to launch a newspaper for the Boer War was in full swing and, as always during wartime, there was a large demand for the latest news from the front. In fact, in the very first issue there was a stirring account of a British attack on Bloemfontein. But an even bigger story was to break a few weeks later when, on May 19, the *Express* was able to announce the news that Mafeking had been relieved. The paper's normally restrained presentation was enlivened slightly by a banner headline asking: 'When shall their glory fade?—History's most heroic defence ends in triumph—The Boer's last grip loosened—Mafeking and Baden-Powell's gallant band set free'.

The paper had shown initiative by despatching a reporter to Baden-Powell's family home where he was met by the great man's sister who received the news with much incredulity and a display of controlled emotion which went down well with the Victorian public. The *Express* had also scoured London in order to obtain reactions from every sector of the public. From the House of Commons, Clubland, Suburbia, Fleet Street and Islington came descriptions of unconfined joy, with much throwing of hats into the air and shouting of 'Bravo, Baden-Powell!'

However, even this occasion of national rejoicing did little to persuade Pearson to illustrate his paper. By modern standards it looked bleak indeed. On page 6 there were a few miserable line drawings (it was just a little too early for photographs) and that was all. Nothing else was allowed to break the columns of print. Apart from the banner headline on page 1 all the other headings were puny—only about a quarter of an inch high. Yet, strangely, the *Express* already had a name for 'yellow journalism'. It seems incredible that this large, wordy and almost unillustrated journal was regarded with the sort of scorn which nowadays readers of *The Times* might reserve for the *Sun*. For Pearson's taste for sentiment, gush

Gradually there were signs that Pearson and his staff were grasping the basics of layout and presentation. The photograph at the top of the page catches the eye and leads it to the surrounding dramatic headlines.

and flag waving was popular but hardly respectable by the standards of late Victorian England. Yet if one looks beyond the main stories at the bulk of the paper it appears to be sober and innocuous in the extreme. There were reports on the Stock Market and on sporting occasions, some theatre announcements and a weather forecast. Not the sort of thing to set the world alight. Yet this was another tradition which was to remain unbroken. For in the years since 1900 the *Express* has always occupied the middle ground between the solid comment of the 'heavies' and the shock tactics of the sensational Press. In taking such a course it has had to contend with the view that somehow, in some vague and scarcely definable way, it has never quite achieved respectability. It has catered for a class of people who, although literate and politically aware enough to require a serious newspaper, also want something lighter and more readily digestible than the political and economic comment which dominates the pages of the quality Press.

Pearson knew this class well. He designed his paper specifically to reach them. The hallmark of the 'heavies' at that time was a penchant for obscure quotations, preferably in a foreign language. The quotes were usually not particularly appropriate and contained only such information as could quite well be expressed in English but to understand them was a mark of belonging to that magic circle of people with a classical education. Arthur immediately outlawed that sort of writing from his newspaper. 'Never forget the cabman's wife', he instructed his

Left *The death of Scott at the South Pole was enough to make even the most staid newspaper break forth in pictures and a rash of large type.*

Right *War is always good for newspaper sales and encourages a more exciting approach. At last the Express was experimenting with a variety of type styles and sizes. Even so, all the text was still set in regular columns like soldiers on parade.*

journalists. Unless the paper could be read and enjoyed by a literate, but not deeply educated, person it was no good.

To be able to broadcast one's opinions to the public at large is a temptation so great that there must be few people at any time since printing was invented who could resist it. Arthur Pearson was not going to be an exception. Whatever intentions he had when he began the *Express*, it was very soon to become the propaganda sheet of a political faction. He had read two books by Ernest Williams which made a profound impact on him, they were, *Made in Germany* and *The Foreigner in the Farmyard*. The gist of Mr Williams' argument was that the days of free-trade, as advocated by Cobden, were over. Germany's rise as an industrial power meant that Great Britain should erect a tariff barrier against foreign competition. Here was just the thing the *Express* needed; it had already declared itself a patriotic paper with the interests of the Empire at heart and now there were economic arguments which could convert that view from a piece of sentimentalism into a hard and well-defined political philosophy.

Williams was hired to write protectionist articles in the paper. His views are encapsulated in an article he wrote on the taxation of West Indian sugar: ' . . . we look forward longingly to a great British Empire Zollverein some day which would be able to hold its own in any tariff war against the whole world, and which the world could not afford to boycott or defy'. And the final article in the series contained this passage: 'With protected markets here and in the colonies, we could afford to disregard the German menace; and even the attacks of the mammoth American trusts. Under the stimulus of protection, industry would expand and be strengthened, and we should be in a position to hand down to our children a well secured and glorious imperial heritage. Is it not worth while to protect ourselves?'

These stirring words were useless without some political force to put them into action. It was Joseph Chamberlain who was to provide that force. He launched

DEE and ESS
COCOA ESSENCE
British *Made*
No increase in price
4½d. per ¼lb. tin

Daily Express

NO. 4,528.   LONDON, MONDAY, OCTOBER 12, 1914.   ONE HALFPENNY.

Saved from the ruins of Termonde
BELGIAN LACE SUCCESS.

THE REGENT STREET HOUSE
OF PETER ROBINSON, LTD

"I am the Instrument of the Most High"—The Kaiser.

HOW ANTWERP FELL.

HEROIC LAST STAND OF THE BELGIAN TROOPS.

FORTS BLOWN UP

BRILLIANT WORK OF BRITISH MARINES.

2,000 OF OUR MEN TAKE REFUGE IN HOLLAND.

DESIGNS ON OSTEND

[70th Day of the War.]

The fall of Antwerp, announced in a late edition of the "Daily Express" on Saturday morning, is the crown of Belgium's sacrifice on the altar of honour and independence.

After an heroic resistance, in which a British naval brigade bore honourable part, the city was evacuated by the allied forces. Of the terrors and miseries inflicted on the innocent and suffering Belgians, whose only crime it is to have resisted the word of German statesmanship, the whole civilised world will read with horror and indignation.

An insolent proclamation has been issued by the German general who has occupied the city. This contains the customary threat to lay Antwerp in ruins if any hostile acts are committed by a maddened and distracted people.

THE FOUR-WEEKS' BATTLE.

GERMAN REPULSE NEAR GHENT.

RETIREMENT TOWARDS BRUSSELS.

DEADLY FRENCH FIRE.

By PERCIVAL PHILLIPS.
"Express" Special Correspondent.
(Copyright.)

REPEATED ATTACKS.

MARINES BACK FROM ANTWERP.

TERRIBLE EXPERIENCE UNDER GERMAN FIRE.

BELGIANS BLOW UP THEIR FORTIFICATIONS BEFORE EVACUATING ANTWERP.

GRAPHIC DESCRIPTION OF THE FINAL SCENES IN THE RUINED CITY.

GERMAN SHIPS IN THE SCHELDT DESTROYED.

By EDWIN CLEARY,
"Express" Special Correspondent in Antwerp.
(Copyright.)

From Hansweert (on the frontier), by telephone to the Hague, Saturday, Oct. 10.

IN THE TRENCHES: Men of the Naval Brigade awaiting the German onslaught

NAVAL BRIGADE CUT OFF.

LARGE FORCE ESCAPES INTO DUTCH TERRITORY.

RESCUE OF THE GUNS.

[OFFICIAL]
(From the Press Bureau.)
Oct. 11, 12.30 a.m.

RUTHLESS ATTACK.

ARRIVAL AT OSTEND.

THREAT TO DESTROY.

GERMANS' PROCLAMATION IN ANTWERP.

OUR SAILORS IN THE TRENCHES.

BRITISH MARINES' AID FOR ANTWERP GARRISON.

UNDER HEAVY FIRE

COMRADES IN ARMS.

ADDITIONAL FORCE.

MR. CHURCHILL'S MESSAGE.

MARCHING ON OSTEND.

GERMAN EFFORT TO CAPTURE THE KING.

THE HAGUE, Oct. 10.

QUEEN OF THE BELGIANS.

KING ALBERT SAFE.

MR. EDWIN CLEARY.

"ABOUT THE BRAVEST MAN I EVER MET."

THE KAISER'S OBSESSION.

"I AM THE INSTRUMENT OF THE MOST HIGH."

"Express" Correspondent.
PARIS, Oct. 10.

"ENORMOUS SUPPLIES" TAKEN.

AMSTERDAM, Sunday, Oct. 11.

Daily Express

FOR AUCTION ANNOUNCEMENTS
See Page TEN.

NO. 4,706.   LONDON, SATURDAY, MAY 8, 1915.   ONE HALFPENNY.

BRAND'S MEAT LOZENGES. WORLD-RENOWNED

The World's Greatest and Foulest Crime.

NO WARNING GIVEN.

LUSITANIA TORPEDOED & SUNK IN EIGHT MINUTES.

WAS THERE A CONVOY?

QUESTIONS RAISED BY THE GREAT DISASTER.

GREAT LINER GOES DOWN IN EIGHT MINUTES.

GRAVE MESSAGES.

BETWEEN 500 AND 600 SURVIVORS LANDED AT QUEENSTOWN.

MANY HOSPITAL CASES.

German piracy reached its climax yesterday when the great Cunard liner Lusitania, with 1,978 souls on board, was sunk without warning by a submarine twenty-three miles west of Queenstown.

Up to a late hour last night only the scantiest details of the outrage had been received in London. Between 500 and 600 survivors, many of whom were injured and were taken to hospital, were landed last night at Queenstown. Some others have been landed at Kinsale. As the liner sank eight minutes after she was torpedoed there may have been considerable loss of life. Many prominent persons had booked passages in the Lusitania, including Mr. Charles Frohman, Mr. Alfred Vanderbilt, Mr. D. A. Thomas, Sir Hugh Lane, Lady Mackworth, and Lady Allan, wife of Sir Hugh Allan, of Montreal.

While the incident may impress the imagination by reason of the size of the liner, it will in no degree impair the courage of the nation, and will not have the slightest effect on the course of the war. It is simply an act of piracy and nothing more.

SPEED AND ROUTES.

STOPPING TO PICK UP A PILOT.

"COME AT ONCE."

LINER'S LAST MESSAGE FOR HELP.

"Come at once. Big liat."

FOR MURDER!

EXCITEMENT IN NEW YORK.

COLLAPSE OF THE STOCK MARKET.

FOR RESCUE.

ALTERED VIEWS.

OFFICIAL ATTITUDE.

THE PASSENGERS.

FAMOUS PEOPLE WHO WERE ON BOARD.

PREVIOUS DISASTERS.

THE BRITISH FLAG.

THE LUSITANIA.

The sinking of the Lusitania *caused a national outcry and did much to fuel anti-German sentiment.*

the Tariff Reform League in 1903 and Pearson was elected chairman, a post he held for almost two years. Alfred Harmsworth, now a business rival of the Pearson organisation, was also a supporter of Tariff Reform but, as in all political causes with which he was connected, his support was never constant and therefore Chamberlain came to rely on Pearson for his Press campaign.

He put an enormous effort into this work and even started each day with a visit to the League's office before going on to the *Express* building in Shoe Lane. Chamberlain came to refer to Pearson as 'the greatest hustler I have ever known'. It was intended as a compliment but contained a note of alarm for the methods of a successful journalist and entrepreneur are not the same as those of a politician. Pearson had been driving Chamberlain hard, not only by committing him to speaking engagements in favour of Tariff Reform, but also by trying to launch a scheme whereby gramophone records of the speeches would be circulated, thus increasing the size of the potential audience. Such an idea is tame enough by our standards but, at the turn of the century, the use of a new-fangled device like the gramophone for political ends smacked of gimmickry and Chamberlain would have none of it.

Arthur tried to dragoon his own magazine, *Pearson's Weekly*, into serving the cause but, as he should have predicted, his readers were not really interested in such matters and the idea was soon dropped when it became clear that circulation was being badly affected by this policy. Pearson now started to move away from the *Express*; he acquired two more papers, the *Standard* and the *Evening Standard*, and harnessed them to the same old plough of protectionism. But eventually the whole campaign came to nothing. In 1905 there was a general election and a win by the radicals put an end to the hopes of the protectionists.

Arthur Pearson left his post as chairman of the Tariff Reform League, giving as his reason pressure of work—though there must also have been an element of disillusionment in his decision. There was also another cause. His eyesight, always poor, now failed and he went completely blind. Even so he continued to work tirelessly for the rest of his life. After the First World War he ran St Dunstan's, a home for soldiers blinded in the conflict. Though it is no part of this story, his work for disabled servicemen won him as much fame towards the end of his life as his business successes had done previously. His eventual death was as a result of a stupid accident. On December 9 1921, whilst taking a bath, he fell, knocked his head and subsequently drowned. His death was nationally mourned but the enterprises he had set up continued to function.

The *Express* had not been dependent upon its proprietor for some time. Even while he was still active in business Pearson had left control of the paper in the hands of its editor, Ralph Blumenfeld. 'Blum', or R.D.B. as he was universally known, was a journalist of great ability and had, at a very early age, been the representative in London of Commodore James Gordon Bennett, an American newspaper tycoon of formidable personality and considerable eccentricity. R.D.B. had obviously liked London and took the opportunity to stay there as long as possible. He wrote a diary of his experiences from shortly after arriving, at the turn of the century, up to the First World War. This journal reveals not only a

A busy and interesting layout with visual interest heightened by the addition of maps breaking the columns irregularly.

highly enthusiastic young man with a great natural curiosity about life but also, ironically for a journalist, a great reactionary who was wrong about almost every development of his time. When the underground train came to London, R.D.B. commented that it was hell on Earth and could not last. Golf he dismissed as 'rubbidge', little knowing of his own country's future involvement with the game. Even the pneumatic tyre was viewed with deep suspicion!

Blumenfeld's early career was one of considerable brilliance but it was all conducted in the whizz-kid style which has always characterised the American approach to business. No one who observed his early days would have thought that he was not only to join the *Express* but also to stay long enough to become its elder statesman.

Chapter 2

Enter the demon king

By the time of the First World War the *Express* was a dull, not entirely respectable journal which clung on to the middle ground of daily journalism—it was neither taken seriously as a 'quality' paper, but nor was it a sensation-seeking rag. In that condition it would have been unlikely to survive for long. Fortunately, the paper had attracted the attention of Sir Max Aitken, later to become Lord Beaverbrook, and from that moment it was to undergo revolutionary changes.

Beaverbrook's character and achievements have been the subject of more assessments than those of almost any other man this century—an obvious exception being his great friend, Churchill. He has been dubbed both angel and demon king, politician and shady trickster, great newspaper proprietor and shabby manipulator of the Press. And yet the man had enormous charm, great wealth and a large, but not accurately quantifiable, influence on the public life of this country. Since almost everyone who ever had any dealings with him seems to have dashed off to write their reminiscences, no very deep study of his life outside the *Express* will be attempted and interested readers are referred to A.J.P. Taylor's excellent *Beaverbrook* which supplies answers to most of the questions about his long and complicated life.

The familiar face of Beaverbrook is of a little man with twinkling, mischievous eyes and a large, rubber-lipped satchel mouth. 'Puckish' is an adjective which most writers seem to fall back on; but that is only justifiable if one bears in mind that Puck was not only a creature of mischief and fun, but also a malicious little devil.

However, the conventional description cannot be allowed to pass without some argument. Taylor maintains that, in spite of the fact that people referred to him— behind his back—as 'the little man' he was 5 ft 9 in, a perfectly respectable average height. No doubt it was the large head on a rather small body which gave acquaintances the impression that they were dealing with some overgrown child. It was a dangerous misapprehension for, though he could use charm and generosity in abundance when they suited his ends, he functioned best only in the position of a dictator and as such he was completely ruthless and could pursue his schemes with remarkable singleness of purpose as long as they continued to interest him. Michael Cummings, the *Express*'s long-term political cartoonist has said that the general misunderstanding of Beaverbrook's character always shows in the way people draw him. 'They always draw him as though he were rubbery,' he said. 'They don't notice that he also had a spiky quality which was an important clue to his personality. Look at the Sutherland portrait—that's the *real* Beaverbrook.'

Max Aitken was born in Canada at Maple, Ontario, on May 25 1879. His father was a Presbyterian minister who had emigrated to Canada in 1864. It is intriguing to note how, in many ways, Pearson and Aitken were so alike. Both the sons of clergymen, both prodigiously active and with wide-ranging interests, both adept at business life and capable of amassing large fortunes at an early age, and, finally, both acquired a daily newspaper after a spurious retirement from public life, and used it as a propaganda sheet to fight for the same political cause.

Eventually the Aitkens moved to Newcastle, New Brunswick, and the five children, of whom Max was the youngest, were followed by a further five. Max went unnoticed in such a large family and it seemed during his childhood that he would never do much to distinguish himself in any way. He was rebellious, quarrelsome, moody and very much of a loner. At school he showed no great ability and had the sort of butterfly mind which is not suited to the hard slog of academic study.

However, he did show some interest in the money-making possibilities of newspapers. At first he sold them in order to make pocket money and later, typically, he organised a group of other boys to do the selling while he made a profit from directing their efforts. In 1893 he launched his first paper, *The Leader*, which lasted for only a few issues and then collapsed. Even in the course of the paper's short life it managed to insult several members of the local community, both adults and children. The editor commented, 'Newspaper editing is a very funny business. If you give a man a puff he never sees it; but let one line against him appear and he sees it before the paper is off the press; and while he would not have time to stop on the street and say "thank you", he has time to run all over town to denigrate the editor who seeks to print all the news'. Never mind. The publisher and manager of the paper, W. Max Aitken, was only 14 and it was to be another 22 years before he would make a second and more successful attempt to enter the newspaper industry.

After school Max was faced with the challenge of earning his living in the real world. At first he worked as a student-clerk with a law firm in the town of Chatham. He was not a great success and went on to law school at Saint John, where he also did not do well. Eventually he moved to Calgary and got a job selling insurance. It was not a well paid post and Max found he had to live very economically in a single room. This experience did nothing but sharpen his entrepreneurial talent. He borrowed some money and, in company with another lad, set up a bowling alley. However, it was only after he sold the alley and moved to Edmonton that he started his first real business, transporting cargoes of meat. From then on he began to get the hang of the business and on his 21st birthday he claimed to have had a sort of divine revelation. But it was Mammon, not God, who spoke to him. The result of this experience was a profound conviction that he must work much harder and more systematically at his commercial affairs. If this sounds like a rather tame sort of good resolution then, for most people, it would have been. But not for Max. Thereafter his business enterprises were conducted with an energy and complete dedication which very few young men could have matched. His fortunes changed and he started to acquire considerable wealth, though his popularity by no means increased in proportion. His most famous, or infamous, deal involved the buying of cement companies and their amalgamation into the Canada Cement Company, a giant monopoly. He paid $16½ million for the companies and sold his monopoly for $29 million. It was alleged that as a result of this smart move the price of cement went up from $1 to $1.50 per barrel. His personal gain was rumoured to be in the region of $5 million. As though that were not sufficient to infuriate his business competitors, he was then given a knighthood in King George V's Coronation honours list and set out with a title, a personal fortune and wife (whom he had recently married) to conquer England.

It is a strange fact that Aitken always had a powerful attraction to Great Britain. Throughout his life as a newspaper proprietor he favoured various political figures and causes, but his undying passion was always reserved for the British Empire. It must be said that on his arrival here the compliment was in no way returned. For Sir Max had been preceded by his reputation and London in the early 20th century was not a place likely to welcome a get-rich-quick colonial with a flashy title and reputation for slightly shady deals.

If the world of 'old' money, 'old' titles and 'old' school ties thought it was going to close ranks and keep the interloper out, it was mistaken. In later years the then Lord Beaverbrook wrote some articles on the subject of success which were eventually published in book form under the title *Don't Trust to Luck*. Although the aim was to teach success, much as one might teach football or golf, Beaverbrook ignored the fact that such things cannot be taught and poured into the book those ideals and precepts which he held to be responsible for his own victories. One of his first instructions was: 'The bitterest thing in life is failure, and the pity is that it is almost always the result of some avoidable error or misconception. There need be no such thing as failure'.

Clearly Max Aitken had no intention of failing in his new country. One of the first things he did was to cultivate the friendship of Bonar Law, the Tory MP for Dulwich. The two men had much in common—they were both Canadians from New Brunswick who had emigrated to England, they both had considerable financial interests and they both sought to gain influence in public life. Law was of great use to Aitken because he was already accepted at the highest levels of British society and the fact that he had chosen Max as a friend helped considerably to diminish the bad reputation which had attached itself to the newcomer. However, the friendship was quite genuine on both sides and was not merely a matter of convenience. Law was especially loyal in the early days when many people warned him that Max was not the sort of companion he should choose. It is said that when his sister remonstrated with him on the matter he replied quietly, 'Do let me like him'. Mary Law had to give way in the face of her brother's devotion, and soon others started to follow suit—though there were always many who were unwilling to become converts to Max's cause.

Not long after Max Aitken arrived in England a general election was called. He was, at that stage, not even eligible to vote in a British election but he volunteered to help Law fight his seat (in fact, on this occasion he had given up Dulwich in favour of the less safe seat of North-West Manchester). However, not content to help from the sidelines, Max announced that he would also fight a seat and managed to become accepted as the Tory candidate for Ashton-under-Lyne.

Ashton had been for many years a bastion of Free Trade; rather typically Max decided to fight his campaign in favour of Tariff Reform and Imperial Preference. He won the battle by sheer energy and efficiency. Whereas, until his arrival, British politics had been a game for gentlemen, he turned it into a business enterprise, he managed his own campaign down to the last detail and whipped the local Conservative Party organisation into unprecedented activity. His victory was a narrow one, he had a majority of only 196 votes, but it was sufficient to get him into the House of Commons, an essential step for an ambitious man. In fact Max was not over keen on Parliament, he was too much of an autocrat to be bothered with party politics. Even his much-publicised love of the Empire was rather incomplete. As A.J.P. Taylor points out, for Aitken the Empire meant not much more than Canada—he certainly would not have shared the British affection for, say, India. Why then should he have any desire whatever to enter Parliament? Power. Aitken had a good grasp of two fundamentals of public life, one was money and the other was power. If he wanted to be able to exercise power then political, as well as commercial, influence would be necessary.

He set about making a career for himself as a political fixer and his first objective was to replace A.J. Balfour as Conservative Party leader. He thought that his friend, Bonar Law, would make an excellent successor and put all his enormous energy into the intrigue.

In typical British style the whole issue was to be settled at a meeting in the Carlton Club. Law was not even a front runner in the contest and it was really a fight between Walter Long and Austen Chamberlain. However, if neither man could get unanimous support, then they would both withdraw in favour of some third candidate. But who could that candidate be? *The Times*, under Northcliffe, who was by now one of Aitken's cronies, suggested Law. The idea caught on and eventually Long and Chamberlain withdrew from the contest; in fact, when it came to the vote, Long proposed Law and Chamberlain seconded him. Naturally the vote was unanimously in favour. Aitken's part in all this did not go unnoticed. Jack Sandars, who was Balfour's private secretary, got wind of what was going on and told his boss, though by that time it was too late for Balfour to do anything about it. Sandars wrote:

'. . . Bonar Law's own methods are open to much criticism. In the struggle I am told he has been run by Max Aitken, the little Canadian adventurer who sits for Ashton-under-Lyne, introduced into that seat by him. Aitken practically owns the *Daily Express*, and the *Daily Express* has run Bonar Law for the last two days for all it is worth'.

This last charge was quite untrue. However, R.D. Blumenfeld had become aware of Max and had been persuaded to support his campaign in favour of Law. What is more the *Express* had been loaned £25,000 of Max's money and R.D.B. had been promised that, should he get the sack for supporting Law's campaign he would be 'looked after'. Aitken actually went so far as to buy an ailing paper, the *Globe*, just in case he had to make good his promise and find Blumenfeld a job. As it was this did not become necessary and Aitken was left with a useless paper on his hands. Eventually he was forced to pay someone to take it from him.

At the outbreak of the First World War, Aitken was well established in the business and political life of the country. True, he did not yet hold any high office, but he had influential friends and had shown himself to be adept at political intrigue. However, he was also a man of great energy, never content to remain long at one occupation. He managed to acquire for himself the post of Canadian Record Officer and went to the front as an official witness. Immediately he set about doing battle with the bureaucrats and Generals who were trying to keep the conduct of the war a secret from the public. Aitken could not accept that people should be told nothing but comfortable lies. He even went to the lengths of starting his own wartime newspaper, the *Canadian Daily Record*, which was printed until July 1919 and distributed free to the troops.

Quite soon Aitken showed that he really had great talent as a war reporter. He had been given some pointers by his friend, Rudyard Kipling, before he left for the front, but his talent was largely inborn and had been waiting for just such an opportunity to come to the surface.

Not even a World War could hold his attention for very long. Soon he had another political intrigue underway and this time it was a big one. He intended to replace Asquith, the Liberal leader of the wartime coalition, with Lloyd George. Asquith was everything that Max was guaranteed to dislike. He was clearly a member of the 'old school' and rejected élan and dash in favour of sober and serious consideration of the issues. Lloyd George, on the other hand, was the Welsh Wizard, a man who, like Aitken, had risen from obscurity by his own wits and had about him the same slightly dubious air of a self-made man.

The actual details of the campaign are complicated and have no place in this story, having been well recorded elsewhere. Suffice it to say that eventually, and after much intrigue in which Aitken played a leading part, Lloyd George replaced Asquith as Prime Minister. From the point of view of the *Express* the important aspect of the affair was what happened after it was all over. Aitken had been expecting a plum job as his reward for supporting Lloyd George; President of the Board of Trade would have suited him nicely. But it was not forthcoming. For once Sir Max had been used by someone even smarter than he was himself. For, while Lloyd George was only too happy to have Aitken's most valuable support, he knew that his colleagues would never accept the 'little Canadian adventurer' as an important member of the government. So he did exactly what Aitken would have done if the situations had been reversed, he dropped his erstwhile ally like a hot potato. He was offered some very minor post which he could not accept without serious loss of face and then, when he had turned it down, he was offered a peerage. To have come out of the fight with nothing to show for it would have made him look ridiculous in the eyes of his local Tory Party; he had already intimated that he was destined for high office. So, to cover his embarrassment rather than for any love of the House of Lords, he accepted the title of Lord

Beaverbrook in 1916. He had contemplated refusal, indeed Bonar Law had urged him to refuse. However, Law then promptly changed his advice and told his old friend to accept the offer quickly; it seemed that, by a stroke of supreme irony, his seat at Ashton would be required for the new President of the Board of Trade, a man called Stanley.

Even then the affair was not quite over because the King became irritated by the way Lloyd George was dispensing honours without consulting him first. However, it was too late to change things, the new peer had already been told and the King could hardly reverse the decision, though he acquiesced with no very good grace.

Thus in 1916 we find the new Lord Beaverbrook (the name came from Beaver Brook, a stream where he had bathed as a boy) rich and successful in business but thwarted in his quest for political influence. It was not an entirely comfortable situation. Beaverbrook was a new brand of Tory with a strong belief in a man's right to haul himself up by his own bootstraps. Free enterprise, yes. Hereditary titles and privileged minorities, no. And yet he had been forced into membership of the House of Lords, a position from which it would be difficult to exercise any direct influence.

However, Beaverbrook was not finished in his quest for power. He had always had a great regard for the Press as a means of influencing the way people think and it therefore made sense for him to acquire a newspaper. What is more, news-paper ownership would give him just the sort of power he desired, power without responsibility. In politics one is constrained by the other members of one's party and by the voters, but the proprietor of a national newspaper could, in those days, push his opinions, prejudices and mere foibles as much as he liked. For this was the era of great Press magnates such as Northcliffe, Rothermere and the Berry brothers.

The *Daily Express* was, by 1916, in financial difficulties and had urgent need of money in order to purchase a supply of newsprint. Blumenfeld went to Beaver-brook and told him that he would be able to purchase a controlling interest in the paper for £17,500, a trifling sum. Even so, Beaverbrook was hesitant to take this entirely new course in his life. However, at that time he was suddenly put in quarantine as a carrier of spino-meningitis. By the time his quarantine was ended he had become interested enough to take the advice of his friend, Lord Rothermere. The advice, delivered in Rothermere's usual cautious financier's phrases, was to go ahead. However, his brother, Lord Northcliffe, who was also one of Beaverbrook's cronies, was not so encouraging, he asked: 'How much are you worth?' Beaverbrook confessed to having over $5 million. 'You will lose it all in Fleet Street', was the sour reply. Certainly it took courage to acquire the *Express*. At that stage its circulation was slightly more than 200,000. Also the £17,500 needed to buy the paper would not be the end of the story as far as financial outlay was concerned. There were already outstanding losses of £40,000.

It was many years later that Beaverbrook admitted publicly—to the Royal Commission on the Press—his sole reason for owning newspapers: 'I run the paper for the purpose of making propaganda, and with no other motive'. Propaganda was one of the many things he was good at and therefore it was not surprising that, in 1918, Lloyd George should ask him to become Minister of Information. It was by no means a popular appointment for Beaverbrook still had plenty of political enemies.

Probably the most eye-catching front page to date. Pearson was not slow to grasp the importance of grabbing the attention of women readers.

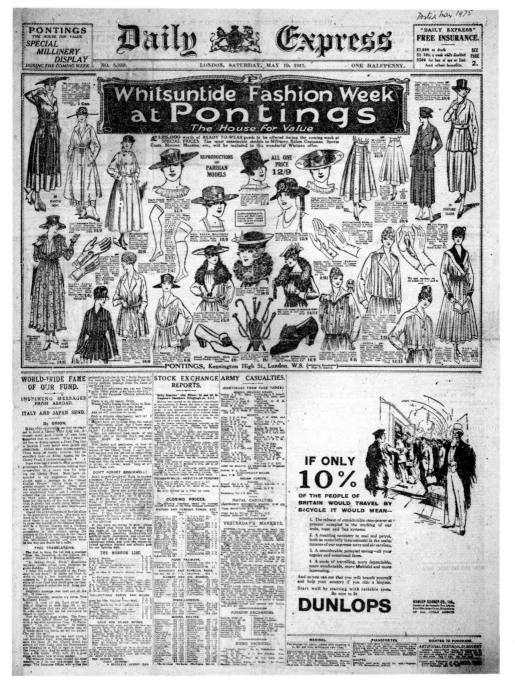

1914.   [THEN AND NOW.]   **1919.**

Above *An early Strube cartoon livens up an inside page. Beaverbrook was quick to see the advantages of the political cartoon as a means of disseminating his ideas.*

Below *By the end of the First World War the Express was at last recognisable as a modern newspaper. By this time it was in Beaverbrook's hands and had been put on a professional footing.*

Chapter 3

New brooms

What sort of paper did Beaverbrook take over? If we look at the issues from the First World War period, and especially from 1916, the year in which ownership changed, the most surprising thing is the way in which the *Express* continued to resemble those early issues produced by Pearson.

The heavy black mast-head set in undertaker's Gothic print and graced by a coat of arms was still dominating the front page. True, there was still news on the front of the paper but, whereas this had been a daring innovation when Pearson had thought of it, 16 years later the novelty had faded. There were still acres of microscopic type set in long, almost unbroken columns. There was still a dearth of large, dramatic headlines or crossheads. Worst of all, where were the photographs? Certainly there were *some*, but they were so few as to be swamped by the great ocean of dull print. At a time when the *Daily Mirror*, for example, was making huge strides in photo-journalism and bringing views of the far-flung places of the Earth into people's homes, the *Express* was looking very drab indeed. The age of the newsreel was about to dawn and the *Express* seemed firmly stuck at the relief of Mafeking.

Readers could have been excused a certain lethargy when perusing their *Express*. In Europe the greatest event in the history of the world to date was taking place and yet their newspaper, although full of reports of the various happenings, had little idea of how to present them as *news*. What the paper desperately needed was some new blood. R.D.B. had been at the helm for many years but there was every reason now to change the style of the paper and make it a brighter, more exciting journal which the public would rush to buy in their millions, instead of the miserable couple of hundred thousand who bought it now.

However, before acquiring new staff, Beaverbrook decided to acquire a new paper. He badly wanted a Sunday newspaper and had his eye on the *Sunday Times*. The Berry brothers had been willing, just before the end of the war, to sell it for £200,000. However, Beaverbrook was still a member of the government and Lloyd George stepped in personally to prevent the transaction. He had taken a great deal of criticism from people who thought that the Press Barons were wielding an undue influence on the government, especially in the case of Beaver-

Overleaf *These attractive photo-features were symptomatic of the way in which the* Express *was developing into a popular family newspaper which aimed to capture the vital middle ground of daily journalism.*

Daily Express

LONDON, MONDAY, SEPTEMBER 21, 1925.

CHILD ATHLETES FIGHT FOR "DAILY EXPRESS" TROPHIES.

MISS A. BREIGNAN, a Hampshire competitor, in the long jump contest.

SCHOOL CHILDREN ATHLETES AT THE CRYSTAL PALACE.—The Schools' Athletic Association, founded by the "Daily Express," held its first meeting at the Crystal Palace on Saturday. A girls' team from London is seen marching past before the events.

ADMIRAL SIR S. FREMANTLE takes the salute as the young athletes march past.

M. DRURY, a Kent competitor, broke the record in the 220 yards race.

AT THE FIRST HURDLE.—Girl competitors in the hurdle race straining every nerve to win.

POLICEMAN'S "MAGIC CIRCLE."—Policemen on point duty at dangerous cross-roads at Bournebrook, Essex, stand inside a white circle for protection.

NOT A SUBMARINE.—This picture was taken just after Mr. Compkin's yacht Tritonella capsized in Teddington Reach during a club race. He clambered out, righted his craft, and sailed on.

MAYORAL PINEAPPLES.—The Mayor of Tunbridge Wells makes a hobby of growing pineapples and bananas. He is seen examining some juicy specimens in the gardens attached to his house.

A HAPPY CASUALTY.—This girl entrant suffered a minor mishap during the contests. Nearly a thousand children competed.

AMATEUR "FIREWOMEN."—Members of a London firm's private fire brigade practising for next Saturday's contests.

MIMIC WARFARE.—Soldiers with pack-horses on the march near Salisbury Plain. The Army manoeuvres begin to-morrow, and soldiers of all ranks will live under active service conditions for four days.

ISLAND OF ROMANCE SOLD FOR £150,000.—Sir Arthur Wheeler, the Leicester financier, has purchased Brownsea Island, in Poole Harbour, for £150,000. The left picture shows the castle which was built on the island in Henry the Eighth's reign. (Right) An island beauty spot.

Daily Express

LONDON, THURSDAY, SEPTEMBER 24, 1925.

ARMY MANŒUVRES : TOY DOG SHOW : WEDDING FILM.

A NEW USE FOR TANKS.—These dragoons, who are taking part in the Army manœuvres, find that a tank can be put to good domestic use.

THE GRIFFON CONDESCENDS TO POSE.—A remarkable photograph of Castleharen Noel, owned by Mrs. C. M. Oster, which won seven special prizes and four "firsts" at the Toy Dog Society Show at the Crystal Palace yesterday.

SCENES FROM THE "SEAT OF WAR."—The spectre-like figures in the left picture are really members of a Lewis gun team photographed in the evening light. (Right) Ten for (more than) two.

FIFTY DAYS' FIRE.—A vivid picture of the great oil fire at Bakırzout. The fire blazed for fifty days, but has now been extinguished. It is estimated that the damage amounts to hundreds of thousands of pounds.

SCHOOLBOY'S LUCK AT WEMBLEY.—Master F. Leach, a ten-year-old schoolboy, who won the Wembley prize of £100, is enthusiastically "chaired" by his schoolfellows. He is one of a family of ten.

BRIDAL FILM.—The marriage of Mr. Robert Tritton to Miss Blanche Hope Sinclair at St. Martin's-in-the-Fields yesterday was "filmed" for the benefit of absent relatives and friends.

MISS EILEEN JACKSON, aged fifteen, of Manningtree, Essex, who climbed the Matterhorn in five hours forty-five minutes. She was accompanied by a guide.

WILL THEY EVER RIVAL "STEVE"?—L.C.C. girl pupils perform a "jockey" dance at a dancing display given by Hackney schoolchildren.

LAST NIGHT'S NEW PLAY.—A scene from "Easy Money," produced at the St. Martin's Theatre last night.

FUR GARTERS are stated to be the latest fashion. Many new styles will be seen at the Fur Ball at Covent Garden on November 2 in aid of the Middlesex Hospital.

brook with his official post as Minister of Information. By the time he was free of government commitments, the *Sunday Times* was no longer for sale.

The solution was to launch his own Sunday paper and so, in December 1918, he founded the *Sunday Express*. Typically he was supremely optimistic about the launching of the new project. He regarded the paper as no more than a Sunday extension of the weekday *Express* and thought that the regular staff could probably knock the thing together in overtime!

The *Sunday Express* was to be an expensive venture and it cost its owner £150,000 in its first year and £300,000 in its second. The circulation had started at a quite reasonable level of 300,000 but was quick to fall off. Beaverbrook then had no alternative but to take personal responsibility for the running of the paper. For the *Sunday Express* he acquired James Douglas (of the *Star*) as editor. He commented that, 'Douglas brought the human sympathy that was needed. I was lacking in that human sympathy'.

Two other characters were now to enter the story of the *Daily Express*. Both were Canadians and both were the sort of self-made men (or, at least, would-be self-made men) whom Beaverbrook admired. One was Beverley Baxter and the other E.J. Robertson. Between them they were to begin the major change in the organisation which would convert the paper from a stuffy and tedious journal into a modern newspaper.

Arthur B. Baxter had an unusual background for a newspaperman having previously worked as a piano salesman. He had tried once before to get a job with Beaverbrook when he was in England near the end of the First World War, helping to train Canadian cadets. At that time he was unsuccessful but, when going home after the war, he happened to find himself on the same ship as 'the Beaver'. The legend is that Baxter entertained his fellow passengers with songs from *HMS Pinafore* (he was something of an enthusiast for amateur opera) and that Beaverbrook had commented drily: 'On hearing you sing, I am convinced you should be a journalist'. Though his pride may have been wounded he had at last got his job on the *Sunday Express*.

At first Baxter was no great adornment to the paper. He worked in the features department and must have been reasonably competent because he then became managing editor. But when he was left in charge one Sunday he managed to create an edition with a grand total of seven headlines all referring to coal! Beaverbrook took him in hand until such time as he could cope alone and, from then on, he would hold regular Friday night and Monday morning conferences to discuss the paper.

In 1924 Baxter went to the *Daily Express* to work under Blumenfeld. This was the beginning of R.D.B.'s replacement as editor. However, in those early days of Fleet Street it was not yet common merely to sack and compensate senior employees who were superfluous. Blumenfeld was 'kicked upstairs' to become editor in chief and, in 1929, Baxter was left completely in charge. Though R.D.B. was no longer at the helm he remained with the organisation in a largely powerless but advisory post for many years to come and was frequently consulted when crises loomed.

Right An early hint of the circulation war which was to follow ten years later. Already it was thought necessary to entice readers with offers of free insurance.

Sweeping Change
in
"Daily Express"
Free Insurance.

We recently announced a re-arrangement and development of *Insurance Benefits* designed to give wider scope and the fullest possible satisfaction.

* * *

We stated that a careful analysis of the advantages derived from the various insurance benefits offered by the news-papers led us to the conclusion that they did not give the complete satisfaction to readers which it was our desire to achieve.

* * *

The "Daily Express" is now able to announce that it has completed Insurance contracts whereby *registered* readers, present and prospective, will secure the widest range of benefits, far exceeding any that have yet been devised and as free from disappointment as it is possible to design.

* * *

No other Free Insurance will compare with the "Daily Express" development. Details will appear later.

Below A lively and interesting page. The art of mixing subjects up and presenting a lively selection on the front of the paper was being practised with growing success.

PICTURED HOMES. PAGE ELEVEN TO-DAY.

 Daily 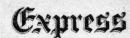 Express

NO. 7,422. .... LONDON, SATURDAY, FEBRUARY 2. 1924. ONE PENNY.

"Not so Dusty"
ZIG-ZAG CIGARETTE PAPERS

SOVIET RUSSIA RECOGNISED.

COMPLETE TREATY WITH MOSCOW.

ALL QUESTIONS TO BE COVERED.

PROPAGANDA, DEBTS, AND CREDIT.

PRELIMINARY NEGOTIATIONS IN LONDON.

THE Russian Soviet Government was officially recognised yesterday by the British Government.

They have been invited to send representatives to London to discuss debts, treaties, and other matters, and to draw up the preliminary bases of a complete treaty which will settle all outstanding questions.

Italy has also decided to recognise the Russian Government forthwith. A treaty between the two countries will be signed on Monday.

BRITISH OFFICIAL NOTE.

THE PREMIER AND THE PRINCE.

SIDE BY SIDE AT A DINNER.

U.S. AND BRITAIN.

MR. WILSON DYING.

WHAT HE SAID WHEN HE HEARD THE NEWS.

"I AM READY."

SUDDEN CHANGE IN THE NIGHT.

CITY CONSERVATIVE TRIUMPH.

SIR T. BOWATER WINS BY A 7,000 MAJORITY.

DEARER PETROL TO-DAY.

ALL GRADES ADVANCED 4½d. A GALLON.

THE HIDDEN BODY.

MOTHER AND SON IN THE DOCK.

WOMAN'S CRY.

"OH, GOD! HAVE MERCY ON ME!"

Baxter would seem a strange sort of newspaper editor to a modern journalist. He was noted for drifting into the office late at night still in his dinner jacket and fresh from the theatre, the opera or an expensive restaurant. Often he would bring some equally elegantly dressed companions with him to show them how a national newspaper was put to bed. The phrase 'dinner-jacketed nonentity' has been used, most unfairly, to describe him. He was *not* a nonentity—if he had been he would not have lasted long as an editor under Beaverbrook. However, Baxter did represent a sort of journalism which was soon to die. Eventually he was to see that not only was the style of national newspapers changing but that he was growing away from Beaverbrook and had started to develop political ambitions of his own. When the parting finally came, he went into Parliament—supported by the Empire Crusade, of which more later.

An anonymous *Express* reporter once summed Baxter up in this lampoon, sung to the tune of 'Burlington Bertie'*.

> 'I'm Beverley Baxter,
> The Empire's wise crackster
> At golf I'm a bit of a don.
> When I meet the Beaver
> I take my hat off,
> But at other times keep the thing on.
> I'm fair, fat and rosy,
> I never am prosy,
> And this you can safely bet on—
> I'm Bax, Bax,
> Just you ask Max
> If I'm not his pride and his joy.
> I'm Beverley, Beverley,
> Rising so cleverly—
> Beaverbrook's white-headed boy.'

The other Beaverbrook discovery was E.J. Robertson. He had first been noticed before the First World War when he was working as a bell-boy in the Queen's Hotel, Toronto. He was working his way through college and had carried the Beaver's bags for him. When asked if he wanted a tip he said he would prefer a job. Like Baxter, he did not get his wish straight away, but during the war he joined the Army and ended up in a British hospital suffering from spino-meningitis. (One of his visitors was Lady Beaverbrook.) He worked for the Beaver in the Canadian War Records Office and then was asked to join the staff of the *Express* in 1919.

With reliable and able assistants to do the donkey work, Beaverbrook now had to look for ways in which to improve his newspapers. One method, which relied entirely on luck, was the *Express'* reputation as a source of good racing tips. In June 1920 the tipster predicted a run of winners and the paper's reputation began

*Quoted from Arthur Christiansen's *Headlines All My Life*.

to spread. In that month 33 winners were tipped and the circulation shot up from 530,000 to 700,000. Unluckily the run was not sustained and when the tips began to fail the new readers all deserted in search of more reliable advice.

However, sheer quality of journalism did produce a slow but steady increase in sales, and advertisers were attracted to the paper in increasing numbers. There is a story that Beaverbrook one day discovered his wife reading the *Daily Mail*. Somewhat piqued he asked her why it was so much more interesting than his own paper. The answer? Drapers' advertisements—in which the *Express* was deficient. Beaverbrook was quick to rectify this shortcoming. One particular customer he persuaded to take advertising space was the American, Gordon Selfridge, owner of the department store. He was a personal friend of Beaverbrook's and the newspaper proprietor took the unprecedented step of handling all the advertising for the store personally. What is more, Selfridge became a member of that exclusive inner circle of people who were never, under any circumstances, to be criticised in the Beaverbrook Press.

As the *Express* and the *Sunday Express* continued through the '20s they developed into an important segment of British journalism. However, if Beaverbrook thought that his papers were going to give him the political influence which he had been unable to gather by other means, he was quite wrong. In the later years of the decade he launched his Empire Crusade which was aimed at putting into effect the Imperial Preference policies he had advocated for so long. He rushed about the country making speeches, candidates were put up at elections, the *Express* even started to include in its pages an enrolment form which (without demanding any fee) made those who completed and returned it, full members of the United Empire Party. Naturally Baldwin and the Tory Government were angered by all this nonsense. The Beaverbrook campaign whipped up a certain amount of popular xenophobia and it waved a lot of flags but, as a serious political movement, it was a flop.

However, there were more serious developments afoot. In 1927 a Manchester edition of the *Daily Express* was started and this was followed, the following year, with a Scottish edition. Then, just as success seemed in sight, Beaverbrook dropped out! He wrote: '. . . I have put eight years of my life into making the *Daily Express* whatever it is. I am the creator of the structure . . . But my share in the work is done. I am like a shipbuilder who has built a ship but will not be her captain. As the vessel glides down the slip-way he says "Farewell" . . . I planned the *Daily Express* . . . but the staff are more competent that I am to manage it. I can conceive and create but I cannot conduct. This has always been my case . . . So on the very last day of the month of November, 1927, I said "Goodbye" to the *Daily Express* office for ever . . .'.

Two further statements, both equally amazing, were to come. He wrote to the *Morning Post* that he was no longer engaged in the management of the *Express* and that, although he was still the major shareholder, he no longer controlled policy. Then, later, another announcement appeared: 'Lord Beaverbrook has made a gift of his controlling share interest in the London Express Newspaper Company to, and for the benefit of, his elder son, William Maxwell Aitken'.

Could it be true? Could the Beaver be about to abandon the empire he had built? Rubbish! This was merely an early example of a ploy which he was to use, with great success, for the rest of his life. He would publicly distance himself from his newspapers but, in private, would be in complete control of every ha'penny of expenditure and of every full stop and comma of print which appeared in his columns. However, when criticism of his journals became an embarrassment (such as when it came from political colleagues with whom he did not wish to fall out in public) he would stick his tongue firmly in his cheek and exclaim with an air of injured innocence that, although he was the principal shareholder, he would not, of course, interfere with the complete freedom of his editors.

Chapter 4

The back streets of Derby

The *Express* under the Canadian triumvirate of Beaverbrook, Baxter and Robertson was impressive enough, though circulation was still quite modest. But it was to be another man, Arthur Christiansen, who would take control of the newspaper and bring it to the height of its power and popularity. Born in Wallasey, but of Danish extraction, Christiansen was to be called by Beaverbrook 'The foreigner who edits my chief newspaper'.

He arrived at the *Express* via a number of provincial papers including the *Wallasey and Wirral Chronicle*, the Liverpool *Evening Express* and *Daily Courier* and the *Liverpool Express*. This was, and still is, the normal route for an aspiring journalist on his way to Fleet Street. The main advantage to be gained from this sort of training is that it leaves the young journalist with a very clear idea of the sort of people he is writing for. It would be only too easy if he had only ever been involved with the important news which comes flooding into a Fleet Street paper, to forget how hopelessly remote politics, high finance and international affairs can seem from the lives of the ordinary reader. Christiansen had two slogans which sprang directly from his experiences: 'Remember the people in the back streets of Derby' and 'What is the man on the Rhyl promenade thinking?' The phrases were interchangeable but they were so hammered home to the journalists of the *Express* that, when Christiansen retired, he was presented with two photographs, one of each of these favourite places.

After some considerable difficulty he managed to get himself taken on for Saturday night work as a sub-editor on the *Sunday Express*. The sub-editor has to take the various pieces of raw copy as they come in, combine them into one well-written and grammatically accurate narrative and compose the headlines. If this sounds easy, it is not. National papers work under such high pressure and at such great speed that a good sub is worth his weight in gold. If he makes a mistake he can turn an important story into gibberish or even lay the paper open to an action for libel. To a large extent a good sub can set the tone of the paper. News may appear to be quite straightforward but, by a skilful combination of items, it is possible to produce a quite unexpected effect. Christiansen recalled in his memoirs how, on his first day, he had taken two stories, one about a man who had been fined £10 for dangerous driving at Bow Street and another about a man who had been given one month's imprisonment on a similar charge at the Mansion House and, by combining them under the headline 'Two Voices of the Law', he had injected interest into something which was apparently dull.

By 1926 'Chris', as he was always called, was a regular attender at the *Sunday Express* and so he became involved in the production of the 'scab' edition at the time of the General Strike. Beaverbrook had reacted to the strike in typical fashion: he would produce papers come hell or high water. And he used his friends and some senior staff to help him get the paper out. Blumenfeld, by now a revered grand old man of the organisation, became head printer. The works manager was set to working the Linotype machine and the chief sub-editor found himself working in the machine room. It was a feature of the strike that the middle and upper classes combined to defeat the efforts of the recalcitrant workers and, in the case of the *Express*, two of Beaverbrook's friends, Lady Louis Mountbatten and the Hon Mrs Richard Norton, lent their assistance to the effort.

Chris had been a member of the National Union of Journalists since he started in the business but, because of the union's very confused attitude towards the strike, he resigned and helped with production of the paper. He was not the only one. Francis Williams, later to be a peer, actually drove a horse and cart loaded with newsprint through the picket line at the end of Shoe Lane and into the *Express* printing works. Later in life Williams was to become an influential left-wing journalist and to embrace views diametrically opposed to those of Beaverbrook. In fact he even went so far as to pillory Chris, during a television debate, for his loyalty to the old man's policies.

However, after the strike was over, Beaverbrook came round in person to meet some of his staff. It was to be the first of many meetings between Chris and 'the little man' and it is worth quoting the description which Chris wrote many years later:

'. . . Lord Beaverbrook has changed little in appearance and in character not at all. He had a little "pot" around the middle then, and he has the same little "pot" now. He wore blue serge suits then and he wears blue serge suits now. He wore brown shoes with his blue suits then, and he wears them now (although nowadays he occasionally goes around at home in brown open-toed sandals). He wore black trilby hats and drab black overcoats then and does so now. He wore buttons on his shirts then, having no patience with cuff-links, and he still wears buttons now. He wore white shirts then and still does. He did not care if his collars were frayed then, nor does he now. The knot of his tie was loose and care-less then and is now. Sartorially little or nothing has changed'.*

History is full of great partnerships between men who, though they had great ability on their own, ony achieved their true potential as part of a partnership. Certainly Beaverbrook was a remarkable man and he ran his own empire (as distinct from the British Empire which, to hear him talk, you might think he also owned) with enormous skill. However, when it came to his favourite newspaper he found that Christiansen was the man who really made it go with a bang. A large factor in this magical combination of personalities was that they complemented each other rather than competing for control. Chris had political views which were broadly in agreement with those of his proprietor; he never

*Arthur Christiansen, *Headlines All My Life*.

During the General Strike of 1926 Beaverbrook and his friends produced these 'scab' issues themselves, with the help of sympathetic staff.

Daily Express

No. 8125.   LONDON, SATURDAY, MAY 8, 1926.   ONE PENNY.

TO-DAY

*PUBLICITY TRIUMPHS
A CHILDISH ARGUMENT
EVERYONE HELPING
UNION LIABILITY*

FOOD BLOCKADE THREAT

PUBLIC SERVICES TO CONTINUE AT ALL COSTS

TO THE ARMED FORCES

PUBLIC MEETINGS

MAGISTRATES EMPOWERED TO PROHIBIT THEM

RUSH OF VOLUNTEERS

FALSE RUMOURS

NO TROOPS IN ACTION

NO FOREIGN SUPPORT.

SOVIET OFFERS HELP.

FOODSTUFFS IN FIVE DAYS OR £350,000

THE KING'S PLANS.

THE CHURCHES UNITED.

THE MINERS' REFUSAL

IMPROVED RAILWAY SERVICES

SIXTY-SIX MEN REMANDED

THE WEATHER

DAILY EXPRESS

No. 8126.   LONDON, WEDNESDAY, MAY 12th, 1926.   ONE PENNY.

THE STRIKE WITH ITS BACK BROKEN.

IMPORTANT HIGH COURT DECISION.

Strike Contrary to Law.

UNION FUNDS CANNOT BE DEPLETED BY PAYMENTS.

LADY TERRINGTON.

DECREE FOR A FORMER PEERESS M.P.

AMUNDSEN OFF TO THE POLE.

ABD-EL-KRIM BEATEN.

A GREAT PEOPLE.

MINERS' LEADER IN THE DOCK.

CHARGE AGAINST BIRMINGHAM JUSTICES.

WOMEN'S WORK IN THE CRISIS.

OTHER NEWS IN BRIEF.

STRIKE CERTAIN TO END THIS WEEK.

Trade Union Leaders Admit Defeat.

T.U.C. RESPONSIBLE.

ATTORNEY-GENERAL PLACES THE BLAME.

TRAIN OVERTURNED.

THREE PERSONS KILLED, EIGHT INJURED, AND FIVE GASSED.

THE MYSTERY DERBY.

GAOL FOR RIOTERS.

SHORTAGE OF BEER.

WEATHER FORECAST.

Rain at times. Cold and unsettled.

YESTERDAY'S CRICKET.

Printed and Published by the London Express Newspaper, Ltd.

found himself so deeply in disagreement that it became a serious issue between them. He was also a superlative craftsman and was made all the better by Beaverbrook's help and encouragement. If this sounds cosy, it was far from it. For most of his working life Chris was given hell by the Beaver. Nothing was sacred, the old man felt the right to 'phone him at any hour of the day or night, no matter where he was or what he was doing. He would praise extravagantly and criticise furiously. The pressure under which Beaverbrook's top executives were expected to live was quite exceptional and it is small wonder that, when Chris finally left, it was as the result of a heart attack—a lesser man would have been dead years before.

However, in 1926 this was all very much in the future. James Douglas, editor of the *Sunday Express*, offered Chris the post of news editor at the salary of £12 a week. He accepted with alacrity and began a career with the Beaverbrook organisation which was to last for most of his working life. That in itself was no mean achievement, for in Fleet Street getting fired is a damn sight easier than being hired and most journalists of any note have been bounced around from one paper to another in their time. Chris only managed to get fired once, and fortunately it was not to be permanent. On the night in 1927 when Lindbergh flew the Atlantic alone, Chris made a mess of presenting the story. On hearing that he had been responsible for the disaster Blumenfeld merely said: 'Sack him. He's too good looking to be any use'. Fortunately for Chris and for the organisation, John Gordon, the chief sub-editor of the *Express* who was on loan to the Sunday paper, managed to persuade Blumenfeld that it was unfair to put the blame on a junior when people higher up were responsible.

Gordon went on to become editor of the *Sunday Express* and under him Christiansen was to learn much about journalism and about survival in the eccentric world which was Beaverbrook's empire. One useful technique—for those bold enough to employ it—was always to tell the Beaver exactly what you thought, either directly or by the more devious route of unburdening yourself in front of people who would report your words. Gordon went in for this kind of criticism frequently. Christiansen recalled a typical Gordon tirade: 'The little man thinks we should use Arnold Bennett in the Thing. What good's Bennett at a shilling a word? But the little man's the capitalist millionaire proprietor, so let him have the Thing and we'll get on with selling the Thing ourselves'. The meaning may seem a trifle obscure until you know that the *Sunday Express* was what Gordon meant by 'the Thing'. It was his own catchphrase which, interestingly, has persisted through the years so that it is still possible to hear of employees of Express Newspapers referring to their distinguished journals merely as 'the Thing'.

Chris got his first chance to make something of a really big news story in 1930 when the R101 disaster struck. It was October 5 and he had already gone home after a hard Saturday on the paper. He was preparing for a holiday with his wife and had, with difficulty, put all thoughts of his newspaper out of his mind. However, at 1 am the 'phone rang and he was given the news that the R101 was down

Opposite *The R101 disaster. It was this event which gave Christiansen his first moment of true glory.*

Daily Express

TO-DAY'S WEATHER: Rain at Times.

NO. 9,493.　　MONDAY, OCTOBER 6, 1930.　　ONE PENNY.

The R101 Crashes And Is Destroyed: Lord Thomson, Sir Sefton Brancker And 44 Others Burned To Death.

THE TRAGIC AFTERMATH.—Dead bodies shrouded in sheets near the wrecked airship.—*Special "Daily Express" Picture.*

GREAT AIRSHIP STRIKES A HILL AFTER BATTLE WITH A STORM.

SLEEPING PASSENGERS ENVELOPED BY SWIFTLY RUSHING FLAMES.

THE giant airship R101, which left Cardington at 7 p.m. on Saturday for India, crashed on a hill near Beauvais, France, at 2.5 a.m. yesterday, and 46 of those on board—including Lord Thomson, Minister for Air, and Air Vice-Marshal Sir Sefton Brancker—were burned to death.

A quarter of an hour before the crash those on board had no warning of danger, although the weather was stormy. At 1.30 a.m. they received a message from the French Air Ministry, telling them they were one kilometre from Beauvais. They replied "Thank you"—nothing more.

The next few minutes sufficed to produce the worst disaster in aviation history. Low-lying clouds had prevented the R101 rising, and the storm, which left masses of rain-water on the top of the envelope, forced her down until she struck a low hill by a wood near the village of Allenne.

A few moments and the whole airship was a mass of flame. Many of the victims were killed in their sleep, so swift was the rush of the fire when the hydrogen of the R101 was ignited.

Some of the survivors owed their escape to the fact that the water tanks broke, and the flood washed them through the flames to safety. Rain became was displayed by three of the survivors who, though injured, returned to the burning wreck in the hope of finding some comrade to help.

One survivor's last glimpse of the wreck was Flight-Lieutenant Irwin standing at his post quietly giving orders. He was still there when the flames enveloped him.

Lord Thomson was considered by many to be the Government's nominee as next Viceroy of India. Flight-Lieutenant Irwin, the captain of the airship, was among the victims, who include a number of distinguished officers and experts.

Biographies of victims are on Pages Two and Ten.

LATEST NEWS.

An emergency meeting of the Air Council was held at the Air Ministry last night to hear Air Chief Marshal Sir John Salmond report on the disaster in which five chiefs of the Ministry perished.

It is announced by the Ministry that a public inquiry will be held in this country, subject to coordination with the arrangements which are being made by the French Government.

The bodies of the victims will be brought to England for burial. They will be carried across the Channel in a warship.

Engineer H. J. Leech was in a cabin with two other engineers when the crash came. "We shook hands," he said, "and once we would not be burned to death, but that somehow we would make our way out. We had no idea how." All three escaped.

Mr. H. J. Greenwald's full story of the disaster and rescue stories is on Page Three. Survivors' narratives are on Page Eleven.

"A DRUNKEN, REELING MONSTER."

By HAROLD PEMBERTON

"Daily Express" Special Correspondent

(who flew from London at dawn yesterday to the scene of the disaster).

BEAUVAIS, Sunday, Oct. 5.

LET me tell the story of the most terrible disaster in the history of British flying as simply and as faithfully as possible. Let me reconstruct an accurate picture of how brave men of estate high and low met their death in the fabulous palace of the air.

It needs no gloss. No mind could conceive a drama more pitiless than the one unfolded to me by eyewitnesses in this stricken and terrified town, a few short hours after the flaming sky had lighted terror in a thousand eyes.

From my aeroplane flight over the wrecked R101, and stories told to me by survivors in having something of divine Providence about them, it is from these that I reconstruct for you a narrative of facts that stood near the wreckage.

Beauvais, a small French town some forty miles from Paris, was sleeping peacefully when, about 2 a.m., the great ship appeared above the housetops.

It was a fearful shadow, for the

WHAT WAS THE CAUSE?

AIRSHIP IN PERIL THREE MONTHS AGO.

LEAKING GAS BAGS.

"Daily Express" Air Correspondent.

I am able to reveal the complete details of an alarming experience which overtook R101 during her flight over Hendon during the Air Pageant last July which now casts a mysterious shadow across the terrible disaster of the airship yesterday morning.

There were elaborate precautions against the publication of the following facts and, until now the secret has been kept successfully.

The destruction of the great air liner, with its toll of forty-six lives, however, makes it vital that the truth should be held at once before the public.

Officials have carefully concealed the fact that disaster almost ended the career of R101 on the day that was made her public appearance at the Royal Air Force display.

The airship began her cruise on that day shortly after noon, and spent a considerable time hovering over the vast crowd before starting for London, so that she would arrive over the flying field at her appointed time.

Directly on leaving Hendon, after being in the air for more than four hours, the officers in control of the vessel discovered that she continued to lose height.

Members of the crew who examined the gasbags found that the small balloons, which fly scores of goldbeaters' skin, were chafing against the metal framework. A report was immediately made to the whole matter, and by all folks at once for Cardington and ordered all available speed from his engineers.

R101 returned safely and was moored. The airship, however, was saved solely by the swift action of Flight-Lieutenant Irwin, the captain, who dropped her entire water ballast and two tons of many of fuel, and employed every other possible means of reducing weight.

HOLES WORN.

Shortly afterwards R101 was taken from the mast and you only her shed for repairs.

It was discovered on examination of the deflated balloons that more than sixty small holes had been worn through the gas containers.

The re-dressing of the airship's hull, which meant inserting another bag and renewing fresh fabric, was not subsequently undertaken, and it was understood in some quarters that a new method had been introduced for the arrangement of the gas bag inside.

The theory of yesterday's disaster which, however, is a recurrence of the gas trouble which the R101 experienced on the day of the Air Pageant.

THE PRINCE INFORMED.

Air Ministry officials at Beauvais were in constant touch with the Prince of Wales throughout the day. It is possible that he may fly to Beauvais to-day.

The Last Message: "Going To Bed."

The last of a series of wireless messages received at Le Bourget from the R101, states Reuter, was timed 1.59 a.m. Sixty minutes before the crash. It read as follows:—

"At the moment, the passengers, after an excellent meal and after enjoying a number of cigars, are getting ready to go to bed."

The King immediately on hearing of the disaster sent the following telegram to the Prime Minister:—

"I am horrified to hear of this national disaster which has befallen Airship R-101, and the consequent serious loss of life, including that of Lord Thomson, my Air Minister.

"The Queen and I sympathise deeply with the relatives and friends of those who have perished in the service of their country, and also with the injured survivors.

"GEORGE R.I."

LATE NEWS.

REVOLT AGAINST BRAZIL GOVERNMENT.

NEW YORK, Sunday, Oct. 5.

According to despatches received here to-night, Brazil is in the throes of revolution. Practically the entire State of Rio Grande do Sul has revolted against the Federal Government, while outbreaks are also reported in the States of Parana, Minas Geraes and Rio de Janeiro. Owing to the strict censorship the extent of the uprising is not known.—*Reuter.*

Broadcasting Programmes on Page 13

NUNS' VIGIL OVER BODIES.

BEAUVAIS, Sunday, Oct. 5.

While the rude beat down on the smoke-blackened girders of the wreck of the R 101, the Sisters of Mercy of the Beauvais convent gathered in the little schoolroom where most of the victims' bodies lie, to begin an all-night vigil.

They will spend the night in prayer. The schoolroom is too small to accommodate all the bodies, and eleven are to remain in a field outside, protected by tarpaulins.—B.U.P.

TRAPPED MAN'S ESCAPE.

Mr. A. Bishop, wireless operator, failed to escape by tearing and flung his way through the fabric. He could work his way back easily, he said. He became exhausted, then suddenly fell through "a raging torrent of fire," and found himself safe on wet grass.

(HALF SCOTT IN THE R 101.)

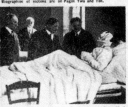

M. LAURENT EYNAC, the French Air Minister, talking to Rigger W. G. Radcliffe, one of the survivors, in Beauvais Hospital.

in flames at Beauvais. This was a major disaster, quite unlike anything which had happened before. The airship was still considered to be the shape of things to come as far as air travel was concerned and on this particular flight there were several dignitaries including Lord Thomson, the Air Minister, and Sir Sefton Brancker, the Director of Civil Aviation.

Legend has it that Chris arrived back in the office in 20 minutes flat, wearing his pyjamas under his coat and clutching his wife's handbag in which he had found change for the taxi. Unfortunately the story is entirely untrue—he *did* manage the journey in 20 minutes and he *did* borrow the taxi fare from his wife, but the other details are just part of Fleet Street legend. If the general public often feel that they suffer from the attentions of journalists who care more for a dramatic story than for the truth, they should take some small consolation from the fact that the journalists practise the same arts of dramatisation upon themselves. There is no well-known figure in Fleet Street who is not surrounded by a myth much greater than the man it contains—as we shall see in later chapters.

Chris then actually set about doing what every journalist always wants to do; he stripped down the paper to its bare essentials and went about re-creating it in an entirely different form with a really sensational story. Special trains had to be hired to take the new papers out all over the country and exchange them for the old edition. All night Chris and the *Sunday Express* staff worked to bring the story to the public in subsequent editions as more details were known. By the morning everything which could be done had been. Then Beaverbrook 'phoned. They had not spoken since the days of the General Strike four years before. Beaverbrook said: 'You have secured a wonderful feat of journalism. I am proud to be associated with a newspaper on which you work. Goodbye to you'. No reply was asked for or needed. In fact, the 'goodbye to you' was the hallmark of Beaverbrook's telephone conversations and frequently left people feeling nonplussed on the other end of the line. When taxed about this on one occasion, by someone who thought him rude, he merely pointed out that he had finished what he wanted to say and could see no point in taking the conversation further. This was, of course, a typically disingenuous remark. The little man knew full well that his dramatic endings gave him a powerful edge when dealing with others.

It was subsequent to this piece of good fortune that Chris was invited to go and see Sir George Sutton, the managing director of Associated Newspapers, the organisation which owned the *Dispatch*. After some preliminary questions about his age, experience and present salary—he was 26 and earning £37 a week—Sir George left the room. When he came back he had the Hon Esmond Harmsworth, Lord Rothermere, with him. Between them they then offered him the editorship of the *Sunday Dispatch* at a salary of £3,000 per year. Chris was rather taken aback by this sudden offer of power and riches and, being a rather cautious character, he asked for time to consider. This was granted on the condition that he would not use the offer as a bargaining counter to jack up his salary at the *Sunday Express*.

On returning to his office he told John Gordon what had happened. The result was that both he and Gordon were quickly on their way to Stornoway House, Beaverbrook's London home, to see his lordship. Chris' own account of their conversation is as follows: 'I am told,' said Lord Beaverbrook, 'that you have been offered the editorship of the *Sunday Dispatch* at a salary of £3,000 a year. Now that is a big job and it is a lot of money. But I want you to know that you are regarded by me as one of the young men on my newspapers with a bright future. We have many young men growing up whose opportunities will come. I would naturally like you to stay on the *Express*. Which is it to be? Are you going to stay on the sunny side of the street, or are you going to cross to the shadows?'

Chris agreed to stay, whereupon the Beaver decided to raise his salary to £3,000 per year. Chris objected that he had promised he would not use the *Dispatch* offer in this way but the Beaver would have none of it. He insisted that Chris had made the decision to stay *before* the salary increase and that therefore he had not broken faith with Rothermere.

It was not long after this that Chris was sent north to work on the Manchester edition of the *Daily Express*. That paper was in trouble and it needed drastic alterations if it was to succeed. Chris was persuaded to go—and John Gordon cajoled into relinquishing him—by a promise that he could return to London as soon as he had put 100,000 on the sales in Manchester. He was not totally happy with this situation. He had struggled hard to leave the north and make his way to Fleet Street and he hardly relished the prospect of being sent back, albeit in a position of some considerable influence. However, the power of the Beaver was such that he could not be denied. Chris went.

The period at the Manchester office was a great success. Christiansen, being a northerner himself, appreciated that the London edition of the paper would never do for the hardbitten northern counties during the Depression. He set the *Express* campaigning on behalf of Lancashire cotton workers who were on strike against substantial wage cuts. It must have been one of the very few occasions when the paper actually backed a workers' strike. Even though it was a lost cause the fact that the campaign was bold, vigorous and popular did the *Express* a lot of good.

Chris introduced other innovations such as a children's colour comic and a racing section (compiled by his father). He even had a go at printing a few of the illustrations in the paper in rather lurid colours. Some of these experiments worked and some did not, the important thing was that the Manchester edition was now a separate entity especially tailored for northern tastes and, as a result, sales began to rise dramatically.

However, Chris was overworking to such an extent that his health was affected. In the *Express* organisation a rising young executive was expected to damn nearly kill himself in the service of his paper. Nor did things necessarily change after Beaverbrook's death. Even in recent times Jocelyn Stevens, one time deputy chairman of Express Newspapers, was accused of working his executives into an early grave—though it would be fairer to say that he expected them to work as hard as he did himself. In any case, Chris had to take a rest but, when he had recovered, he was at once ordered back to London to become assistant editor of the *Daily Express*.

This appointment was not universally popular. For a start, the *Express* already had an assistant editor, a man named Vaughan Wilkins. Not only would he not be delighted to have a bright newcomer invading his territory, but he and Chris did not much like each other in any case. In order to avoid the conflict, Chris offered to stay in Manchester, but the Beaver would have none of it. Christiansen was to go to London and work in a position junior to that of Wilkins. However, this situation never came to a head as Wilkins resigned and became a highly successful novelist.

The controversy over the new appointment did not end there. Baxter was still the editor of the *Express* and his 'dinner jacket' attitude to journalism was quite at odds with Chris' outlook. Chris was one of the new breed of Fleet Street men who were much more down to earth than their predecessors and who were able to feel the pulse of the general public. Baxter belonged to the age of the god-like editor—the two did not mix. Baxter's interview with the Beaver over this matter has been much quoted but is amusing enough to be brought out for a re-run.

Beaverbrook: 'I want you to know that Christiansen is coming to London as assistant editor of the *Daily Express.*'

Baxter: 'If that is so, then I resign as editor.'

Beaverbrook: 'Just the same, Christiansen is coming to London as assistant editor.'

Baxter: 'In that case I withdraw my resignation.'

Chris had arrived at the *Express.*

Chapter 5

The give-away war

The 1930s are famous for many things: the Depression, the rise of fascism and the start of the Second World War. Few people not connected with the Press would remember another sort of struggle which took place during this period—the newspaper circulation war. At that time the market was over-supplied with papers and the competition for circulation was fierce. It was soon to become cut-throat.

The struggle which broke out between the newspapers was conducted by means of free gifts and cheap offers. For a number of years the country was literally plagued with canvassers who were sent out by the papers to get people to agree to take out subscriptions. The bait was very varied. Every imaginable kind of inducement was offered—from canteens of cutlery to complete sets of Dickens' works, from clothing to free insurance policies.

It is often said that this was one of the lowest points for British journalism (of course, this was before the 'great bingo war' of the '80s, of which more later). While the war lasted the quality of journalism came a poor second to the gimmicks thought up by harassed circulation managers. Presentation of the news was no longer the main aim of the paper and was replaced by emphasis on the latest stunt to persuade potential readers to subscribe. However, from the public's viewpoint this was far from being a sorry episode. When *Express* readers were asked to share with us some of their memories of the paper in its early days we expected to get a great variety of reminiscences about favourite columnists, cartoonists and so on. Not a bit of it. Every last living soul who read the *Express* in the 1930s remembered the gifts and nothing but the gifts. What is more, some of them were jolly good ones too. There are still road atlases, encyclopaedias, dictionaries and mountains of other goodies left over from the 'war' being used in homes throughout Britain today. This leads inevitably to a somewhat mischievous thought. Large numbers of little old ladies sent in the insurance policies which were issued to them free by the *Express*. In the intervening years many of these policy-holders must have become entitled to claim. What would happen if they all did so now? We only asked.

So great was the public enthusiasm for the free gifts—it must have been rather like living under an unpopular government near election time—that some people told us that the *Express* actually started publication in the '30s. Until the free gift campaign they had been totally unaware of the paper's existence. So, although one cannot deny that Christiansen and his staff did an enormous amount to put the paper on the map journalistically, it is as well for newspapermen to remember just how little effect their efforts actually have on the public at large. Give us cutlery, give us tea services, give us dictionaries—and write how you please!

If the campaign seems funny, in retrospect it was no joke for Beaverbrook and his fellow proprietors. They brought themselves to the verge of a very dangerous financial situation with this suicidal attempt to gain readers. However, the whole affair was not very different from a real war—nobody could afford to be the first to give in. Also there was one man who was so obsessed with the struggle for supremacy that he was prepared to take enormous risks in pursuit of his goal. His name was Josiah Elias, the proprietor of the socialist *Daily Herald*. In spite of his ownership of a left-wing paper, Elias was not averse to using all the weapons in the armoury of capitalism to achieve victory. He had already been attempting, with some success, to poach the best talent on the *Express*. Hannen Swaffer, for example, was one of the greatest journalists of his day but, unluckily for his employers, he was also a convinced socialist and when he was offered a job by Elias he accepted with alacrity.

The Newspaper Proprietors' Association was by now so worried about the situation that it convened a special meeting to call for a cease-fire in the free gift war. Elias was informed that he would be opposed by all the other proprietors acting in unison if he refused to co-operate. It was agreed that newspaper canvassing could continue but that only competitions and free insurance should be offered as inducements. There were to be no more free gifts or cheap offers.

However, Elias was not in the same position as the rest of the Press. They already had their circulations firmly established—he was struggling to build up a readership at their expense. Eventually he came up with a scheme which he hoped would help him get round his agreement whilst remaining technically within it. He would produce cheap books, produced on the latest binding machinery which cut costs dramatically. These books could then be offered to the readers at apparently 'reduced' cost, thus the other papers could not accuse him of having broken the agreement.

The works he concentrated on were the *Home Doctor*, the *Handyman* and the complete works of Dickens. They were a vast success and Elias was fiercely reviled by all the other proprietors. At last a meeting was arranged at the Savoy Hotel which was to be attended by representatives from the *Express*, the *Mail*, the *News Chronicle* and the *Herald*. Elias suggested a compromise solution but Beaverbrook was not interested—he would settle for nothing less than the complete withdrawal of the Dickens offer. Elias could not and would not agree. Beaverbrook, it is said, advanced towards him in a rage, drew an imaginary sword and ran him through with it, saying, 'Elias, this is war—war to the death. I shall fight you to the bitter end'.

Suddenly the whole situation degenerated from comedy to farce. The other papers began to distribute sets of Dickens without regard for the cost. The country was blighted with improving works of literature. But it did not end there, for now it was considered that the original truce was at an end and the free gift war was resumed with increased vigour. After some hectic canvassing (during

Above *Britain's decision to come off the gold standard was greeted with jubilation because our currency would no longer be subject to control by foreigners.*

Below *A typical Beaverbrook message to his readers. More work and more prosperity—never look back!*

Top left *As the circulation rose the paper was not slow to proclaim its 'triumphal progress'.*

Bottom left *The brand new Express building was a talking point in London. It was designed by Ellis and Clarke with Sir E. Owen Williams as consulting engineer. The builders were Trollope & Colls who were to play a substantial part in the organisation's future.*

Right *A dignified symbol of a most undignified episode. This insurance policy is a relic of the great circulation war which nearly ruined the newspaper industry in the 1930s.*

Overleaf *Gandhi, a pet-hate of Beaverbrook's because of his desire to gain independence for India, is arrested, much to the delight of the Express.*

Page 53 *The photo-feature was still a popular item, but here it also carries a political message.*

IMPORTANT NOTICE.

This Insurance Policy will not be valid until the day upon which your Newsagent begins to deliver the "Daily Express" to you, upon your instructions.

Daily Express Free Insurance

Certificate of Registration

Mrs A.E. [signature]

The Manager of the "Daily Express" Insurance Department is in receipt of Registration Form from the abovenamed, who has accordingly been registered as a regular reader for the purpose of the Free Insurance, the Benefits and Conditions of which are as printed overleaf, or as published from time to time in the "Daily Express."

INSURANCE REGISTRATION DEPARTMENT, GREAT ANCOATS STREET, MANCHESTER.

JUNE 29 1936

Daily Express

TO-DAY'S WEATHER: Cloudy; Very Mild.

NO. 9,878. MONDAY, JANUARY 4, 1932. ONE PENNY.

GANDHI ARRESTED AT 3 A.M.

Watching Thousands See Police Call On Their Sleeping Leader.

FACTS ABOUT THE BEST FREE INSURANCE.

"DAILY EXPRESS" PAYMENTS TO READERS ACHIEVE A RECORD.

NEW 1932 BENEFITS.

SPECIAL PROVISIONS TO SAFEGUARD CHILDREN.

THE GIGANTIC AND UNPARALLELED NEW 1932 FREE INSURANCE ANNOUNCED BY THE "DAILY EXPRESS" MAKES IT IMPERATIVE THAT EVERY READER SHOULD AT ONCE COME INTO THE "DAILY EXPRESS" INSURANCE GROUP.

Moreover, he should persuade all his friends to come in, too. If this is done the results will be twofold :—

1.—The total payments in respect of the group will be increased.

2.—The individual payments of benefit to each claimant will also be increased.

These are the results that have happened hitherto as the group of "Daily Express" readers has constantly expanded. Distinguished among all national newspapers by being the only one to maintain three complete printing and publishing centres in Great Britain, the "Daily Express" is every day making a wider appeal.

TEN YEARS' PROOF.

The facilities for printing late news and for ensuring efficient distribution from the centres in London, Manchester, and Glasgow leave the newspaper without a rival in efficient production. As the group of readers constantly spreads and widens, so the scope and amount of insurance payments have steadily expanded.

DURING THE LAST TEN YEARS THE TOTAL AMOUNT PAID OUT IN BENEFITS BY THE "DAILY EXPRESS" IN RELATION TO THE NUMBER OF REGISTERED READERS HAS BEEN GREATER THAN THAT OF ANY OTHER NEWSPAPER IN THE COUNTRY.

The continual expansion of the business now enables the "Daily Express" to expand its benefits still further. The moment that an opportunity offered to recast the insurance scheme with the conclusion of the year 1931, the "Daily Express" immediately raised its benefits to correspond with the expansion of its group.

CARE AND ANXIETY BANISHED.

Splendid new safeguards against accident to life and limb have been drafted so as to achieve the maximum result in banishing care and anxiety from the homes of its readers. Just as a great insurance company at the end of a year or a three-year period reconsiders its bonus in the light of the expansion of its business, so to-day for the New Year the "Daily Express" has declared an increased insurance bonus for its readers.

But there is no reason at all why the bonus should stop at its present level. In fact, it will not stop there. The benefits will grow bigger and better with the growth of the group which they cover.

If you are a regular reader, come into the group at once. Go out and bring your friends into it. In his own interests, every reader can be a canvasser for the newspaper, and he will find no difficulty in recommending it with success. For in its facilities for news-gathering and news-printing the "Daily Express" has no rival. Its features are the best. Its policy is sound. Its spirit is a morning tonic.

The immense extensions which are now made in the insurance benefits have been particularly designed to safeguard the young lives in the family. While all existing benefits to adult registered readers are maintained, and in some cases doubled, the scheme now opens up a great new sphere of helpfulness in protecting the children and the young folk at just those points where experience shows that they are most vulnerable to risks.

Outstanding among the new plans for the safeguarding of family welfare is the splendid benefit which will ensure that

PAGE TWO, COLUMN FIVE.

"GILBERT IS JUST WONDERFUL," declared ELSIE JANIS, the actress and spinster of forty-four, on her arrival in New York from Hollywood. She was referring to Gilbert Wilson, a young film star, her marriage to whom she admitted is "quite probable."

PERRY WINS TRIPLE TENNIS CROWN.

AGAIN TOO GOOD FOR BOROTRA.

ENGLISH GIRLS' RIVIERA BATTLE.

"Daily Express" Correspondent.
PARIS, Sunday, Jan. 3.

BRITISH lawn tennis is definitely on the up grade.

F. J. Perry, now ranked as Britain's No. 1 player, to-day beat the redoubtable Jean Borotra by 3–6, 7–5, 6–1, 6–4 in the final of the International covered courts championship here, while two English girls, Sheila Hewitt, daughter of Admiral Hewitt, and Muriel Thomas, fought out the final of the Beaulieu singles at Cannes, Miss Hewitt winning by 8–10, 6–2, 6–4.

Perry has swept the boards in the Paris tournament. On Friday he won the mixed doubles title with Mdlle. Sigart as his partner, and yesterday, partnered by Christian Boussus, he won the men's doubles.

F. J. Perry.

His victory over the "bounding Basque" confirmed form in last season's Davis Cup matches, when Perry beat the Frenchman in the challenge round.

"It's a wonderful thing for me to beat Jean, especially on covered courts," Perry told me after the match, "and I was jolly lucky. But he gets tired rather quickly nowadays, and cannot keep it up as long."

This explanation does Perry less than justice. He won by magnificent verve, doggedness, and determination not to be over-awed.

PERRY RECOVERED.

The first set went to Borotra, playing in his old style, and the second went up to 5–4 in his favour. He even had set point, but he put the ball into the net.

Then Perry made a magnificent recovery with unplayable shots across the court, and managed to pull up to 5–all, and then on to 7–5 for the set.

At Cannes Miss Hewitt should have met Mrs. Satterthwaite in the semi-final, and Riviera "fans" were looking forward to a battle royal between a famous player and a new challenger for honours.

But Mrs. Satterthwaite caused keen disappointment by scratching because she was suffering from an injured heel.

Miss Hewitt, who is seventeen, won the British girls' championship at Wimbledon in September last, beating Miss K. Stammers, the Hertfordshire senior champion, in the final within twenty-four hours of an operation on a dislocated toe. She played throughout with her foot tightly bandaged.

THE EX-KAISER HAS INFLUENZA: SOME ANXIETY.

"Daily Express" Correspondent.
DOORN (Holland), Sunday, Jan. 3.

The ex-Kaiser has contracted influenza, and has been ordered to remain in bed.

Some anxiety is felt by his medical advisers. The ex-Kaiser will be seventy-three years of age this month.

CALLING IN THE DOCTOR
Is an all-too-familiar domestic necessity.
What of the nation—does it need the doctor, too?
See PAGE TEN To-day
for the first article in an altogether new and invigorating series of interest to young and old alike.
To-morrow: Sir Philip Gibbs

GOVERNMENT SWOOP ON REBELS.

Gandhi's Last Act To Buy British Watches For London Detectives.

TROOPS MOVE IN INDIA.

BOMBAY, Monday, Jan. 4.

GANDHI WAS ARRESTED TO-DAY ON A MAGISTRATE'S WARRANT. HE WILL BE INTERNED WITHOUT TRIAL UNDER THE ORDINANCE ACT OF 1827.

Within a few hours he and two other prominent leaders of the Indian revolutionary movement were seized and swept off to gaol.

This is the first dramatic stroke of the Government of India, following the Viceroy's refusal on Saturday to negotiate with Gandhi as long as his extremist organisation threatened widespread violence.

Gandhi, who has been imprisoned several times in the past ten years, was received by the King at Buckingham Palace a couple of months ago. He is sixty-two.

He had avoided arrest earlier last night by failing to catch a train.

TRAIN ARREST PLANNED.

Plans had been made to arrest him on his journey from Bombay to Ahmedabad, where he runs a training camp. [illegible] was travelling, was to have been "slipped" halfway between the two cities. There two other officers were to board the train, present the warrant to him, and effect his arrest.

The extremist leader decided at the last minute not to catch his train, but to remain in Bombay.

The train arrest plan thus fell through.

Throughout the night thousands of people had squatted round Gandhi's house, in expectation of the arrest.

They had spent the previous night there, too, and when their leader appeared yesterday morning he was hailed with shouts of "Victory!"

Throughout the day he held court outside his house, sitting with his wife and with the bundles of blankets and loincloths and the packets of dates which, with Mr. Ramsay MacDonald's book "Wanderings and Excursions," he proposed to take to prison.

SUPPER AND SPINNING.

Gandhi, after supping at nine o'clock, began his twenty-four hours of silence, which he observes every Monday.

He continued at his spinning wheel until eleven o'clock, when he retired to rest.

At 3 a.m. to-day (Indian time is in advance of Greenwich) the police arrived and arrested the extremists' "Holy Man."

One of Gandhi's last acts in preparing for his departure was to purchase two watches for presentation to the two Scotland Yard detectives, Sergeant William Evans and Sergeant William Rogers, who were his bodyguard in England at the recent Round Table Conference.

A secretary brought a large selection of Swiss watches, but Gandhi insisted that best English lever watches only should be sent.

When it was pointed out that this purchase was inconsistent with the campaign to boycott British goods, Gandhi said: "When I made the promise to give these watches the truce was still in force, and the boycott therefore does not stand in this instance."

The watches are inscribed, "With love, M. K. Gandhi."

The police pounced on another rebel leader last night, Vallabhai Patel, president of the Indian National Congress, who went quietly off to gaol—not for the first time.

He and Gandhi were taken by car to Yeravda, in Poona, a military fortress at which Gandhi was a prisoner for several months in 1930.

A few hours earlier Subhas Bose, late Mayor of Calcutta, who has been imprisoned more than once for sedition and rioting, was arrested.

The Government of India is expected at any moment to sweep all the other revolutionary leaders into prison, to confiscate their political funds, and suppress their organisations in order to stop open incitement to rebellion.

The Government is already on the move in other directions. Five hundred troops were sent to-day to northern Madras, where fifty extremist leaders have been warned to cease their "no-rent" campaign.

The stern telegram of the Viceroy yesterday, refusing to see Gandhi so long as the extremist "Indian Congress" threatened widespread violence, has taken the wind out of the sails of the wild men.

"BARBARISM."

But Gandhi, in spite of his protestations of "non-violence," fanned the flames to the last.

"India will survive the worst type of Government barbarism," he declared yesterday.

In an address to his training camp followers he said:—

"The fight is imminent. Endure its hardships. Welcome bullets. In your hands rests the honour of India."

He also issued an appeal to the 1,750,000 Indian Christians to join the rebellion.

In an amazing message to the American nation, he invites them to intervene in Empire affairs.

"On the eve of embarking on a deadly struggle," he writes, "I would expect American friends to watch its progress and to use the influence of a great nation for oppressed humanity."—Reuter.

GANDHI.

FIVE REGIMENTS FIGHT A BARRACKS FIRE.

"Daily Express" Correspondent.
FOLKESTONE, Sunday.

THE officers' mess and adjoining buildings, including the silver room, of the 1st Sherwood Foresters, stationed at Risborough Barracks, Shorncliffe, near here, were burned to the ground early to-day in a blaze which lit up the entire camp, and was fought by fire pickets from five regiments.

Officers and men dashed through the flames and saved the King's and regimental colours, the Army Football Cup, which the regiment won last season, the Inter-Arms Fencing Trophy, and a large amount of plate intimately connected with the history of the regiment, which dates from 1741.

All silver plate used in the dining hall to-day, however, was lost, and the total damage is estimated at several thousand pounds.

The fire started in the silver room shortly before 3 a.m., and within four hours the whole of the buildings were completely burnt out, only the chimney stack being left standing amid the smouldering debris.

The fire was discovered by Private Quilt, who was sleeping in the silver room. Within a few minutes the whole of the camp was roused by the sounding of fire calls by buglers.

In the brilliant glare of the flames, which flood-lit the drill-ground a short distance away, the battalion was paraded. Officers and N.C.O.s detailed men to various tasks, while in the barrack rooms on the other side of the square a draft of men were getting their kit together to leave for India.

The fire had almost died away when the draft marched out of barracks, [illegible]

TWIN BABIES AND FATHER KILLED.

MOTOR-CAR SKIDS INTO A PRAM.

"Daily Express" Correspondent.
REIGATE, Sunday.

TWIN babies and their father, who was wheeling them in a perambulator at Kingswood to-day, were killed in a collision with a motor-car.

The twins were the five-month-old daughters of Mr. Albert Kinge, of Kingswood.

They were being wheeled along a path by the road when a motor-car skidded into them and threw Mr. Kinge, the perambulator, and the babies into a ten-foot dip at the roadside.

The babies were killed instantly. The father died later in hospital.

The motor-car dashed into a large tree overlooking the bank and was badly damaged.

"It all happened in a flash," said an eye-witness. "The babies were hurled over the bank in different directions, falling several yards from one another."

U.S. GOLD FOR PARIS.

PARIS, Sunday, Jan. 3.

The liner Bremen arrived at Cherbourg to-day with a shipment of gold from New York worth 200,000,000 (approximately £12,500,000 at par).

The consignment is for Paris.—Central News.

SIX POLICE SHOT DEAD BY BANDITS.

RAIN OF MACHINE GUN BULLETS.

ALL-DAY SIEGE OF FARMSTEAD.

"Daily Express" Special Correspondent.
SPRINGFIELD (Missouri), Sunday, Jan. 3.

SIX men—a sheriff, a deputy-sheriff, and four detectives—were killed and three policemen were wounded in a fierce battle with four hill bandits trapped in a farmhouse near here to-day.

Almost by magic the four men escaped under cover of darkness—supposedly through a secret tunnel.

The victims were mown down by pitiless machine gun fire that barked from windows as the officers were attempting to storm the farmhouse to effect the arrest of one of the bandits, Harry Young. He has been wanted for two years

LATE NEWS.

Broadcasting Programmes on Page 13

Daily Express

OVERTIME THE OUTCOME OF PROMPT INCOME-TAX PAYMENTS.

NO DAY'S REST was possible yesterday for the staff employed in the West Ham income tax office. They were kept busy with arrears—not of the more usual kind—but of work caused by the rush of payments. All over the country taxpayers are rallying to the aid of the National Exchequer.

THE PRINCESS ROYAL, Countess of Harewood, with the Hon. Mrs. Edward Lascelles, at the meet of the Bramham Moor Hunt.

MAROONED HOUSES in one of the districts flooded by the River Mississippi. Many people are living in box cars shunted to railway sidings.

ATHLETES OF THE SNOW—Oxford and Cambridge ski-ing teams practising near Quebec, Canada.

REHEARSING A STAR. Binnie Hale going through a part with John Murray Anderson, the producer, for to-night's production of "Bow Bells," twice postponed at the London Hippodrome.

THE NEW DEAN OF EXETER, the Rev. Canon Matthews, wearing black robes, walking with the bishop in the procession to the cathedral for his installation.

ANCIENT FOR MODERNS—Sandals and socks

TRIBUTE IN IMMORTELLES. Members of the Royal Antediluvian Order of Buffaloes placing wreaths on the Cenotaph yesterday.

which the leader of the race changed several times) the *Herald* came out in front of the field and was the first newspaper in the world to achieve a circulation of two million copies a day. Although this was a great achievement it proved more difficult to sustain than it had been to gain the circulation in the first place. The *Express* had not relied totally on the free gift campaign and had invested considerable sums of money in improving its news services. In the long term this paid off and the circulation surpassed even that reached by the *Herald*. In 1937 the *Express* had a circulation of 2,329,000 and the *Herald* was still stuck at two million. The *Mail* only had 1,580,000 and the *News Chronicle* had a mere 1,324,000.

Elias was finding it hard to hold on to his readership and the cost of doing so was crippling. Eventually he was faced with losses of £10,000 per week and, had the outbreak of the Second World War not intervened, the results would have been catastrophic for the *Herald*. As it was the start of the war, with the consequent limitations imposed on resources, brought the crazy circulation war to an end.

Although the entire episode has frequently been deprecated by historians of the Press, it should be borne in mind that it did have its beneficial side-effects. For example, it was largely responsible for the high level of newspaper reading among the British public and, although the readers were bought at a high price, the cost was probably justified in the long term. For the British now consume more newspapers than any other nation on Earth and, though the cost of buying a paper has continued to climb dramatically, this is still one of the few countries in the world where a daily paper is regarded—even by people with little education—as a necessity rather than a luxury.

However, that is the view with benefit of hindsight. More typical of informed opinion at the time was this pronouncement from Sir Emsley Carr who, in 1933, was President of the Institute of Journalists:

'Is there anyone who will admit that a free distribution of washing machines, pyjamas, pillow-cases, silk stockings, fountain-pens and even more elaborate gifts, such as gold wristlet watches, to capture any and everybody, is consonant with the traditions of British journalism? We have given up selling newspapers— we give away mangles and ask people to accept the paper as a favour.

'The purse is the chief weapon in this insane competition; and what the actual cost will be is difficult to estimate. Some authorities have placed it as high as at the rate of three to three and a half million pounds a year and, as the united profits of the papers concerned last year amounted to little more than half this sum, the gravity of the conflict can be realised'.

Chapter 6

The Red Crusader

It was at the height of the circulation war, when the *Express* was selling two million copies per day, that, on July 17 1933, the famous Red Crusader appeared on the paper's mast-head for the first time. Its purpose was to represent Beaverbrook's Empire Preference policies to the readers. Since these opinions were never taken up by any government the Crusader became something of a futile gesture—in fact, after the Second World War, the figure was put in chains until such time as a government favouring Empire Preference should be elected and thus release him. It was a typically melodramatic gesture from the Beaver and typically lacking in any sense of the political realities.

The *Express* was badly in need of bright new ideas if it was to prosper in the struggle against the other major dailies and the Beaver was to put great emphasis on youth in his struggle to make his paper bright and different. Chris was by no means the only bright young man working on the paper and Baxter had an article written by a member of staff who dubbed these young men 'the eaglets'. The tone was one of optimism and enthusiasm:

'This astonishing string of newspapers, with their vast circulation and their three centres of production, is, in great measure, an achievement of youth. One of the greatest revolutions of our time in Britain was the decision to put youth in charge of the *Express*. It was a big risk. Many shook their heads at the experiment. But it was made by a man who likes risks for their own sake—and who is often seeing a little deeper, or quicker, when he seems to be most daring. And there it is. The revolution is in being. In Europe, the youth are giving the Fascist salute and hailing one Caesar or another. In Britain they are producing the *Express* and hailing themselves'.

After that it should have come as no surprise that, when Baxter finally decided to retire, a young man was to be chosen to fill the post of editor. It *should* not have been a surprise—but it was. There were still plenty of older, more experienced men working on the paper who felt that they had a claim to the job.

Baxter's relations with the Beaver had slowly become strained. There were political differences between them—for example, Beaverbrook was devoted to the ideal of the British Empire in 'splendid isolation' whilst Baxter was an internationalist and a strong advocate of the Leage of Nations. When he was offered a job at £10,000 a year as public relations counsellor to the Gaumont-British Film Company, Baxter accepted. It is probable that his departure was not ultimately because of any political squabbles but was a result of having lived under the

The future begins to look doubtful and Beaverbrook puts forward his isolationist views. His hatred of the League of Nations was legendary.

thumb of the old tyrant for too long. Life with the Beaver was a constant battle for survival and the prospect of some quieter and highly paid employment must have been irresistible.

For Chris it was to be a lucky year. He was only 29 and had just become the father of twins—then he was made editor of the *Express*. Because of his youth and comparative inexperience he was given George Gilliatt, an older Fleet Street hand, as a temporary 'nanny' until he found his feet, but this arrangement did not last long and soon he was in sole charge of one of the largest and most powerful newspapers in the world.

As soon as he took over, Chris was faced with the urgent task of establishing his own style. Nothing is more important to an editor than to be seen to be doing something which makes his paper different from the others. Of course, being different is not enough on its own—the difference must have public appeal and must increase circulation, otherwise the editor's career will be a short one.

Chris' style was being watched carefully by his Fleet Street rivals and, in particular, Hugh Cudlipp of the *Mirror* was to make some pointed comments about the *Express* in its new form. He described it as a 'brilliant sub-editors' newspaper in which style and rewriting were everything. Information and opinion were served piping hot and pre-digested, a form which might not stimulate the brain but was pleasing to the palate'. However, he also went on to comment

Onward and upward! Circulation rises inexorably and Beaverbrook loses no chance to push his love of the Empire.

that, under the Beaverbrookian code of morality, the paper was seriously handicapped in certain areas. Divorces, for example, were reported as avidly as in other papers but the reasons for them were always carefully glossed over.

'Political and financial brigandry were lavishly and exultantly reported; national disasters, particularly adventures or rescues at sea, enjoyed 'saturation coverage' in crisp, shampooed English. But the subtler and baser foibles of human nature did not, so far as the *Express* was concerned, exist. The policy was energetically pursued. The paper was aiming at the man with a car in a garage. Or with a car without a garage. Or with a garage without a car. At any rate, their target was the chap who *wanted* a car *and* a garage.'

Cudlipp goes on to describe Chris and his staff as 'these bright young men with their rubber gloves and white coats in the glasshouse news clinic'. However, Cudlipp was also a bright, ambitious young man who was working for one of the *Express'* bitterest rivals so, though his criticisms are illuminating, they should not be taken literally.

Whatever the pros and cons of the paper's literary style, it was not long before it was being put to use on some sensational news. Reports started to arrive from America that King Edward VIII would marry Mrs Wallis Simpson, an American divorcee. This was more than just the usual speculation about the royal family by foreign journalists for the headline, 'KING *WILL* WED WALLY', appeared in

Daily Express

TODAY'S WEATHER : FAIR.

RADIO PROGRAMMES : PAGE 19.

No. 11,403

TUESDAY, DECEMBER 1, 1936

ONE PENNY

CRYSTAL PALACE CRASHES IN FLAMES

Orchestra Escape As Roof Collapses; All London Watches : Gas Alarm Given

AS THE ROOF FELL IN.

His 'Home' In Ruins

"There will never be another one," said Sir Henry Buckland, general manager, last night, watching the destruction of the building that meant so much to him.

His daughter Crystal—named after the Palace—was with him. "I am heart-broken," he said. "My Crystal Palace is finished."

TANKS SPEED TO FRONTIER

Daily Express Correspondent

NEW DELHI, Monday.

400 Firemen Save Television Tower

Daily Express Staff Reporters

THE CRYSTAL PALACE, MOST FAMOUS EXHIBITION BUILD-ING IN THE WORLD, WAS A TANGLED MASS OF RED-HOT IRON AND SHATTERED AND MOLTEN GLASS AN HOUR AFTER FIRE HAD BROKEN OUT THERE ABOUT EIGHT O'CLOCK LAST NIGHT. WITHIN 30 MINUTES THE ROOF OF THE GREAT TRANSEPT HAD COLLAPSED WITH A CRASH THAT WAS HEARD FIVE MILES AWAY.

The building, towering to a height of 550 feet above sea level, cracked and fell to pieces like an eggshell. Its girders crashed to the ground like gigantic, charred matchsticks. There was no stopping the trail of ruin, though 56 engines and 400 firemen fought the flames desperately.

The two tall towers still stand. In the southern one, which was protected by firemen's hoses, is valuable television apparatus belonging to the Baird Company. This is safe. But one of the transmitters in the South Transept has been destroyed, as well as a few television sets.

As the fire died down in the early hours of this morning the crowds of spectators who packed every road round the Palace were warned to move away: waves of gas released from broken pipes were sweeping the whole area. People living all round were ordered from their houses in the early evening when it was feared the towers might fall.

The Duke of Kent, accompanied by Lord Herbert, his equerry, motored from the West End. He wore evening dress and a black overcoat. As he was watching the firemen playing their hoses on the flames a puff of wind blew a cascade of water over him and he laughed as he pulled out his handkerchief and wiped his face and head. Later he

PAGE TWO, COL. TWO

THE WORLD LAST NIGHT

MESSAGES from Daily Express correspondents abroad reached last night :—

Madrid : War Flames

D. Sefton Delmer, telephoning from Madrid after midnight, said: "The city is resounding to the thunder of the strongest night attack yet."

Story on Page Two.

Rome : Duce Trots

Mussolini led 400 MPs at a running trot through Rome to his office in the Palazzo Venezia after a meeting of the Italian Parliament. Announced: Training mobilisation of half of the 1914 air force class.

Vienna—No Pact

Chancellor Schuschnigg bluntly told Hungarian Regent Admiral Horthy at the end of a two-day State visit to Vienna that Austria would not join the German-Japan anti-Communist pact.

Reason: It might create bad feeling in France and Britain.

U.S.A. : Shun Europe

President Roosevelt revealed his speech for the Pan - American Conference at Buenos Aires today. He aims to withdraw from Europe's troubles by setting up an inter-American court of justice.

Story on Page Seven.

Page 10— They called it a white elephant in glass.

Page 11— Pictures of the Duke of Kent watching the fire.

Page 20— More vivid pictures of the scenes.

£6,000 NETTED BY 8-1 HORSE

Daily Express Staff Reporter

BACKERS who sent last-minute telegrams from post offices all over the midlands and Home Counties brought off another great starting-price racing coup yesterday.

The horse they backed was Royal Pilgrim, owned by Mrs James Field [formerly Miss Audrey James, younger daughter of Mrs Willie James, famous Edwardian hostess, then Mrs Dudley Coats, then Mrs Marshall Field], and trained by Mr Harry Brown, the King's trainer.

The race was the Buckfield Selling Handicap Hurdle of 4/156, run at Birmingham at 1.30 p.m.

Royal Pilgrim last won at Cardiff in 1934, and Mrs Field, "fed up with paying his training bills," herself backed him for only £25 and instructed the trainer to sell him.

The stable had only £100 on the horse.

He won by three lengths at 8—1, and it is estimated that the total of

PAGE TWO, COL. SIX

JIM RACING TIME

JIM McMILLION and his co-pilot, Edouard Corneillon-Molliner, planning to reach Kisumu, Kenya Colony, from Khartoum by six o'clock this morning, must make an all-day 2,000-mile dash at well over 200 mph if they are to keep to their schedule and reach the Cape by this evening.

The Dorothy had averaged only about 180 mph when she reached Cairo from Tunis at 3.36 GMT yesterday morning.

There Jim said : "It's been beastly so far. For 45 minutes we circled Alexandria in the dark before I remembered that Cairo had promised flares for us. We got down here.

with just enough petrol left, about five gallons."

A little sleep and the fliers were following allegations made during the Khartoum.

It took them nearly 13 hours. Jim has won't the resource after-day, and began drafting their report.

B.B.C. Inquiry Asks For More Evidence

Daily Express Political Correspondent

More evidence is to be heard on Thursday by the special board of inquiry set up by the Prime Minister to investigate allegations made during the "Talking Mongoose" case yesterday.

Members of the board met Wednesday, and began drafting their report but found that clarification of certain points was necessary.

Left *The shutters click as Crystal Palace burns. Some of the most arresting photographs ever taken resulted from this event.*

Right *Beaverbrook was always eager to impress his public with the success of his newspaper empire. This announcement was quite typical of the sort of trumpet-blowing which appealed to him.*

Overleaf *The death of George V ushers in the short reign of Edward VIII.*

Pages 61 and 62 *The Abdication Crisis looms. Beaverbrook became engrossed in the hidden intrigues but his support of Edward VIII did nothing in the long term to endear him to the royal family. This was the start of a rift which would affect the* Express *for many years.*

the *New York Journal* and the originator of the news was William Randolph Hearst, the American newspaper magnate, who had recently been a visitor of the King's at Fort Belvedere. The *Journal*'s allegation was quite clear: 'Within a few days Mrs Ernest Simpson of Baltimore, USA, will obtain her divorce decree in England, and some eight months thereafter she will be married to Edward VIII, King of England . . .'.

The British Press was in considerable difficulty over such rumours. They knew as well as their American counterparts that the King had taken Mrs Simpson for a cruise on his yacht but, in the mid-1930s, there was enormous pressure on the newspapers not to delve into the private life of the royal family. Chris played for time by showing a picture of the King but cutting out Mrs Simpson.

Daily Express

No. 11,134   TUESDAY, JANUARY 21, 1936   ONE PENNY

DEATH OF THE KING

THE KING IS DEAD—   —LONG LIVE THE KING

KING GEORGE THE FIFTH

The Queen And The Prince At His Bedside

"THE KING'S LIFE MOVED PEACEFULLY TOWARDS ITS CLOSE": THE LAST BULLETIN

Illness That Began At Christmas

WITH deep regret the Daily Express announces the death last night of his Majesty George the Fifth, by the Grace of God, King of Great Britain and Ireland, and of the British Dominions beyond the Seas, Defender of the Faith, Emperor of India, in the seventy-first year of his life and the twenty-sixth year of his reign.

The King died at Sandringham House, his country home in Norfolk, where he and the Queen had been staying since December 21, and where the Royal Family Christmas party was held.

At 9.25 last night this bulletin was issued : "The King's life is moving peacefully towards its close." Then, later, came news of the end.

The Queen was with the King when he died. With her at Sandringham to console her in her great sorrow are her sons, the Prince of Wales, the Duke of York, the Duke of Kent, and her daughter, the Princess Royal.

The Prince of Wales and the Duke of York flew back to Sandringham yesterday from London. On Sunday night they had conferred with the Prime Minister, Mr. Stanley Baldwin, and it was decided to set up a Council of State to take over the King's State duties.

That Council was set up yesterday morning. The Privy Council met in a sitting-room adjoining the King's bedroom. While the meeting lasted the door of the King's room was wide open, so that, in accordance with constitutional precedent, the Council was held in the presence of the King. The King was propped up in bed with pillows.

Then, the meeting over, Lord Dawson of Penn, the royal doctor, took to the King the paper setting up the Council of State. He handed the King a pen, and the King signed, "George R.I."

The King had not been well since Christmas Day. After his address to the Empire on the radio he had to keep to his room.

First public indication of the illness was given last Friday morning. It was announced that the King had a cold, and was remaining indoors.

In the evening came graver news : a bulletin which said that he was suffering from bronchial catarrh, accompanied by heart weakness which gave cause for "some disquiet."

On Saturday the bulletin said that the cardiac weakness and the embarrassment of the circulation had slightly increased and gave cause for anxiety.

On Sunday the King passed a quiet day. Last night a grave announcement was made: "The King's strength is diminished."

Three doctors and three nurses, at his bedside almost constantly since the illness began, did all that they could do. In vain. The King became unconscious; passed from unconsciousness to death.

So passed a great King, a great man.

—LONG LIVE THE KING

KING EDWARD THE EIGHTH

THE PRINCE OF WALES RULES AT THE AGE OF 41

HIS ROYAL HIGHNESS EDWARD ALBERT CHRISTIAN GEORGE ANDREW PATRICK DAVID, PRINCE OF WALES AND EARL OF CHESTER, BECOMES KING EDWARD THE EIGHTH AT THE AGE OF FORTY-ONE.

He is the first bachelor King of England since George the Third, who ascended the throne in 1760 and married a year later.

King Edward the Eighth is better known to his people at home and over the seas than any monarch has ever been.

He has journeyed to almost every part of the Empire as Prince and as Ambassador.

He has shared the sorrows and the joys of the nation in war and in peace. He is loved as a comrade; he is loved as a Prince among men.

He ascends the throne at once, but his Coronation, in accordance with precedent, will probably not take place for another twelve months.

King George became King on May 6, 1910, and was crowned on June 22 in the following year.

Little Princess Is Now Second In Line To Throne

NINE - YEAR - OLD PRINCESS ELIZABETH, ELDER DAUGHTER OF THE DUKE AND DUCHESS OF YORK, IS NOW SECOND IN THE LINE OF SUCCESSION TO THE THRONE. ONE DAY SHE MAY BE QUEEN ELIZABETH OF ENGLAND.

Now that the Prince becomes King the line of succession is:—

First: Duke of York.
Second: Princess Elizabeth.
Third: Princess Margaret Rose.
Fourth: Duke of Gloucester.
Fifth: Duke of Kent.
Sixth: Infant Prince Edward, son of the Duke and Duchess of Kent.
Seventh: Princess Royal.
Eighth: Viscount Lascelles.

After these comes the Hon. Gerald Lascelles, younger son of the Princess Royal and the Earl of Harewood.

It was laid down in the Act of Settlement that an elder brother's child is preferred in the succession to a younger brother.

That is why Princess Elizabeth stands in front of her uncles, the Dukes of Gloucester and Kent, and her aunt, the Princess Royal.

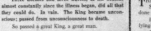

PRINCESS ELIZABETH

IF KING MARRIED

It was by reason of this provision that Queen Victoria ascended the Throne in 1837 instead of the Duke of Cumberland, who was the eldest surviving brother of the dead King William IV.

Various circumstances may affect Princess Elizabeth's position.

The birth of a son to the Duke and Duchess of York would place her one back in the line. She would always be behind any brothers she might have just as the Princess Royal ranks behind all her brothers, although they are younger than she is.

A royal marriage made by the new King might influence the whole order of succession.

Any princes or princesses of whom the Prince of Wales was the father would rank precedence of the Duke and Duchess of York and their children.

Only thus exception of England from the grave danger of the Confusion to the present day have remained unrecorded testament that no elder brother's child Elizabeth is the outstanding.

Edward V. was murdered in the Tower at the age of thirteen, and Edward VI. died aged sixteen. William II. lived to the age of forty-three, and never married.

Silence On The Air Today

The Stock Exchange will be closed today. Lombard-street and Mincing-lane will be without their usual bustle.

There will be no normal broadcast by the B.B.C. today.

The transmitters will be silent for twenty-four hours except for the repetition at intervals of the announcement of the King's death. Other announcements in the interest of safety, such as gale warnings, will be broadcast if necessary.

The B.B.C. will resume broadcasting tomorrow with the morning service.

Theatres are expected to close tonight. This action is voluntary. When King Edward died West End managers agreed to keep theatres closed until after the funeral, but they were reopened by order of King George.

"DECENT MOURNING"

ON the death of King Edward VII. in 1910 the Duke of Norfolk, Earl Marshal, gave notice that the public were expected " to put themselves into decent mourning." A similar announcement may be expected today.

Mourning for men consists of a black tie and/or a black armlet. Women may wear black, black and white, grey or mauve.

Lying-in-State In Westminster Hall

THE body of King George will be brought from Sandringham to London by road. This will be done privately.

It will be taken to Westminster Hall for the lying-in-state.

By day and by night Yeomen of the Guard and Gentlemen at Arms will keep watch over the body. It will be draped in Coronation robes, the Royal Standard and the Union Jack, surmounted by the Coronation Crown, Orb and Sceptre.

The burial will take place at Windsor, in the vaults beneath where lie Henry VIII. and Charles I. and King Edward VII.

The proclamation of the new King by heralds will take place today immediately after he has taken his oath at the first Privy Council.

LATEST NEWS
Telephone : Central 8000

Daily Express

TODAY'S WEATHER: FOG   RADIO PROGRAMMES: PAGE 23.

No. 11,411   THURSDAY, DECEMBER 10, 1936   ONE PENNY

CABINET SUMMONED IN PREMIER'S ROOM LAST NIGHT: DEFINITE DECISION TO BE ANNOUNCED TODAY

ABDICATION IS FEARED

QUEEN MARY SEES HER SON AT WINDSOR

Message From Fort Belvedere Read To Cabinet

DOUBLE POLICE FORCE ON DUTY IN LONDON TODAY

HISTORIC DRAMA IN PARLIAMENT

A COMMUNICATION FROM THE KING WAS READ TO A SPECIAL MEETING OF THE CABINET CALLED SUDDENLY AT THE HOUSE OF COMMONS LAST NIGHT. IT WILL BE ON THE BASIS OF THIS THAT MR. BALDWIN WILL MAKE A DEFINITE AND CONCLUSIVE STATEMENT TO PARLIAMENT ON THE CONSTITUTIONAL ISSUE THIS AFTERNOON ABOUT 3.15.

The turn that events took yesterday means that the question of the King's abdication can no longer be ruled out, as seemed likely two days ago, when Mrs. Simpson's message that she was willing to withdraw from "a situation that had been rendered both unhappy and untenable" was issued.

IT WAS FEARED, INDEED, THAT ABDICATION IS ALMOST INEVITABLE.

If the King, unhappily, should decide to abdicate the Throne, it is understood that he will retain the revenues of the Duchies of Cornwall and Lancaster, which amount to £113,000 net annually, as well as other revenues which are the inherent property of the Prince of Wales.

Mr. Baldwin's statement in Parliament today will cover the whole position, giving the facts leading up to the decision he will announce, and any resulting steps. If, as expected in the Lobbies, it is necessary to consider legislation concerning the Throne, both Houses will be asked to pass immediately a measure naming the new King, settling the further succession, and allocating revenues to the outgoing monarch. All other business would be swept aside for the present; Parliament might even have a Saturday sitting.

King Edward's assent would be necessary to make the Bill an Act of Parliament. This would be his last official act as King: as soon as the assent had been signified in the House of Lords he would cease to be Sovereign. His successor would be proclaimed next week.

LEGISLATION AT ONCE

All legal formalities that may be necessary have now been completed, and party leaders who were consulted last night agreed that there should be no delay in passing any legislation that may be brought forward. No meeting of the Cabinet has been summoned for today, but Mr. Baldwin will see his leading Ministers before he speaks.

It is expected King Edward will send a message to both Houses of Parliament, but is not yet certain that it will be delivered today. If King Edward abdicates, all M.P.s and peers will be resworn immediately after the new monarch has been proclaimed.

In the Lobbies last night there was keen satisfaction, writes the Daily Express political correspondent, that the King has avoided precipitating a constitutional crisis. He has, up to the present, only signified his wish for the guidance of the Cabinet on his marriage plan. Not until he rejected their formal advice would a constitutional crisis arise.

The Cabinet have formally advised him on only one

☞ PAGE TWO, COLUMN ONE

THE PRIME MINISTER LEAVING DOWNING-STREET FOR THE HOUSE OF COMMONS AFTER YESTERDAY'S EARLIER CABINET MEETING.

THE KING KEEPS SECRET RENDEZVOUS

IT was revealed in the Court Circular last night that Queen Mary visited the King yesterday, leaving London shortly after luncheon. Every precaution was taken to ensure the secrecy of her visit; only a few of those closest to her at Marlborough House knew of it.

She was accompanied by the Princess Royal and the Earl of Athlone. Mother and son had not met since last Thursday night, when the king went to Marlborough House from Buckingham Palace before going to Fort Belvedere.

The meeting of the King and Queen Mary took place in the presence of the Duke of York and the Duke of Kent, at Royal Lodge, the Windsor home of the Duke and Duchess of York. The lodge, which is in the middle of the Great Park, was hidden by thick fog, and it was only with difficulty that the royal cars found their way through the gloom.

Queen Mary was the first to arrive at 2.15. The Dukes of York and Gloucester followed immediately. The Duke of Kent came in his own black car. The King, who had not left Fort Belvedere for six days, drove to the lodge by the private road by way of Virginia Water.

THE BRIDLE PATH

An old bridle path leads from the Fort, running under the main Ascot road. It is about fifteen to twenty yards long and is wide enough to take a motor-car. The path emerges at the side of Virginia Water, then joins the private road through Windsor Great Park.

No turn Royal Family reunion had taken place since the death of King George. It lasted two hours. Police patrolled all entrances to the Lodge.

At the end of the meeting the King said good-bye to his mother, and, driven by Ladbrook, his first chauffeur, returned to Fort Belvedere, an entirely as he had left.

The Duke of York arrived at his home, 145, Piccadilly, at nine o'clock last night. He looked pale and worn. The Duchess and his two daughters were awaiting him.

PEACE PLAN FOR SPAIN

BRITAIN and France have jointly asked Germany, Italy, Portugal and Russia to join them in an endeavour to end the Spanish civil war. . . . . PAGE THIRTEEN.

. . . . PAGE THIRTEEN.

Fourteen people were killed, three injured, three houses set on fire when a Royal Dutch air liner crashed soon after leaving Croydon yesterday. . . . . PAGE FIVE.

LUGGAGE LEAVES THE FORT

AT eleven o'clock last night the shooting brake used as a conveyance for royal luggage drove at speed down the main drive of Fort Belvedere and on to the London road. It had baggage in the back.

About 9.30 one of the King's motor-cars, driven by Wagstaffe, his second chauffeur, left Buckingham Palace with parcels and suitcases.

Half an hour later the same car, empty, left the Palace by the same exit. It returned at 10.10.

Mrs. Simpson giving up her London home . . . . Page 2.
When a monarch abdicates . . Page 2.
The Empire awaits news . . Page 4.
Revenues of the Duchies . . Page 4.

TODAY'S WEATHER: UNSETTLED

Daily Express

FOUNDED BY LORD BEAVERBROOK

NORTHERN EDITION

NO. 11,412   FRIDAY, DECEMBER 11, 1936   ONE PENNY

The King Abdicates: Duke Of York On The Throne:
Baldwin Tells Commons The Whole Sad Story

KING GEORGE THE SIXTH
To Be Crowned On May 12—In Place Of Brother

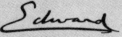

LATE NEWS

THE eighth King Edward of England, who is 42, renounces the throne and becomes plain Mr Windsor.

His abdication was announced yesterday in a message to Parliament in which he said :—

" After long and anxious consideration I have determined to renounce the Throne . . . and I am now communicating this, my final and irrevocable decision . . .

The message is given in full on Page Two.   The Abdication Bill, which gives effect to King Edward's decision, is on Page Six.

DUKE OF YORK, who is 41 on Monday, and is the second son of King George and Queen Mary, will be proclaimed King tomorrow. He will most probably take the title King George VI—his full name is Albert Frederick Arthur George.

His accession makes the Duchess of York Queen, and 10-year-old Princess Elizabeth the Heir Presumptive to the Throne.

The life story of the Duke and Duchess is told on Page Eight; whole page of pictures Page Eighteen.

MR WINDSOR
TO BROADCAST AT 10 TONIGHT
Exile Tomorrow

Fifteen other pages tell the story of yesterday's drama. Highlights are:

Page 7—Scenes from the ten months' reign.

Begins on Page 3—Full report of the Commons drama.

Page 9—Firms count Coronation trade losses.

Page 12—Love Story that will be told for ever.

King Phones
Mrs Simpson

Daily Express Staff Reporter

CANNES, Thursday,

MRS SIMPSON heard of the King's intention to abdicate several hours before it was known in London. The telephone rang in the villa. Lord Brownlow answered it.

" The King, madam."

Mrs Simpson went to the 'phone. As she answered quietly in monosyllables her eyes filled with tears. The conversation went on for 20 minutes. Tears rolled down her face.

" Yes" and " No" was all Lord Brownlow and Mr and Mrs Herman Rogers heard.

She hung up the receiver, gave no explanation, said nothing, but for some time sat quietly waiting in the corner of the armchair.

Every one in the house knew that the King had spoken to her.

ATE NOTHING

All day she had been silent and tearful, eating nothing, smoking rapidly, unable to read.

"I, EDWARD VIII of Great Britain, Ireland and the British Dominions beyond the Seas, King, Emperor of India, do hereby declare my irrevocable determination to renounce the Throne for myself and for my descendants, and my desire that effect should be given to this instrument of abdication immediately.

"In token whereof I have hereunto set my hand this tenth day of December Nineteen Hundred and Thirty-Six, in the presence of the witnesses whose signatures are subscribed—EDWARD R.I."

Sitting at his study desk in his country home, Fort Belvedere, with his three brothers—the Duke of York, the Duke of Gloucester, and the Duke of Kent by his side—King Edward at ten o'clock yesterday morning signed this " instrument of abdication" which later was read in every Parliament of the British Empire.

At that moment in the silent house where, in the words of the message which accompanied the announcement of his decision, he had spent so many days of " long and anxious consideration " the flag of the Duchy of Cornwall flying from the battlements was lowered from the masthead.

With a stroke of the pen Edward Albert Christian George Andrew Patrick David had resigned his many titles and dignities to his brother, Albert Frederick Arthur George, Duke of York, and became plain " Mr Windsor."

ON THE RADIO AS A "PRIVATE PERSON"

The shortest reign—325 days—in 453 years of England's history has been ended by the first of the Kings to give up his Throne voluntarily. The Act of Abdication, as passed by both Houses of Parliament today, will be taken to Fort Belvedere for King Edward to sign this evening.

That will be his last act as Monarch.

The BBC announced last night that it was King Edward's desire, immediately he ceased to be King, to broadcast " as a private person owing allegiance to the new King." The broadcast has been fixed for about 10 o'clock tonight. He may broadcast from Sunningdale. His

PAGE TWO, COLUMN ONE

THE NEW KING motoring to his home in Piccadilly at midnight
'Daily Express' picture.

MULTITUDE CHEER THE
NEW KING

WHEN the new King returned from Fort Belvedere to his Piccadilly home late last night he was greeted by a multitude which completely blocked the road. As his car drove into the forecourt cheer after cheer was raised, and there were shouts of " We want the King."

After the new King had stepped from his car he turned to the crowd and raised his hat several times.

Motorists " saluted " by continuously sounding their hooters.

After the new King had gone into his home a thud in the crowd started the song the National Anthem. Immediately hundreds of people took it up.

Men and women climbed the railings round the house and all other points to try to catch a glimpse of the King.

A few minutes after midnight the new King went to see his mother at Marlborough House.

As the new King entered at Marlborough House the scene was one of tense excitement. Queen Mary's detective was on duty at the gate.

Thinking
Cheerfully

Naturally if there were to be any decent intrigue the Beaver would want to be part of it and it was not long before he was seen scurrying between the palace and Fort Belvedere. However, Chris had to tread carefully with his boss. If he waited for news of Beaverbrook's missions to be cabled to America he could then quote reports put out by the American International News Service, but he could not appear to be including the news in the *Express* as soon as it became available here.

Chris' task became no easier when the Beaver took a stance as a firm supporter of the King, in spite of the fact that the public were largely unsympathetic to Mrs Simpson. Although Beaverbrook had never had much time for the monarchy, and had personal reasons to dislike the previous King who had tried to block the granting of the Beaver's peerage, here was an occasion on which his passions were wholly on the side of the lovers. For what Beaverbrook loved above all else was a chance to give the establishment a good kick in the pants. Respectable opinion was against the King marrying a divorced woman, therefore Beaverbrook would be for it. What is more, the woman in question was no society belle but an American which, as far as the Beaver was concerned, at least on this occasion, was almost as good as being a Canadian.

To give some idea of just what difficulties faced the Press at this time, Chris recorded in his memoirs that, whilst talking to Herbert Wilcox, the film director, about a forthcoming film biography of Queen Victoria, he was informed that it had only very recently become possible to make such a film. Previously the Lord Chamberlain would not have permitted the portrayal of the private life of a monarch. Ironically the ban had been lifted by none other than Edward VIII!

Eventually Mrs Simpson issued a statement that she was willing 'to withdraw from a situation which has been rendered both unhappy and untenable'. Chris saw this as the solution. He told the Beaver that it could be a way out for the King and he was not put off by Beaverbrook's reply: 'You are entitled to take that view—if that is your view'. Accordingly the *Express* went ahead and published a splash headline: 'END OF CRISIS'. It was not. As is now well known the King finally decided to abdicate rather than lose the woman he loved. Beaverbrook told Chris sourly: 'How often have I said that you should not prophecy for tomorrow, only for six months hence!'

Chapter 7

No war this year, or next year either

Optimism has been, quite intentionally, a keynote of the *Express* throughout its history. It sprang from Beaverbrook's own enormous and unconquerable energy which drove his employees and himself ever onwards and upwards. Defeat, depression and despair were not words which played any part in the Beaverbrookian vocabulary. He was devoted to the ideal of a Britain which was the hub of a mighty empire, sitting in splendid isolation from the troubles which beset less fortunate nations. Within Great Britain he advocated high wages, unbridled free enterprise and an end to the class system which dictated a man's future purely on the facts of his birth. However, this forward-looking attitude could get both himself and his newspapers into trouble from time to time. We have already seen that the result of the Abdication Crisis was wrongly predicted in a burst of excessive optimism. That occurrence cannot be laid at the door of Beaverbrook since he was too close to the facts to be badly misled. But when it came to the prospect of a European war he was as unwilling as any of his staff to believe that such idiocy could be allowed to interfere with the growth of national prosperity.

In the period immediately prior to the Second World War the *Express* could boast that it had the world's largest daily sale of 2,329,000 copies. Its influence at that time was immense, for it was not then a paper devoted purely to the interests of the Tory middle class but had a readership which extended right through the social spectrum. As A.J.P. Taylor put it in his *English History*: 'The *Express* drew its readers impartially from every group—about a third of each of them. Beaverbrook, its Canadian proprietor, was not confined by the English social system and had the New World view that there was no difference between the rich and poor except that the rich had had more money. The *Daily Express* was what England would have been without her class system'.

Thus the Beaver was in an ideal position to push the view that Great Britain should not involve itself in the affairs of European states. He said: 'My sole and only object is to serve the public interest and advance the cause for which I stand—the united British Empire, strong, resolute and determined in the pursuit of peace'.

The *Express*, as always, reflected faithfully the views of its proprietor. In April 1938 it stated: 'It is impossible that the British Government should pledge us to

Opposite *The peace propaganda continues. As the Germans occupy Czechoslovakia, the* Express *determinedly follows a policy of isolation.*

Daily Express

WORLD'S LARGEST DAILY SALE

No. 11,971   Saturday, October 1, 1938   One Penny

Premier home, tells cheering crowd:

"IT IS PEACE IN OUR TIME, YOU MAY SLEEP QUIETLY"

Mussolini invites him for new talks in yacht next week

STEP BY STEP TO WORLD PEACE

LEANING OUT OF A WINDOW AT NO. 10 DOWNING-STREET LAST NIGHT THE PRIME MINISTER SAID TO A GREAT, CHEERING CROWD:—

"This is the second time in our history that there has come back from Germany to Downing-street peace with honour. I believe it is peace for our time. We thank you from the bottom of our hearts. And now I recommend you to go home and sleep quietly in your beds."

The Cabinet met later and approved the Munich pact.

By GUY EDEN
Daily Express Political Correspondent

SIGNOR MUSSOLINI, I understand, has invited Mr. Chamberlain to confer with him on various questions of interest to Britain and Italy.

Mr. Chamberlain intends to take a short holiday after he has met Parliament next week, and he will probably spend some of it yachting in the Mediterranean.

M. Daladier, the French Premier, is likely to join in the talks, some of which are expected to be held in the yacht.

The demobilisation of the German Army may be expected as soon as the peace plan is well under way.

ABLE TO RELAX

This will enable other countries, including Britain and France, to recall the precautionary measures taken in the last few days. The Government are anxious to resume mobilised men as soon as possible.

Parliament will not be asked to pass the many emergency measures already in the preparation of several Government departments.

Three were to have included a Bill to share all citizens of the Repeal of the State for any service consideration measures for the benefit of industry...

"We thank you from the bottom of our hearts."—Mr. Chamberlain at a window of No. 10.

'WE SHALL NEVER GO TO WAR AGAIN'

WHEN the Prime Minister landed at Heston he read out to the crowd this pact, which he and Herr Hitler had signed a few hours before in Munich.

"We, the German Fuehrer and Chancellor, and the British Prime Minister, have had a further meeting today and are agreed in recognising that the question of Anglo-German relations is of the first importance for the two countries and for Europe.

"We regard the agreement signed last night and the Anglo-German Naval Agreement as symbolic of the desire of our two peoples never to go to war with one another again.

"We are resolved that the method of consultation shall be the method adopted to deal with any other questions that may concern our two countries..."

Midnight German march in

BERLIN, Friday.

WELL-INFORMED German quarters announced tonight that the march of the German troops across the Czech frontier would begin at midnight. The troops are expected to enter the Sudeten zone north of Passau and Linz, in Upper Austria.

Already reports are coming in from the Belgian region of withdrawing eastward with anxieties faces...

The International Commission set up by the Four-Power Conference at Munich to supervise the taking over of Germany of the Sudetenland began deliberations at the German Foreign Office this evening.

AN HOUR LATE

Those present at the start of the Commission's meeting were the British Ambassador, Sir Nevile Henderson; the French representative, M. François-Poncet; the Italian Ambassador, Signor Bernardo Attolico, and Herr Weizsaecker, German Secretary of State.

The fifth member, Dr. Vojtech Mastny, Czecho-Slovak Minister in Berlin, arrived about an hour late, having only just landed at the Tempelhof Airport from Prague...

Wall-st. and London soar

Markets in Britain and America surged yesterday.

IN LONDON Czecho-Slovak bonds jumped 20 points to 86—a rise in two days of 43 points. German bonds jumped 11½ points to 88, and there a total jump for the two days of 21½ points. Shares reported more vigorous orders than at any time for the last two years.

ON WALL-STREET nearly all major stocks moved, with rises of up to eleven points.

Belgians 'demobbing'

BRUSSELS, Friday.—The Belgian Government decided today to put the Army on a peace footing again.—British United Press.

QUEEN MARY ILL

Laryngitis

THE following statement was issued from Marlborough House last night:—

"Queen Mary is suffering from an attack of laryngitis, and will be unable to fulfil her engagement at the West Herts Hospital, Hemel Hempstead, tomorrow.

"In consequence, the Duchess of Kent will lay the foundation stone of the children's ward and open the extension of the nurses' home on behalf of her Majesty."

Laryngitis is an inflammation of the larynx, or windpipe. It is usually produced by exposure to cold, either directly or through a catarrh, or by the inhalation of irritants, or the swallowing of very hot fluids.
Queen Mary is seventy-one years old.

'Terriers' go home from air raid duty

Demobilisation of Territorials of anti-aircraft and coast defence batteries, called up on Monday, began last night. Most of those in the London area returned home late last night.

The War Office announced: "A limited period of leave is being granted to personnel of the anti-aircraft and coast defence units of the Territorial Army.

"All equipment will remain in position with the necessary guards and sentries."

Murdered on birthday

SHANGHAI, Friday.—Tong Shao-Yi, first Prime Minister of the Chinese Republic, was murdered in his Shanghai home today—his seventieth birthday. Two men slashed him with axes.—Exchange.

Poles menace Czech peace

POLAND and Hungary, drawn by Germany into partnership last week to put pressure on Prague, forgotten by Hitler as soon as his own claims were settled, were looking hungrily across the frontier into Czecho-Slovakia last night.

In both these countries the man in the street had been led to believe that Polish and Hungarian minority areas in Czecho - Slovakia would be surrendered on the same day that Hitler marched into Sudetenland.

Now, under the Munich Peace Plan, they are told that they must wait three months before their demands are considered.

Poland, with an imposing military force on the Czech frontier, has sent a "virtual ultimatum" to Prague calling for an immediate reply.

"DANGEROUS"

Every effort was made in Warsaw last night to represent the situation to the Russian area which Poland claims as becoming "hourly more and more dangerous."

Through the Polish Government radio stations at 8 p.m. after a long conference between President Moscicki, Marshal Smigly-Rydz, Premier Slawoj-Skladkowski, and Foreign Minister Josef Beck, a message was sent off saying that "Poland is determined to settle the conflict with Czecho-Slovakia independently."

Should the Czech answer contain no agreement to immediate cession of the disputed territory the Polish Government will instantly...

➤➤ PAGE TWO, COL. FOUR

Cheered by 10,000 people: Mr. and Mrs. Chamberlain on the Palace balcony last night, the King on one side, the Queen on the other.

GET A DAILY EXPRESS
MODEL GLIDER
FOR THE CHILDREN

Special 5 a.m. Edition

Daily Express

FOUNDED BY LORD BEAVERBROOK

NORTHERN EDITION

BEAR BRAND'S *Slimming* Sy-metra TRUE FASHIONED Stockings

No. 11,970   Friday, September 30, 1938   One Penny

The Daily Express declares that Britain will not be involved in a European war this year, or next year either

Mussolini draws up frontier

PEACE

Commission to decide plebiscites

LATE NEWS
Phone: Manchester Central 1112.

AGREEMENT SIGNED AT 12-30 a.m. TODAY

German troops march in tomorrow: then occupation gradually until October 10

FRONTIER GUARANTEED

By SELKIRK PANTON

MUNICH, Friday morning

This is the issue which Beaverbrook and Christiansen never lived down. Even now other newspapers are not averse to referring to the infamous 'no war' headline.

fight to hold together the ramshackle state of Czechoslovakia'. However, this position did not come to Chris without some twinges of conscience. When Neville Chamberlain described Czechoslovakia as 'a far-away country' Christiansen had felt revulsion at such an attitude and had expressed his doubts to Beaverbrook. The Beaver merely said, 'Well, isn't Czechoslovakia a far-away country?' and Chris had been forced to admit that it was.

One of the criticisms which was levelled against Christiansen most often, and the one which hurt him most deeply, was that he always acted as the Beaver's lackey in political matters. He always maintained that since he was primarily a newspaperman and not a political animal, and since Beaverbrook was both a newspaperman *and* a political animal, it made sense to let the Beaver get on with the politics. Indeed, since on most issues their opinions coincided pretty closely, there was little reason for them ever to squabble.

What Chris was employed for was to produce a bright exciting paper which appealed to all tastes. He was far more concerned with the opinions of the famous 'man on the Rhyl promenade' than with political prognostication. According to Christiansen's description, the man from Rhyl must have been a difficult character to please. He did not know the difference between the Civil List and the Privy Purse, he did not like anything to appear in French in his newspaper, not even common phrases like *'bon mot'*, and he had no patience with foreign cooking or with any sort of sophistication not found in the vicinity of Rhyl. Chris had the task of interesting, amusing and informing this touchy and demanding customer, and, above all, ensuring that he went on buying the *Express*. His watch-word was, 'Mix it up. Cater for all tastes'. It is small wonder then that he had no time to bother about an impending world war.

Beaverbrook, on the other hand, was not constrained by the need to provide popular journalism for a mass audience, and he was a man with a deep interest in the political life of the country. Yet he would quite blatantly support political positions which were known to be unpopular. He advocated the return of the German colonies which had been taken from them in the First World War. He was against Zionism and the founding of a national homeland for the Jews. He was against the League of Nations. He was against chain stores and the Co-op, but in favour of small shopkeepers. What is more he was proud of the fact that, in spite of the unpopularity of these policies, people would still read the *Express*. He even burst into print with the above list of unpopular opinions and used it as evidence that his papers did not need to embrace safe, popular opinions in order to attain a huge daily sale.

Thus Beaverbrook was only too willing to state publicly his view that there should be no British involvement in the affairs of Europe. The *Express* was soon full of pronouncements on the issue and these were all to be raked up again after the conflict by the enemies of the Beaverbrook Press. Here is a selection which shows the tone of the paper and its proprietor at the time:

'I am a pacifist and no one more than I abhors the prospect of another war.' (June 2 1931.)

'The President [of the USA] has no power to involve the American people in European entanglements. The people will not have it. Any treaty involving US participation in a European war would not be ratified by Congress. The Monroe doctrine still prevails—and in the hearts of the American people.' (May 24 1933.)

'Mr Eden is attending the meeting of the League of Nations for the purpose of meddling in a dispute between two foreign countries. If we had never belonged to the League we would never have been involved in these concerns.' (July 30 1935.)

'Britain will not be involved in war. There will be no major war in Europe this year or next year. The Germans will not seize Czechoslovakia. So go about your business with confidence in the future and fear not . . ..' (May 23 1938.)

'Why all this gloom? You escaped war—if you were ever in danger of it—and you were happy for a day or two. Then you made yourselves miserable again by talking to one another about the dangers to come. The inevitable war. The destruction of London. And other nonsense. What is it all about? Is it anxiety about Germany? But Britain should not have any quarrel with Germany. There is no reason for a German to attack this country, and no possibility of it for a long time to come. (October 14 1938.)

'Many people will say that the Germans will make war on Britain, but I predict that it is peace . . ..' (December 12 1938.)

'I would not be out here if I did believe that war was imminent.' (Quebec, August 11 1939.)

On September 3 1939 Britain declared war on Germany.

Chapter 8

Rosenbloom's war

When war was finally declared it came as no great surprise. The announcement was, of course, made late on the morning of Sunday September 4 1939, so that the newspapers lost the drama of the event to the BBC's radio service. However, Monday's *Express* found plenty to talk about.

In the first place, a German U-boat had torpedoed the British liner *Athenia* with 1,470 people on board, many of them American college girls hastening home to avoid the troubles in Europe. The *Express* led with the story and lost no time in drawing suitable parallels between this atrocity and the *Lusitania* outrage of the previous war.

There were two other major stories on the front page. The first, which must have gladdened the heart of Beaverbrook, was that Churchill had been asked to become First Lord of the Admiralty. With typical brevity the *Express* told its readers: 'WINSTON BACK'. The second important piece of news was that the Navy had begun its blockade of Germany. The message 'Begin hostilities!' had been sent to the Fleet.

Across the top of the paper, lying incongruously between advertisements for Sure Shield Fruit Laxatives and Cremex Shampoo, ran the message: ' "We fight against evil things—brute force, bad faith, injustice, oppression and persecution—and against them I am certain that the right will prevail''—The Premier said'.

Inside the paper there was a strange mixture of war fervour and normality. Amid reports from Poland of the crowds cheering outside the British embassy, and an announcement that Australia, New Zealand and Canada were in the fight too, there were advertisements inviting readers to acquire an electric shaver for six shillings or a pocket watch for three shillings or even, height of extravagance, a vacuum cleaner for 59/6d.

William Hickey, the gossip columnist, had very mixed feelings. On the one hand he felt contrite because, right up to the last minute, he had refused to believe that war would break out. On the other hand, he was jubilant that he had just scored heavily over the journal, *Psychic News*. That learned paper had been claiming that spirit messages received by mediums, especially one claiming to have come from the ghost of Lord Haig, all made it quite clear that war would be avoided. Hickey had been referring to these prophecies with derision and there

Opposite *War is finally declared and the* Express *rises to the occasion in words and pictures.*

Daily Express

6 A.M. EDITION

WORLD'S LARGEST DAILY SALE

No. 12,258   Monday, September 4, 1939   One Penny

> "We fight against evil things—brute force, bad faith, injustice, oppression and persecution—and against them I am certain that the right will prevail."—*The Premier said. Then this news . . .*

U-BOAT TORPEDOES BRITISH LINER

100 American girls were on board

LAST MESSAGE: 'SINKING QUICKLY'

1,150 passengers

A GERMAN U-BOAT TORPEDOED AND SANK THE BRITISH LINER ATHENIA—WITH 1,470 PEOPLE ON BOARD, MOST OF THEM AMERICAN AND CANADIAN—A FEW HOURS AFTER THE START OF THE WAR YESTERDAY.

A hundred American college girls—hastening home from Europe and its troubles—were among the victims of this 1939 "Lusitania" outrage.

An Admiralty report at 5 a.m. said: "The last official information we have received from the Athenia is that the ship was sinking rapidly."

The Athenia was 200 miles west of the Hebrides when she was attacked.

She was a 13,581-ton liner, built in 1923 by the Fairfield Shipbuilding Company of Glasgow and owned by the Donaldson Line.

The crew she carried was 320. On this trip she carried 1,130 passengers—many more than her normal, because of the crisis rush from this side of the Atlantic to the other.

The Lusitania was torpedoed by a U-boat in May 1915, while she was off Queenstown, with a loss of 1,198 lives.

The Athenia left Glasgow at noon on Friday, bound for Montreal. She called at Belfast and Liverpool on the way. Many of the passengers should have sailed on other lines from Continental ports, but because of cancellations travelled to Glasgow to join the Athenia

SEPTEMBER 3 SUNDAY

● AT 11 O'CLOCK yesterday morning Britain declared that a state of war existed between this country and Germany.

Notification of the state of war was handed to the German Chargé d'Affaires in London at 11.15. This constituted a formal declaration of war

At 11.15, ninety minutes after the expiry of the time-limit laid down in the British ultimatum, von Ribbentrop invited the British Ambassador to call on him and gave him the German reply.

This was a refusal by the German Government to give any assurance about the withdrawal of troops.

The reply, it is officially stated, also included propaganda, the sole purpose of which seemed to be an attempt to lay the blame for the present war on Britain.

At 11.30 Sir Nevile Henderson demanded his passport.

● AT 5 O'CLOCK yesterday afternoon France declared that a state of war existed between France and Germany. France presented her ultimatum at midday.

(See Page Two.)

The King's message

For 15,000,000 homes

The King has consented to a copy of the message he broadcast at six o'clock last night being sent to every household in the country as a permanent record. It will be printed, and each will bear his signature in facsimile.

The message is on Page Seven.

HITLER GOES TO POLISH FRONT

BERLIN, Sunday.

HITLER left his Chancellery in Berlin this evening for the Eastern Front, where he is to assume command of the German Armies.

Four bodyguards were on the running board in the car.

In an appeal to the German Army on the Western Front earlier, Hitler said:—

"As an old soldier of the world war and as your supreme commander I am going, with confidence in you on the western front, to the eastern front.

"I trust that our eastern campaign can be brought to a conclusion in several weeks.

"Our honourable enemies will realise that they are now dealing with a different army from that of the year 1914."—British Press and Reuter.

WINSTON BACK

He is First Lord; Eden is the new Dominions Secretary

By GUY EDEN
Daily Express Political Correspondent

ONE of the first acts of the Prime Minister, as soon as Britain's declaration of war became effective yesterday, was to reconstitute the Government and to set up a War Cabinet of nine Ministers.

Mr. Winston Churchill enters the Cabinet as First Lord of the Admiralty—the post he held in 1911—and Lord Hankey, former chief of the Cabinet Secretariat, becomes a Minister without Portfolio. Both have seats in the War Cabinet.

Mr. Anthony Eden becomes Dominions Secretary, without a seat in the War Cabinet, but in order that he may be in the best position to maintain contact between the War Cabinet and the Dominions he will have special access to it.

The War Cabinet will be the supreme executive body responsible for the conduct of every aspect of the war. Its members, whose average age is sixty-one, are:—

PRIME MINISTER.
Mr. Winston Churchill.

CHANCELLOR OF THE EXCHEQUER,
Sir John Simon.

FOREIGN SECRETARY,
Lord Halifax.

MINISTER FOR CO-ORDINATION OF DEFENCE,
Lord Chatfield.

FIRST LORD OF THE ADMIRALTY,
Mr. Winston Churchill.

WAR MINISTER,
Mr. Hore-Belisha.

AIR MINISTER,
Sir Kingsley Wood.

LORD PRIVY SEAL,
Sir Samuel Hoare.

MINISTER WITHOUT PORTFOLIO
Lord Hankey.

Lord Stanhope, former First Lord of the Admiralty, becomes Lord President of the Council, and Sir Thomas Inskip, former Dominions Secretary, becomes Lord Chancellor.

Sir John Anderson, former Lord Privy Seal, becomes Home Secretary and Minister of Home Security.

It was announced last night that Sir Archibald Sinclair, leader of the Liberal Opposition, had declined an offer by the Prime Minister of a post in the Cabinet, on the ground that present circumstances the Liberals could give better service to the nation and the Government by supporting all necessary war measures from an independent position.

FLEET BEGIN THE BLOCKADE

BRITAIN'S Navy started the blockade of Germany last night. Two radiograms of one code word each put the whole Fleet on a war footing. The first proclaimed a state of tension; the second told each commander: "Begin hostilities!"

The Fleet in northern waters, and in the Atlantic are concerned with our first action at sea. There are no German warships in the Mediterranean at the moment at this time.

Before war was declared all ships using the Straits of Dover were warned that they must pass through the Downs—the eight-mile-wide roadstead between Deal and the Goodwin Sands.

Any ship disregarding this order does so at her peril. In the Downs all vessels will be examined. Those bound for Germany or carrying contraband will be stopped.

In the north waters all ships will be boarded in the open sea, which over the weather. Between 1914 and 1918 the twenty-two British blockading cruisers stopped 12,979 merchant steamers in the North Atlantic and missed only 642.

It is believed that some German submarines—not more than fifteen or eighteen—are already at sea. They will have to be hunted down.

From the Panama Canal some a Dutch steamer reports that four German U-boats are fuelling at yesterday.

American Envoy bombed

From SEFTON DELMER
Daily Express Staff Reporter
WARSAW, Sunday.

MR. DREXEL BIDDLE, United States Ambassador to Poland, escaped unhurt when a German bomb dropped near his country villa this morning.

He was in his bathroom, shaving when the bomb fell. His window was smashed, his shaving mirror was shattered and the razor was blown out of his hand.

That is why Mr. Biddle appeared unshaven this evening when addressing the cheering crowds who marched on to his embassy after calling on the British and French Embassies. Warsaw tonight is wild with joy.

► PAGE TWO, COLUMN THREE

Theatres, cinemas closed—may reopen

All places of entertainment are closed for the present. It may be possible to reopen cinemas and theatres later.

Day schools in evacuation and neutral areas are closed but at least those in the war of 1914-19.

► See Page Eleven

Curious, the Dutch colony off with our first action at sea. The convoy system for British merchant ships has already been reintroduced

Poland celebrated her first victory last night. At 18.45 p.m. Warsaw officials declared that the Polish Army had smashed a way into East Prussia and were now fighting on German soil.

The Poles are also reported to have defeated the German effort to drive across the Corridor and cut Poland from the sea.

After bitter fighting, the German have been driven from several towns. The Poles say they have broken through the German fortifications as far as the railway terminus of Deutsch Eylau, Zbaszyn, an important Polish centre, has been recaptured.

Berlin claims "advances on all fronts," but this only three border towns captured yesterday.

Midnight bulletins report extensive damage in confirmed air raids over Poland. Several towns are in flames. The Poles claim sixty-four aircraft shot down.

Banks close today

ALL banks, including the Post Office and all other savings banks will be closed today. BUT THEY WILL BE OPEN FOR BUSINESS AS USUAL TOMORROW.

There will be no money shortage.
Details on Page Eight.

Gort, V.C., will lead our troops

THE Government announced last night that Viscount Gort, V.C., will be Commander-in-Chief of the British Field Forces.

General Sir Edmund Ironside will be Chief of the Imperial General Staff and General Staff, and General Sir Walter Kirke Commander-in-Chief of the Home Forces.

Fifty-three-year-old Viscount "Tiger" Gort will thus take over the post held by Field-Marshal Lord Haig in the war of 1914-19.

General Gort was appointed Chief of the Imperial General Staff in December 1937 at thirty-six. He is the youngest man ever to hold the post.

The War Minister (Mr. Hore-Belisha) said: "This is a soldier of genius," and cut red tape to bring him into the highest place.

► PAGE TWO, COLUMN FIVE

had been some rather acrimonious exchanges between him and the editor. Now that war had broken out Hickey was able to tell his readers that, even though his own prophecies had been quite wrong, they were at least his own and had been made without spooky assistance.

Strube, the paper's cartoonist, responded to the crisis with a cartoon showing a massive British lion rousing itself to face Hitler and von Ribbentrop. The Fuehrer is complaining to his henchman, 'But you told me it was stuffed!'

Erich von Stroheim, who had for years been every cinema fan's idea of the brutal Hun, had just joined the Army, it was announced—the French Army. Apparently von Stroheim was an Austrian, not a German, and had for some years been in disfavour with the Nazis because of his unsympathetic portrayal of German officers.

There were paragraphs of advice on page 9 to tell readers what to do when the sirens sounded. Nearby, at the foot of the page, Rupert and Toby were busy consulting Captain Barnacle about how they might track down the sea serpent which had carried off Algy and Pug. There was trouble all round that day.

Finally, the back page was given over entirely to a feature called 'Photonews' in which policemen and ARP wardens were shown calmly and efficiently preparing the people for air raids. A Private with his kit bag on his shoulder gazes up at the Westminster clock tower. Herr Kordt, the German Chargé d'Affaires is shown shaking hands with his chauffeur as he enters his car and starts the journey home. General Ironside strides purposefully past the German Embassy, chewing on a cigar, on his way to take up his duties as Chief of the Imperial General Staff.

This was one of the last normal issues of the *Express* for many years to come. Paper rationing would soon reduce the paper's size dramatically from 12 pages by stages to a mere four during the worst days of the war and it would remain so for some considerable time. The effect of this would be to enhance the very intricate, dramatic and interesting layout which Christiansen had been at such pains to achieve. For, by 1939, the *Express* did not have 'the world's largest daily sale' by acccident. The paper had become a model of lively presentation, interesting writing and good pictures. It had achieved a formula which was extremely popular and which no other paper had been able to copy with anything like the same success. Stories were short and punchy or, where a longer treatment was called for, would be broken up with pictures or fractured into short, readable paragraphs. Headlines were crisp, catchy and invited the reader to explore further. It has been said, only half in jest, that in a Beaverbrook paper a paragraph consists of no more than six lines—it always begins with 'and' or 'but'. Certainly every effort was made to avoid the stilted English which had plagued the Press in the past. The *Express* wanted, more than anything else, to present a young, energetic and exciting image. If that involved giving some of the rules of grammar a tweak, then so be it.

Opposite *The evacuation of Dunkirk. By this time newspapers were suffering from a shortage of newsprint, but from the immaculate layout and interesting design you would never guess that anything was amiss.*

CREMEX SHAMPOO

BLACK-OUT
TO-NIGHT
UNTIL 4.21 A.M.

Daily Express

No. 12,467   Friday, May 31, 1940   One Penny

ENJOY THE LUXURY OF THIS FINE TOBACCO
MICK McQUAID

Through an inferno of bombs and shells the B.E.F. is crossing the Channel from Dunkirk—in history's strangest armada

TENS OF THOUSANDS SAFELY HOME ALREADY

Many more coming by day and night

SHIPS OF ALL SIZES DARE THE GERMAN GUNS

UNDER THE GUNS OF THE BRITISH FLEET, UNDER THE WINGS OF THE ROYAL AIR FORCE, A LARGE PROPORTION OF THE B.E.F. WHO FOR THREE DAYS HAD BEEN FIGHTING THEIR WAY BACK TO THE FLANDERS COAST, HAVE NOW BEEN BROUGHT SAFELY TO ENGLAND FROM DUNKIRK.

First to return were the wounded. An armada of ships—all sizes, all shapes—were used for crossing the Channel. The weather which helped Hitler's tanks to advance has since helped the British evacuation.

Cost to the Navy of carrying out, in an inferno of bombs and shells, one of the most magnificent operations in history has been three destroyers, some auxiliary craft, and a small steamer.

Cost to the enemy of the Fleet's intervention outside Dunkirk can be counted in the shattering of German advanced forces by naval guns and the survival to of thousands of British soldiers whom the Germans had hoped to capture or destroy.

THE NAVY CARRIES ON

"Ceaselessly, by day and by night . . . operations are continuing," said the Navy's communiqué last night.

Many more men than was expected have already been able to extricate themselves from the perilous position in which they were left by Belgium's king.

A midnight message from Paris brought dramatic news which suggested that the withdrawal was nearing its end:—

"Two divisions of General Prioux's army (who held the Flanders line between Dunkirk and Lille in a desperate rearguard action) have now reached the coast.

"By means of a furious tank battle they have blasted their way out of the German trap. The rest of their comrades are following."

GENERAL CAPTURED?

It is feared that General Prioux himself will not reach safety. He stayed to the last to safeguard the retreat and a German news agency message claims that he and his staff have been taken prisoners.

The armies, navies and air forces of Britain and France have fought as one unit in what military authorities consider the most perfectly executed rearguard action on record.

Casualties have been, heavy, so have losses of supplies and equipment, but German claims of losses inflicted are regarded in London as "fantastic."

German air losses on the other hand, have been great, mainly because of the reckless manner in which the assault on the withdrawing Allied forces has been conducted.

Fierce fighting continued last night on the flanks of the Allied withdrawal behind Dunkirk, where forty German infantry divisions and eight armoured columns—totalling 700,000 men—were flung against the remnants of the Allies' northern army.

But the unfold handling and courage of the Allies in Flanders bear on all sides and outnumbered by three to one, led French military experts to hope that at their men may fight their way to defendable positions on the coast.

There, supported by the heavy guns of the Navy, it is possible that they could check the Stukas, small hills and soft ground that surround the port.

Much of this ground is already fortified—it formed the northern end of the extension of the Maginot line.

HOLDING ON

British forces, helped by one or two French divisions, are believed today to be still holding the famous line of the Yser against German tanks which are attempting to batter their way through to Dunkirk.

The Germans are reported to have captured Cassel Hill (where Prioux's men held out) and are thrusting east for a line of small hills and ridges.

These mounts, which were roughly fortified with tunnels and dug-outs with high gun-down map view furnish good cover for the Allies.

Fighting flared on again last night on the Southern Front, between the Somme Yore guns British and French troops are fighting side by side.

It is believed in Paris that when the Flanders battle has died down the whole German war machine may suddenly be switched on to this front.

See Western Front despatch, Page Two.

How the Allies fought back to Dunkirk, aided by warships and planes. British troops held the left flank. French troops the right flank. Last rearguard action (see inset) fought by French under General Prioux on the hills between Cassel and Ypres.

Tired, dirty, hungry they came back —unbeatable

THREE DESTROYERS LOST
As Navy helps B.E.F.

THE Admiralty issued this communiqué last night:—

The Royal Navy has been and is giving all possible help and support to the British and French land forces which are operating in the vicinity of the French and Belgian coast under heavy enemy pressure.

Warships are giving supporting and covering fire to the troops, impeding the enemy's movements, and have inflicted considerable punishment upon the German advanced forces.

The wounded and a large number of other elements have already been safely withdrawn. These operations are being conducted ceaselessly, by day and night, with coolness and determination in the face of fierce opposition, particularly from the air.

The German High Command has claimed to have inflicted very large losses upon naval units and the transports which they protect. AS USUAL THESE BEAR NO RELATION TO THE FACTS.

Operations of this nature cannot be carried out without losses. The destroyers Grafton, Grenade and Wakeful and certain small auxiliary craft have been lost. Next-of-kin of casualties are being informed as details become available. One small transport, the Abukir (689 tons), has been sunk.

The spirit and conduct of all concerned are beyond all praise.

"J B.E.F. R.A.F. French and German communiqués, Page Two.

By HILDE MARCHANT
SOUTH-EAST COAST TOWN, Thursday Night.

THE Army is coming back from Belgium. It is a dirty, tired, hungry army. An army that has been shelled and bombed from three sides, and had to stagger backward into the sea to survive. An army that has been betrayed, but never defeated or dispirited.

There was a touch of glory about these returning men as I saw them tramping along a pier, still in formation, still with their rifles. For this army still had a grin on their oily, bloodied faces.

They were exhausted. They had not slept or eaten for days. Many tramped off in their stockinged feet. Others were in their shirt-sleeves.

Many had wounds. Many had torn uniforms, and their tin hats blasted open like a metal cabbage.

They saluted their officers, who stood with ragged mackintoshes and battered hats, and said "Thank you, sir." Then they fell to sleep.

Here was Belgium's betrayal. But here was no defeat. They had not lost their battle.

GLORIOUS SIGHT

Their eyes, bloodshot and half-closed, still mirrored the spirit and cause of their fight. That has not gone, nor can it be taken away.

How to start telling you of these men? It is the greatest and most glorious sight I have ever seen. They saw them line of all huddled up old tramp steamers, ships of all sorts, even barges in tow.

The ragged legs of transport had been ploughing backwards and forwards. Germans had chased them halfway over the Channel, and in their turn had been chased back.

Young crews volunteered for the job, and the older local skippers who has a the Bhausts matter-that the land. Without fear they went into the sea and bell on the other side.

CURTAIN OF FIRE

Sitting under the curtain of fire that hangs over the wrecked coast, they brought out our boys alive. The soldiers struggled out in the ships. Then, with fire on their tail, they crept out again and dashed for England.

The men came ashore in heaps, scarcely able to stand. They threw themselves on the harbour, and walked to the harbour gates.

I saw one man with a handkerchief tied over his head wound. Another with a torn trouser-leg soaked in blood. Another with his arm tied up to a scarf. There had been no time for bandages.

And as they came through the gates they were met by just one of three Navy cooks with tea and stew.

BACK PAGE, COLUMN THREE

Signposts to be removed

SIR JOHN REITH, Minister of Transport, announced last night that "Ighways authorities indications which would be of value to the enemy in case of invasion. The work was put in hand on Wednesday.

and did not come on deck from her stateroom, although several officials wished to see her.

50,000 car radios to be removed

FIFTY THOUSAND radio sets, now installed in motor-cars in Great Britain, will have to be dismantled soon and removed.

"No person shall use or have to his possession or under his control any radio receiving apparatus installed in any road vehicle."

The carrying of portable radio sets in cars is also forbidden. For the purposes of this regulation a radio set is deemed to be installed even if it is not fixed in position, if, in circumstances in which it can be readily adapted for use.

The exact date on which car radios must be dismantled is not definite at but is not definite at

Seven Germans —in London ARP

Councillor H. E. Arnhold, chairman of Hampstead N.W. Emergency Committee for Civil Defence, said at a meeting of Hampstead Borough Council last night that seven Germans or Austrians were A.R.P. wardens in the borough, that four Germans were air raid shelter marshals, and that a sixteen-year-old German girl was a canteen worker.

The question of their dismissal, he said, was being considered.

Half-term holiday cut

Boarding school children who are usually given a half-term holiday so that they can get home will be discouraged from doing so. The Government has asked preferably hopes that schools will dispense with this holiday this year.

BOMB FEAR STARTS EVACUATION AGAIN

IT was announced last night that the Government had decided to ask parents in all evacuation areas—in Scotland as well as England—who wish their children to be evacuated to register them before the schools close on Monday afternoon.

It may be necessary, the Ministry of Health say, to start during next week the evacuation of schoolchildren from some of the evacuation areas. In addition to the nineteen east and south-east coast towns which children will leave on Sunday.

A Belgian Cabinet meeting held in France yesterday passed a decree saying: "Up view of the fact that the King is in the power of the invader, we declare, in the name of the people, that it is impossible for him to reign."

An appeal to parents to register their children.

In Parliament yesterday Mr. Cann (Soc. Broxtowe) asked whether all central roads covering British cars were being searched for convoys troops by Victor Warrender Financial secretary to the Admiralty, replied: Yes, sir, all neutral vessels entering in which have recently entered, British ports are being subjected to thorough search.

BELGIAN TROOPS FIGHT ON

UNITS of Belgian troops, despite Leopold's "cease fire" order, are still fighting side by side with the Allies. It was officially announced by the Belgian authorities in Paris last night.

A Belgian Cabinet meeting held in France yesterday passed a decree...

Hidden troops hunted in all British ports

Airways staff returning

ROME, Thursday.—British staffs of Imperial Airways depots in Italy today received orders from London headquarters to leave for home.

—Rome rushes home front defence, Page Eight.

FOOD TABLETS READY

Concentrated tablets of synthetic vitamins, similar to those issued to German troops, are being manufactured in Britain.

This was disclosed yesterday by Professor J. C. Drummond, scientific adviser to the Ministry of Food.

The output of the tablets could never equip the nation's larder, necessary, he said, if poorer people were unable to maintain adequate mixed dietary.

Swedish ship seized

The Swedish steamer Lorna 13,396 tons, was seized by the Germans at Bergen on May 24, says the Stockholm radio.

G.E.303-1

However, in wartime Chris and his team were to learn a new art—that of compression. By 1941 it would be normal to fit at least 30 items of news into a single page—any less and the editor would want to know the reason why!

Chris was to continue to edit the *Express* throughout the war years. As a man in his early 30s he was not likely to be amongst the first called up in any case and, as the editor of a national newspaper, his job was of great importance in keeping up morale amongst the civilian population. What is more, the war had hardly started when he fell during the black-out and broke his leg in five places. Even so, he continued to oversee his paper from the select surroundings of Miss Ellis's Nursing Home, where members of his staff smuggled liquid refreshment to him to help keep the creative juices flowing.

Beaverbrook spent the early days of the war in a filthy mood. He stomped around muttering about the 'Unnecessary War' and prophesying that no good could possibly come of getting the Empire mixed up in the squabbles of Europe. However, it would not be long before Churchill would find his old friend something to keep him occupied during wartime.

Several other *Express* men went missing for the duration. Sefton Delmer, who had long ago made a name for himself as an expert on Germany, was now asked by the Government to take part in the broadcasting of black propaganda to the Germans. With his knowledge of the country and the language he was a natural choice and a most effective counter to Lord Haw Haw. A couple of other journalists from the paper had already been taken prisoner. Giles Romilly, who was Churchill's nephew, was captured at Narvik and Selkirk Panton, who had covered Berlin for the paper but had moved to Copenhagen when hostilities started, failed to escape from Denmark when the Germans overran it. Others were called up and posted off all over the place—the paper would have to manage as best it could without them.

Of course, there were consolations. A war may not be much fun, but it is without doubt an exceptionally fine way of selling newspapers. The daily paper, a pleasant but inessential part of life in peacetime, suddenly becomes of vital interest when war is declared. But Chris was faced with keeping the paper going with limited resources, an absent proprietor and a much reduced staff.

In retrospect it was none of these things which he complained about during the war's early days. The thing he minded most was his own failure to grasp the way in which the conflict would develop. He was, in his own phrase, Maginot-minded. This was a reference to the supposedly impassable Maginot line which the Germans had so neatly circumvented during the First World War. To be Maginot-minded meant to have old-fashioned notions about the war. It was an attitude which was forgivable in the general population but should have been avoided in a newspaper.

If the natural difficulties were not sufficient, there was to be the added problem of censorship. In the official panic which followed the start of the war everything suddenly became secret. Of course, there were very good reasons why certain information should have been kept out of the papers. The problem was that the bureaucrats would have liked to have kept almost everything quiet and that would have made for some very dull journalism. During the early days things got to such a pitch that even the heading 'BRITISH TROOPS IN FRANCE' was deemed to be too revealing and was promptly censored. Then minds were changed and the ban was lifted. It was all very trying.

However, there was still room for a little humour. It was discovered that German propaganda was insisting that the editor of the *Daily Express* was a Jew called Rosenbloom and that he had been marked down for personal attention when the Germans arrived in London. The Dane called Christiansen got on with his job.

It must have come as an intense relief to Chris when the old man was asked to join the War Cabinet as Minister of Aircraft Production. It certainly was a sure way to keep him from complaining about the war. At last he was given something important on which he could lavish all his superhuman energy and formidable organisational ability. A.J.P. Taylor made the point that, had it not been for that job, Beaverbrook would have been quite forgotten except as a newspaper proprietor. It was to be, to use the old cliché, his finest hour.

However, if the politicians and civil servants thought that a Beaverbrook in office would be a tamer animal than a Beaverbrook in the wilderness, they were in for a huge shock. He ran his ministry exactly as though it were one of his businesses. He had a deep seated irreverence for top brass, whether military or civil, and took an almost childish delight in upsetting their applecart. The only exception to his rule was Sir Hugh Dowding, the Air Chief Marshal in charge of Fighter Command. He and the Beaver got on well. It was a case of the attraction

GILES SENDS THIS FROM HOLLAND

"Unsociable lot, these Germans, sir"

Although Strube was still alive and kicking it was the newcomer, Carl Giles, who was to rocket to stardom as the paper's war cartoonist.

GILES AT THE BATTLEFRONT

"This is a lovely way to spend an evening . . ."

of opposites; Dowding was quiet, reserved, introverted and Beaverbrook was, well, Beaverbrook!

The friendship with Dowding was soon to have political consequences for the Air Chief Marshal had a belief, regarded by many as eccentric, in the power of fighter aircraft. The orthodox view was that there was no acceptable, effective defence to the bomber so the only answer was to build as many bombers of our own as we could and then we and the Germans would pound each other flat until someone gave in. What this view lacked in elegance it made up for in simplicity.

The next source of irritation was the Air Ministry. It held the view that it alone was competent to decide how many aircraft, and of which type, should be produced. Beaverbrook begged to differ. He demanded to differ. He went to Churchill and got permission to differ. Now Beaverbrook was where he always liked to be—in charge. He even sent his subordinates round to the airfields to padlock all the aircraft storage units. The Air Ministry would now do as it was told. During the Battle of Britain Air Vice-Marshal Park would receive a 'phone call every evening. It would be Beaverbrook wanting to know how many aircraft he needed to replace.

Perhaps one of the most amusing of the Beaver's effects on the Civil Service was only discovered after he left. To quote Taylor's account: 'When on his departure the Treasury put the Ministry on a more regular footing, it found that more than half the typists were still being paid by the *Daily Express*. J.B. Wilson, the publicity officer of the Ministry, had been news editor of the *Daily Express*, from which he continued to draw his salary. Other *Express* men were taken off their journalistic work at a moment's notice to produce "data"—with a short "a"—or write appeals for higher production'.

There is no doubt that Beaverbrook had a decisive effect on the production of aircraft for the war effort. He put in an enormous amount of physical and mental effort himself and he spurred on others to do likewise. His gift for inspiring people to follow wherever he led was seldom better employed. However, he also made full use of his gift for drama and showmanship. He started the campaign to get householders to part with pots and pans from which Spitfires could be made. That effort produced 800 tons of metal, though it is said that it was later found to be unsuitable for the purpose. Also, as housewives were quick to see, the shops had no lack of *new* pots and pans, so why the need for their sacrifice? It was pure drama; everybody was given a chance to feel they were contributing something.

Seemingly more valuable was the Spitfire Fund, which had first been suggested by the *Jamaica Gleaner*. Contributions poured in but the problem was not a lack of money but rather a lack of production capacity. However, with Beaverbrook in full flood, and with his every effort being cheered on from the sidelines by the *Express*, the campaign appeared a formidable one.

Having Beaverbrook otherwise occupied left Chris free to get on with producing the paper in his own way. However, after all these years in the old man's shadow it was difficult to tell how much of the *Express* was produced by each of them. They had evolved a relationship so close that it resembled some form of symbiosis: it was even said that they were like the lion tamer and the lion but that nobody could tell which was which! No one at that time could have imagined that such a relationship would ever be broken.

However, the boss was not going to be the only one to have an exciting war. During the Blitz the chief sub-editor, Bill Knott, was returning to the *Express* building when he saw a parachute descending on Fleet Street. Being a veteran of the First World War he naturally assumed that what he saw was a paratrooper and he decided to capture him at once. Imagine his consternation when he rushed on his quarry only to discover that it was a land-mine. His fellow *Express* workers dismissed his story as mere drunken fantasy until they went outside and found the mine swinging from the telegraph wires some yards from the paper's front door. Because there was considerable danger of vibration from the paper's presses setting the mine off, police ordered that the *Express* should not be printed that

Above *Beaverbrook is found a job by Churchill and, to the vast relief of his staff, joins in the war which he had so hoped to prevent.*

Above *Read the headline. Now read it again, and again if necessary. Notice anything? Christiansen must have hauled some unfortunate sub-editor over the coals for that one!*

Beaverbrook takes control of aircraft production. This was to be the most important job he ever tackled and, although he did it in his own unorthodox manner, it was a very great success.

night. It was to be the only occasion in the entire war when the paper failed to reach its readers.

As the war dragged on one of the most impressive features of the *Express* was the way it maintained its superb presentation. Paper shortage had forced other papers to the most drastic measures—even to printing news in the 'gutter' between two pages. The *Express* would have none of this. The paper was packed with war news, home news, sport, humour and much more—but, with the Christiansen touch, it all looked as though it fitted together quite naturally, like a jig-saw puzzle. The content of the paper, too, remained of a very high standard. Chris was fortunate that several of his 'stars' were not required for war service. Osbert Lancaster, for example, though he was to be of great value to the Foreign Office in Greece at the end of the conflict, spent the majority of the war years keeping up morale with an endless flow of witty pocket cartoons—(Italian soldier showing off his medals, 'And this is the Gold Medal for Spaghetti, Milan International Exhibition, 1908'). Similarly Hickey and Beachcomber remained at their desks and maintained the continuity of the paper.

The individual events of the war need not concern us here. The most dramatic headlines can be found in the picture section. However, one event bears a mention. Among the material sent by *Express* readers and ex-employees during

Daily Express

No. 12,793   Tuesday, May 27, 1941   One Penny

THE NEWS in one minute →

BISMARCK is located and attacked by Fleet Air Arm bombers. Hit scored with torpedo. Warships and planes hunting with 'Sink her or slow her down' order. Daring operation by the Germans believed frustrated.

ROOSEVELT rewrites his speech for tonight, is expected in Washington to answer the warning to America by the Nazi Admiral Raeder that convoying of arms to Britain would be an act of war.

CRETE: Germans lose 11,000 men. R.A.F. make day and night attacks destroy 24 troop carriers, damage many more. Nazi light-weight tanks reported assembling at Maleme for eastward push across island.

BISMARCK TORPEDOED BY NAVY PLANE

LIKELY TO BE ATTACKED AGAIN AND AGAIN...

Warships and bombers still in 'hot pursuit'

ZIG-ZAGGING FOR HOME

THE great battle of naval tactics between the British Sea Lords, working in London, and Admiral Luetjens, in full retreat towards home waters aboard the giant German battleship Bismarck, neared its climax last night when the Admiralty issued at 11.30 this communiqué:—

"The chase of the Bismarck in the Atlantic has been hotly pursued. This evening torpedo bombers of the Fleet Air Arm scored a hit with a torpedo on the Bismarck. The hunt continues."

In the next 24 hours it may be decided whether the Navy can avenge the loss of the 42,000-ton battle-cruiser Hood, destroyed by the 35,000-ton Bismarck's fire on Saturday morning.

British warships have been pursuing the Bismarck and her squadron since that time.

All the forces that can be thrown into the action are being directed every hour of the day by our Naval Staff.

The Bismarck, with her speed of 30 knots, was first damaged in the engagement with Hood. On Sunday night the Admiralty announced that "at least one torpedo hit" from naval aircraft was scored, although it was not specified that the Bismarck was the ship.

THE BISMARCK: "Missing" from her lair five days ago. British staff work found her.

What the back room boys do to Berlin

By HENRY BUCKLEY

LISBON, Monday.

ONE of Britain's beautiful 'back-room' bombs which wrecked a railway station in Berlin, blew in all the windows and damaged many roofs within a half-mile radius. That is the news I received to-night from an American business man on his visit from Germany.

FIRE POWER

BRITAIN 16-inch guns, as carried in the Nelson and Rodney class, throw a salvo of nine shells 2,900lb. each. Maximum rate of fire is 12 rounds per minute per gun. Maximum range is around 30 miles.

PLAN FOILED

TURKS BEAT NAZI PLAN TO GET SHIPS

Express Special Correspondent

ISTANBUL, Monday.

'Suez bombed' claim

WHAT LUETJENS CAN DO

Express Naval Reporter BERNARD HALL

SCHMELING IS CRETE PARATROOP

MAX SCHMELING, one-time world heavy-weight champion, lately the show-place of Hitler's paratroop army, is in Crete. He Nazi radio claimed last night.

Ciano faces the sack

Express Staff Reporter

NEW YORK, Monday.

1,000,000 in new U.S. "call-up"

WASHINGTON, Monday.

RACE FOR HOME

Secret inquest on R.A.F. officer

"Shot" when in car

Nazis lose 11,000 in Crete battle

R.A.F. avenges 'Rotterdam raids'

Express Staff Reporter

CAIRO, Monday.

NEWS of the Battle of Crete tonight suggests that the Germans, despite colossal losses in men and aircraft, are going all out to force a decision. Here are the latest news flashes:—

1. The Nazis have so far lost at least 11,000 men in the fight for the island, according to information reaching the Turkish General Staff, quoted in an Ankara radio bulletin tonight.

2. The R.A.F., making a day and night attack with waves of fighter-escorted bombers, have taken fearful revenge for the Germans' 'Rotterdam raids' on Canea, Retimo and Candia. Twenty-four troop carriers were destroyed, many more badly damaged.

3. The Germans, attacking at Maleme, backed by superior fire of bombers in place of artillery, have bitten a salient out of the British lines covering Canea and Suda Bay, the Navy's anchorage.

25,000 LANDED

THEY FLY TANKS TO CRETE

Express Military Reporter MORLEY RICHARDS

SMALL, snub-nosed German tanks, varying in weight from three to eight tons, are reported to have been landed by air in Crete. So far they have not made contact with our forces.

GUNS PROBLEM

SWEEP EAST

Axis is 'fishing' for Crete news

Express Naval Reporter

SAUSAGES MAY BE RATIONED

British push on toward Bagdad

ROOSEVELT ANGERED BY RAEDER

Express Staff Reporter C. V. R. THOMPSON

NEW YORK, Monday.

PRESIDENT ROOSEVELT, locked in his great White House study, is tonight drafting all over again his speech for tomorrow "in the light of rapidly-changing conditions abroad"—which Washington interprets as including German Admiral Raeder's warning that American convoying of war materials to Britain would be an act of war.

4 A.M. LATEST

CHILIAN 'FUEHRER' FLEES FROM ASYLUM

SANTIAGO DE CHILE, Monday.

ITALIAN PRISONERS IN AUSTRALIA

SYDNEY, Monday.

THREAT TO U.S.

£120,041,000

Wind and rain

Left *Good news for the Allies as the* Bismarck *goes under.*

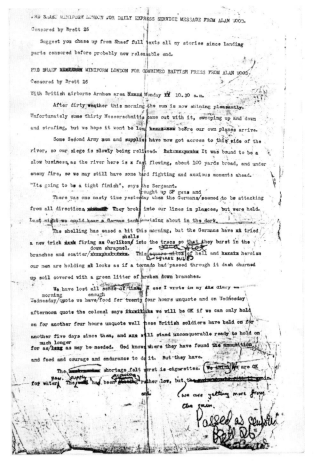

Right *A dispatch from Alan Wood (see below) which was never sent. Wood did not recover from the experience of Arnhem.*

the research for this book was a report written by one of the paper's war correspondents during the battle for Arnhem. The piece had been passed by the censor but, for technical reasons was never sent. The name of the reporter was Alan Wood. At first the name meant nothing—until it was spotted in Christiansen's memoirs. Wood was an Australian who had volunteered to be dropped at Arnhem in 1944. Until that time his chief claim to fame had been that he was undoubtedly the most awkward, griping, difficult so-and-so on the staff. His main complaint had always been that his salary was not high enough and he eventually sent a message back to the paper, from Arnhem, saying 'How about a rise now, Mister Christiansen?'. But, in spite of the joke, Wood never recovered from his experiences. Although he lived until long after the war he was mentally damaged by the events he had lived through and eventually committed suicide.

Unlike some other papers, the *Express* did not clash with the wartime authorities. Beaverbrook and Churchill were the closest of friends and there was no possibility that the Beaver's paper would do anything but praise the conduct of the war—especially since the Beaver himself was largely responsible for that conduct.

Above *The meeting between Beaverbrook and Stalin was to do much to convince the Beaver that the Bolsheviks were only human and could be persuaded by reason. It was a view he was to have difficulty in sustaining in years to come.*

Below *Japan brings America into the war on Britain's side. Note the intricate layout of this front page, reminiscent of a jigsaw puzzle.*

Above *The war in the Far East spreads to Hong Kong.*

Below *The fall of Mussolini called for banner headlines and an exciting variety of type styles.*

Overleaf *D-Day, and the* Express *covers the landings on the Normandy beaches.*

DAILY EXPRESS

No. 13,733 | Black-out 10.58 pm to 4.59 am | WEDNESDAY JUNE 7 1944 | Moon rises 10.58 pm sets 7.17 am (Thurs) | One Penny

MIDNIGHT official—Landings successful: Fighting in Caen streets: Attack on 80-mile front: Losses so far are light

TANKS 10 MILES IN

No longer any opposition on the first beaches

The invasion dispositions indicated on this *Daily Express* map are based on news received yesterday from Germany.

'WE'VE BROKEN THE CRUST': RAMSAY

ALLIED invasion troops, surging into France in mighty non-stop waves, have fought their way into Caen, town ten miles from the coast. Heavy street fighting is going on. The Germans say that the defenders are being "sorely tried." Along the whole front of between 80 and 100 miles from Cherbourg to the mouth of the Seine the offensive is gaining momentum.

Already terrific convoys have been assembled on the one-time holiday beaches. Our tanks are well inland.

Pilots back from the front saw them moving on Caen.

There is no longer any opposition on the beaches. They are completely in our hands. The soldiers are walking around on them without even troubling to bend when there is any fire from inland.

CUT THE WAY

All round Caen fires are blazing. Some were named when petrol dumps went up. The whole battle zone is a maelstrom of hell, says a German front despatch.

Bulldozers are already in action, cutting ways for the tanks and infantry.

By reaching Caen General Montgomery's men have cut the railway running from Paris to Cherbourg, main route for the supply of Hitler's troops in the Cherbourg peninsula.

The Germans report a deep penetration on the Cherbourg peninsula. A strong paratroop formation has a firm grip on the Cherbourg-Caen road, near Carentan, says Berlin.

Paratroops and airborne troops have been dropping in masses all along the front behind the Atlantic Wall. More than 1,000 machines have been used so far in the air descent.

FIRED 2,000 TONS

Off shore is ranged the vast Allied Navy, stretching for many miles in an arc. In only 10 minutes yesterday the Navy fired 2,000 tons of shells into the German coastal batteries.

Both seaborne and airborne troops have reached all the objectives set. Reinforcements to build up the punch are pouring across the Channel in an unprecedented stream.

But headquarters caution that counter-attacks are coming. The next 24 hours will reveal their strength.

The skies are ours. Today the sunlight with an unceasing parade of planes.

Only 50 enemy machines were seen yesterday. Even the German flak dwindled. The lack of opposition so far is described as fantastic.

PLANES LIT UP

Every plane in the great of Ninth Air Force machines that flew the first troops and equipment to the Continent carried coloured lights—yet no flak or fighters opposed them.

Between Monday midnight and eight o'clock yesterday morning more than 10,000 tons of bombs were dropped on coastal batteries. Seven thousand five hundred sorties were made. While the people of Britain were at breakfast 31,000 Allied airmen were in the skies.

Three main waves of Fortresses and Liberators went out from dawn to evening. In the first were more than 1,300

planes. But from these operations only four bombers and seven escorting fighters are missing.

Joining in the most violent air attacks in history, Ninth Air Force bombers, fighter-bombers, fighters, and troop-carrying aircraft flew more than 4,750 individual missions up to 10 o'clock last night.

Two Marauders, three fighter-bombers, and 15 troop-carriers were lost.

At General Eisenhower's headquarters at midnight it was stated that there is a feeling of optimism that all is going well.

All reports indicate that the Germans were caught by surprise. Weather was the chief worry. A strong wind was blowing north-west, raising white horses on the approaches and high waves on the beaches.

President Roosevelt says that the invasion is running to schedule. American navy losses so far were two destroyers and only one tank landing craft of the vast fleet used. Air losses were one per cent.

Midnight communique

Batteries silenced

SHORTLY before midnight on June 5 Allied night bombers opened the assault. Their attacks in very great strength, continued until night.

Between 6.30 and 7.30 on Tuesday morning two naval forces commanded by Rear-Admiral Philip Vian, K.B.E., D.S.O., flying his flag in H.M.S. Scylla (Captain T. M. Brownrigg, C.B.E., R.N.), and Rear-Admiral Alan Goodrich Kirk, U.S. Navy, in U.S.S. Augusta (Captain A. E. Jones, U.S.N.), launched their assault forces at enemy beaches.

The naval forces which had previously assembled under the overall command of Admiral Sir Bertram Ramsay made their departure in fresh weather and were joined during the night by bombarding forces which had previously left northern beaches.

TORPEDO ATTACK

In his firm message from Army headquarters General Montgomery said that he is "pleased with the initial phase of the landings."

Mr. Churchill, in a speech reported on page four, described the operation so far as thoroughly satisfactory. "Troops have penetrated in some cases several miles inland. Lodgments exist on a broad front."

Losses of the airborne forces are so far "very small," the Navy reported "very, very small" losses.

United States naval forces escorted 7,600 vessels across the Atlantic specially for the invasion. Only 10 of them were lost and not one a troop carrier.

A naval officer back from the landings said : "We have broken the crust. One brisk attack by torpedo-boats was driven off. There was no damage."

Many of our troops landed wet through. There was a great deal of sea sickness. It did not interfere however with the schedule.

'PINCER MOVE'

Berlin reports through Stockholm—but not from official Berlin—declare that the invasion front stretches for 240 miles from Calais to Jersey and Guernsey. They add that the Allies have landed at Grainville, on the western side of the Cherbourg peninsula, and are moving forward to isolate the peninsula in a pincers movement.

Here are other Berlin messages: Fighting is grim everywhere. The beaches of Deauville and Trouville are sodden with blood. Calais and Dunkirk were bombed for 18 hours. The bridge-head near Caen is 16½ miles long.

Paris says that a vicious engagement is being fought with paratroops who landed north of Rouen, behind the Atlantic Wall defences.

Further unconfirmed enemy statements are that invasion forces are sailing towards Cherbourg, and that airfields at Calais and Boulogne have been captured.

—BACK PAGE, COL. FOUR

FLASHES

Moscow Yankee Doodles

MOSCOW'S radio played "Yankee Doodle" and British marches last night to round off news of the invasion, green its full. People thronged Moscow's parks to hear the news on the official loudspeakers, and cheered at every pause.

Prisoners arrive

FIRST German prisoners of the first invasion landed in Britain last night. The prisoners were from a sunken craft, once have been seen on the beaches.

Parabombs

THE Germans say the first wave of invasion planes dropped extensive parachute-bombs stuffed with explosives, which were set when the Germans touched them.

Put off 14 hours

THE invasion was planned for Monday, June 5 but was postponed for 24 hours because experts feared the weather, then quite good, would deteriorate. They then produced it would improve in 24 hours. It did not, and so was costly as hoped.

Daily Express steamer for June 7, 1944 : prisoners near Dunkirk and a cross.

Premier flies

MR. CHURCHILL flew from London this announcement in Parliament yesterday to the secret headquarters from which General Eisenhower is directing the invasion. The HQ are a mansion hidden deep in the open English countryside.

In war paint

AMONG paratroop dropped in France were fleet Indians with red and black war paint on their faces. They are members of an American engineer airborne unit.

Final notice

A FEW minutes before the invasion the Furious started a paddle-steamer from North-Western France, warning that the men of the French to leave off the coast.

Secret weapons

MORE secret weapons are being used for the first time.

Mile of fire

FOR only German fighters engaged yesterday were on Mile 10 along the Normandy beaches. The rest of the Luftwaffe was silent.

Man in charge

HITLER is reported to be personally directing the German anti-invasion front.

Cricket as usual

A county cricket's invasion coast yesterday —lookers watched a three-village green.

The town council of Dover from the town have their usual monthly meeting, opening with a minute's silence.

There were two pitch-fire warnings in the Dover area. Children were out walking down the street; women went on delivering milk.

Rain

RAIN in the East Coast late last night. R.A.F. bases covered bound. All now blowing red, green and white navigation lights.

The night shift

As Force flew in over the East Coast late last night, R.A.F. bases covered bound. All were blowing red, green and white navigation lights.

EISENHOWER—WITH SKY-TROOPS

NO FLAK AND NO FIGHTERS

Panzers fought back at planes

Express War Reporter JAMES WELLARD

AT 6.27 yesterday morning I looked down on the invasion beaches of Normandy just as our landing barges were grounding on the sweeping sandy shore.

I had arrived in a Marauder bomber simultaneously with the opening of the Second Front.

It had been planned that my escort move in the vast operation of planes, gliders and men had been planned.

The formation of 36 Marauders I was flying was to be the last to bomb the beaches of Normandy exactly the minute before our infantry arrived. In the numbers that bore a measure they knew would have been off. They might have knocked our sea troops.

One minute after we arrived the town dawn opened. Our tactics pour and the engineer railed over the channel," Route may.

Two minutes later we were heading for home as the first landing barges grounded.

QUIET, DESERTED

I looked down on French and grey countryside, divided and sun-divided into little fields bordered by hedges. It seemed so quiet and undisturbed and peaceful.

Suddenly from a grove of trees, and over water bullets curved upward from towards our guns! It a slow-burning. The white gunner made my swing round and down. His shoulder stood in the rhythm of his pitching gun.

There was a blaze below us. A tank was on fire. More tracers swung past us, and our forces manoeuvred back.

Our formation was flying a squadron of German tanks between them in an area, stretching along the reeds of mixed clear.

FOUR PUFFS

Some enemy fighter challenged us during the approaches to the Normandy coast.

We were not even bothered by flak. Our navigators guided our bomb-morale puffs during the whole point trip.

The German anti-aircraft defences along the coast have been muffled and by air and mud have faded.

From what I saw—it was only a short period of observation—the chance German invaders have similarly knocked out. They

BACK PAGE, COL. THREE

WALKING ABOUT UPRIGHT

From BASIL CARDEW: Front Line R.A.F. Airfield, Southern England, Tuesday night

A SPITFIRE pilot who had just made his third sortie over the Normandy beachhead said this evening: "Our heavy bombers, medium bombers and the guns from our ships seem to have neutralised the enemy's coast defences.

"On the beaches the landing craft worked without hindrance. Like this evening I noticed that the troops were walking about on the beach upright, making no attempt to crouch or dodge enemy fire.

"That showed me how much we dominate the situation in this particular little area.

"The tanks had already gone

100 per cent.

Reports of operations so far show that our forces succeeded in their initial landings. Fighting continues.

Allied heavy, medium, light and fighter bombers continued the air bombardment in very great strength throughout the day with attacks on gun emplacements, defence works and communications.

Continuous fighter cover was maintained over the beaches and the zone distance inland and over naval operations in the Channel.

Our night fighters played an equally important role protecting shipping and troop-carrier forces and by invasion operations. Allied reconnaissance aircraft maintained continuous watch by day and night over shipping and ground forces.

Our aircraft met with little opposition from fighter opposition or S.A.S. gunfire.

Our continued reports of the operations as being very light, especially where the magnitude of the operation is taken into account.

GENERAL EISENHOWER, jaw set, fist clenched, talks with some of his tough, camouflaged paratroopers before they board transport planes for the landings in France.

GOERING: WIN OR PERISH

FIELD - MARSHAL GOERING issued an Order of the Day to the Luftwaffe yesterday. He quoted General Eisenhower's "Nothing less than victory" Order to the Allied Forces, and said:—

"The invasion must be beaten at all cost, even if the Luftwaffe perishes in the attempt. The air personnel must fight to the last shot and to the last man."

Goering has approximately 1,750 fighters and about 500 bombers. More than a fifth of the fighters are in German hands.

Almost certainly he must transfer fighter squadrons from France.

INVASION 4 am LATEST

PARIS TRAINS CANCELLED

All long-distance trains from Paris termini of St. Lazare (Normandy line) and Montparnasse (Brittany line) have been cancelled. Only suburban trains are running.—Paris radio.

'DENMARK NEXT'

STOCKHOLM, Tuesday.—German troops in Denmark are in state of alert. German believe Allied invasion of Denmark may be imminent.—B.U.P.

COL. BECK DEAD

Colonel Beck, Polish Foreign Minister at outbreak of war, has died from pneumonia near Ploesti, Rumania, says Paris radio. He was 34. He concluded German-Polish Pact in 1934, and escaped when Germany attacked Poland in 1939.

BLOW FROM SOUTH FEARED

MADRID, Tuesday.—German mobile units are moving northward from Central France to meet any penetration of the West Wall, and all the German-held Mediterranean area is in the alert for a blow from the south.

WHY LUFTWAFFE KEPT DOWN

German overseas radio denied early today : "Unfavourable weather impeded German air activity yesterday."

German Overseas radio denied that there is fighting in Caen, saying : "No enemy troops have penetrated into the city."

BACK PAGE, COL. THREE

Portugal stops wolfram

WASHINGTON, Tuesday.—Portugal agreed on invasion eve to stop all wolfram for Germany and to stop new mines.—B.U.P.

TO give the maximum amount of news coverage on the historic events of to-day all advertisements have been held over.

This step is made possible by the ready co-operation of advertisers and advertising agents.

Chapter 9

The shackled Crusader

The *Express* emerged from the war with one firm aim—to get Churchill re-elected. Beaverbrook was eager to put the entire resources of his organisation behind the project but, as with his other political aims, it was to suffer misfortune. The first folly was a burst of over-enthusiasm which turned a political squib into a massive conflagration. Unfortunately for Beaverbrook and Churchill it was they, and not their political adversaries, who got burned. Churchill had been hinting darkly that the socialist policies of the Labour Party were a disguised form of totalitarianism. At first this was little more than rhetoric but then something happened which gave it a semblance of credibility.

Professor Harold Laski, chairman of the Labour Party, was reported to have become rather heated at an election meeting in Newark and to have said that if Labour could not have socialist policies by fair means then violence would have to be used to obtain them. At first his remarks were reported only in the *Nottingham Guardian*, but soon they were drawn to the attention of Christiansen by an anonymous correspondent. The implications were frightening; if Laski really *had* said anything so stupid it could well be the ruination of the Labour campaign. Chris rushed to see Beaverbrook and Blumenfeld to ask their advice. At first they were inclined to dismiss the whole affair. They could not believe that a man in Laski's position would say anything so foolish. However, the reporter who had been present was quizzed and his notebook examined and on the basis of that it was decided to go ahead and print the story with the splash headline, 'LASKI UNLEASHES ANOTHER GENERAL ELECTION BROADSIDE: SOCIALISM "EVEN IF IT MEANS VIOLENCE"'.

The *Daily Herald*, which was the Labour mouthpiece, went on the defensive. Percy Cudlipp, the editor, summoned Laski to his office and demanded to know if the allegations were true. The professor denied everything and assured Cudlipp that this was merely a fabrication on the part of the Tory Press. A writ for libel was issued and battle was joined. At this point Chris was greatly in favour with the Tories and there were even some heavy hints dropped that a peerage might be forthcoming.

Brian Chapman, who was assistant managing editor on the *Express*, dreamed up the idea of dubbing Labour the National Socialists, a direct reference to the Nazi Party whose depredations were still fresh in the public mind. However, the whole affair was about to backfire. The public was in a pro-Labour mood and eager for a change of leadership. The idea that the harmless, sincere and rather

DAILY EXPRESS

No. 14,347   Lighting-up: 10.7 pm to 3.49 am   SATURDAY JUNE 1, 1946   Weather: Bright, occasional rain   One Penny

FLOUR: Ministry will draw up scheme at once to put it on points   **MILK: Nearly half of London's supply is threatened by strike of 1,500**

BREAD RATION 'PROBABLE'

May begin in September say official experts

CABINET SEEK WAY OUT

Express Political Correspondent GUY EDEN

BREAD AND FLOUR RATIONING WILL BE IMPOSED UNLESS BRITAIN HAS AN UNEXPECTED WINDFALL OF WHEAT, OR UNLESS THERE IS A GREAT IMPROVEMENT IN THE WORLD SUPPLY.

As neither is likely, Government experts are going on the assumption that rationing is "inevitable," although a final Cabinet decision has not yet been taken.

If ordered, rationing will probably come into force in September or October. For bread, the population will be divided into: Heavy workers (biggest ration); manual workers (next largest), and those with sedentary jobs (smallest). Flour may be put on points, probably with the same grading system.

It was explained in the Commons yesterday that rationing would have two main objects—to save supplies of flour and to give the Minister of Food closer control over wheat supplies so that comparatively small adjustments could be made without elaborate preparations.

Because of the psychological effect on public opinion, the Cabinet will avoid bread rationing if possible. But all Ministers in close touch with the food situation now take the view that it is "next door to impossible."

Strachey makes his first big speech

DECISION IS COMING THIS MONTH

Churchill:

Express Parliamentary Reporter

MR. STRACHEY, the new Food Minister,

JAIL IS PACKED —4 IN A CELL

J.P.s COMPLAIN

Express Staff Reporter

SO bad is the overcrowding at Strangeways Jail, Manchester, that there are three or four prisoners in some cells, declares a report issued last night by 29 magistrates who have been investigating conditions.

The report says that more than 800 men and women prisoners are accommodated in a building designed for between 400 and 600.

Cocoon is expressed at "the maximum employment of

Students marry, leave college

'We are sacked'

Express Staff Reporter

EXETER, Friday.—Mr. Oscar William Ocell, 25-year-old vice-rector for Costa Rica in Exeter, said tonight that he had been "sent down" from the University College in this city because he married an English girl student ten days ago.

His auburn-haired bride, formerly Miss Enid Goodman, of Millbrook, near Plymouth, said she too has been expelled.

Mr. Ocell arrived from San José, Costa Rica, as Consul last year to touch his studies.

His secretary

He has saved day as a student for nine little Goodman and Consul summer interests.

MRS. MARGARET NELSON

MILK STRIKE 'ALL OVER LONDON'

United Dairies men seek rise

Express Staff Reporter

AN unofficial strike last night by 260 men of United Dairies may result in no milk this morning for many people in London. And tomorrow morning nearly half the people in London may be without milk.

Last night, Mr. Tudor Price, managing director of the company's bottling department, said: "There will be some interference with milk distribution in the areas of North and East London tomorrow.

"It is anticipated that on Sunday the whole of the London area will have no supplies from United Dairies.

'Lodger' at her mother-in-law's

Council says quit

The men say—

THE men say, but at last night's Union meeting a Evangelist who we have been able to earn two and three shillings exercise.

"Now that more men are crossing of the Force, the overtime has been reduced and we are not able to make up our wages.

"Once we have applied for increases, giving of hours packet for our deadlock has been taken up.

The meeting was adjourned to

Plan for Empire defence

CHIEFS TO MEET

Express Political Correspondent

A DETAILED scheme of Empire defence is to be drawn up by experts following talks between the Dominions Ministers, the London, Mr. Attlee and the military chiefs of staff.

4 a.m. LATEST

'CLIPPIE' ATTACKED

A bus conductress was attacked and knocked on the head in Holland Park, W., last night. Police rendered the area.

A PREMIER GOES

BAGDAD, Friday.—Tawfiq Suwidi, Iraq Prime Minister, resigned today after opposition in his policy on Palestine.—Reuter.

CENtral 8000

will meet in London and exchange information for the whole country.

DAILY EXPRESS

No. 15,174   Lighting-up: 5.17 pm to 7.10 am   TUESDAY FEBRUARY 1, 1949   Weather: Cloudy, bright periods   One Penny

FREED Costumes, suits and overcoats   **HALVED** Coupons for fur clothes   **SAME** Nylons, shirts, cotton dresses   **WARNED** Two Krupps directors   **ROW** Over teams for U.S.

SUITS OFF THE RATION

Costumes and wool dresses freed too

17 COUPONS TO BUY COTTON

Express Staff Reporter

FROM today nearly all suits, jackets, waistcoats, trousers, overcoats, costumes and woven wool dresses are off the ration. But cotton clothes, knitted garments, socks and underwear stay on the ration.

MR. Harold Wilson, President of the Board of Trade, announced the changes in the Commons yesterday. He said there will be 17 coupons (all the coupons) for the six months after March 1, against 24 last time.

The first effect is likely to be a rapid disappearance of already scarce cotton frocks from the shops. For women, with woollens coupon-free, will want to use coupons to make sure of their summer dresses.

The trade called the changes a "poor effort," said Mr. T. Caves, of the Wholesale Textile Association: "Mr. Wilson should have made a clean sweep of coupon rationing, which he has now thrown out of balance. Today rationing is by game, anyway."

DAILY EXPRESS ENTERPRISE

Tribunal opens the film parade of 1949

THE Film Tribunal is in session again.

The seven wise people whose judgment of the outstanding films and performances of 1948 aroused so much interest have all agreed to serve on the Tribunal for another year.

Its purpose the Tribunal will be the same—to encourage the true art of the motion picture regardless of box office appeal, and to focus International attention on outstanding work no matter what the country of origin.

The Film Tribunal announced in its decisions. The Film of the Year. The Actor. The winners chosen deemed honest work was an award of £1,000 is making records and has been placed for exhibition all over the world.

It will be shown in America. The theatre whom that Tribunal's award brought first the film has caused Mr. David Selznick to issue a decision to enter a theatre in the New York to "See

THE TRIUMPH

The accolade of Actress of the Year awarded to Jean Wyman for her work as the deaf mute in "Johnny Belinda" has resulted in the film running several weeks so far at the Warner Theatre in London—five weeks longer than was originally intended.

And from America has come a constant stream of Transatlantic appreciation and advertising drawing attention to Miss Wyman's triumph.

Possibly the outstanding decision of the Tribunal is the decision to show the French

OFF THE RATION

WOVEN WOOL CLOTH and all garments made from it. Blankets, gaberdines and some jacket utility cloth.

DOWN-COUPONED

FUR GARMENTS, including men's and women's overcoats and capes will be about half their former coupon values.

FUR trimmings, including men's and women's overcoats and capes will be about half their former coupon values. Furs in the shape of a big estate power in East France, now reaches these WOOLLEN coloured dressing-gown woven dressed. Dirt, at look on separate, price for the separate in the first next from an from them, under-clothes lined ones and told for the separate.

In general, only garments made of wool, or partly wool will go coupon-free. Their prices range from 3s at 4d a yard.

STILL RATIONED

KNITTING wool, knitted suits and garments, including socks (tax 1¼), and pants (shirts, 2). Corduroy clothing (trousers, 7) with clothing vests and tropical kit, pillowcases clothing cotton

POCKET CARTOON
by OSBERT LANCASTER

Mrs. Wilson bought this wrap too soon—loses 7 coupons

Oh, Mrs. Wilson—Oh, Mrs. BOTTOMLEY!

ALL ABOVE BOARD at the Board of Trade

Express Staff Reporter

INTO walnut-pastelled Room 806 at the Board of Trade offices in millbank yesterday strode the President, Mr. Harold Wilson—and Mary, his 31-year-old, fair-haired wife.

Mary heard her husband answer questions. But she is a woman with whom official secrets are not shared.

For Mr. Wilson revealed that only three days ago Mrs. Wilson went to the local shops and came back with a new WOOLLEN coloured dressing-gown woven dressed. Dirt, it took no discount from the coupons to get the heavy fresh Mrs. Bottomley, wife of Mr. A. G. Bottomley, Secretary for Overseas Trade, last night made a similar confession.

Said Mr. Wilson: "It's just one of these things.

Husbands 'on loan' urged

Express Staff Reporter

HAMBURG, Monday.—Twice-married, 52-year-old Dr. Dorothea Klaje has started a campaign in Germany to make temporary marriages legal.

She says this is the only way to find husbands for the seven million surplus German women.

At a lecture she told a woman with whom official secrets are not shared.

JUST ASK?

Temporary marriages, she said should be for an agreed period. When the time is up, the couple should be able to dissolve the marriage by a simple application to the town hall.

'MY SISTER AND I ARE NOT WELL OFF'

Legacy to secretary surprises daughter

Express Staff Reporter

A WOMAN waiting to go into hospital learned yesterday that she has been left a fortune by the man whose letters she typed for 20 years.

Mrs. Florence Draper grew up in the City offices run by Mr. Maurice Bauer.

She started as an office girl, earning 15s. a week 27 years ago. Now she is 39.

In the time he died last year—he was rough seas which took him to the River in a dinghy—she—the little office girl, now a woman of 40 and the wife of an electrician—was his confidential secretary.

She worked long hours. She travelled Europe with her men. Even after he retired she stuck on as his personal secretary. He used to tell her that he would remember her work. Apparently—perhaps though, he's

Yesterday the "small amount" was revealed to be a five-figure sum.

With girl of 9

Mr. Bauer, merchant and charitable estate, left £176,906 gross, on which death duties of £72,553 have been paid. His 85-year-old wife is left £2,000 and his office, and the rest to

MOTHER DIES WITH HER 4 CHILDREN

FOUR children, all under six, were found dead with their 30-year-old mother in a gas-filled bedroom at their home in Fenhall-road, Ewell, Surrey, last night.

The home was all-electric last Thursday. Then someone

LAURENCE, PETER and KATHLEEN BECK

Father went mother to India

died a gas ring and gas poker in the front bedroom.

The mother, Mrs. Alma Beck—away for inquiries as "the unnatural mother," had then put in. She smothered to the children.

The father, Laurence Beck, Naval Engineer, was wanted from Singapore on H.M.S. His wife—an Eurasian—in India, where she was a nursing sister.

The children were Laurence, eight; Peter and Kathleen, two; and Linda, four months.

Save-the-cat serum flies

NEW YORK, Monday.—A special serum is being sent to Britain by air today to fight a feline influenza outbreak which could wipe out thousands of cats.

Bread brings illness

Bread is blamed by the public health committee of Tredegar, South Wales, for causing food poisoning at one four families in the town.

The committee, reporting on an investigation into the processing at the Bear Oast bakery, found that the serum much killer, and the Ministry will report.

CENtral 8000

Girls riot at Holloway Jail

AN 18-year-old, 4ft. 10in. girl started a riot in the Borstal wing of Holloway Jail as a concert ended.

She yelled: "Come on, boys," and the girls seized chairs and attacked women police officers.

Six women officers were injured in the attack. It was revealed last night.

4 a.m. LATEST

RIOT LEADERS TO BE 'TRIED'

Three magistrates have been authorized by the riot leaders and "jury" tried by a magistrate on the Home prison and the prison Governor will report to the Home Office.

BLAZE AT DOCKS

London fire brigades rushed to fight big blaze at London docks. Fire started in warehouse in Surrey Commercial Docks, Rotherhithe, Bread bringing.

Bristol institution had made constant protest.

A Home Office report has been received.

This is the second disturbance since Mrs. Mellor took over as Holloway in a munitions factory officers were attacked after Christmas concert. The ringleaders were then punished.

Wife exhumed: 'Rumours'

Express Staff Reporter

POLICE yesterday investigated rumours after the exhumation of a woman, whose body was taken from a cemetery at Great Harwood, Lancs., after dark last night, by police watching the grave and exhumed 71-year-old boring Mr Attlee might in some way be linked with Hitler seemed absurd. The same applied to the equally harmless Professor Laski. Yet the *Express* insisted on using the newly-coined jibe at every possible occasion and it was even printed above a report of one of Attlee's speeches.

The attack drew ridicule from many quarters, not least other sections of the Press. The idea that Mr Attlee was really Hitler in disguise was too ludicrous for words. One of the many attacks which appeared in other journals was that in the now-defunct *Leader* of June 16 1946 under the title 'Chuck it Beaverbrook!':

'The election has taken a surprising turn. The big gun was fired by Mr Churchill, who conjured up a Gestapo-behind-Labour bogy: Lord Beaverbrook then joined in the barrage with an ardour which has made even some of his admirers shudder.

'It is only too clear that Lord Beaverbrook and the men who work with him, have decided that the best chance of stampeding the electors is by an unremitting blackguarding of the Labour leaders as men who are in some mysterious way impregnated with Nazi ideas.

'This plan seems to be based on a statement which was, I believe, expressed by the American journalist, H.L. Mencken, in the following terms: "You can't under-rate the intelligence of the public". That remains to be seen.

'One of the outstanding events of recent weeks was to wake up one morning and stare at the front page of the *Daily Express*, on which was printed an account of Mr Attlee's radio speech, headlined: "THE NATIONAL SOCIALISTS".

'If Lord Beaverbrook's *Daily Express* can produce anything more twisted than this headline, which attempts to delude ignorant readers with the farcical idea that Mr Attlee has some sort of comradeship with the late Hitler, I shudder for the political life of this country'.

There was plenty more in the same vein, a great torrent of abuse heaped on Churchill, Beaverbrook and the entire campaign. What is more, it gave critics of the *Express* an excuse to rake up some rather unfortunate remarks which had appeared in that paper's columns before the war. What had been conceived as a brilliant master-stroke to put Churchill back in No 10 turned into an unmitigated disaster. Chris, needless to say, did not get his peerage.

However, life went on. One of the main saving graces of newspaper work is that yesterday's issue is soon dead and fit only for wrapping rubbish. Beaverbrook had plenty of other issues with which to interest himself. One of his pets was the Cold War. As a man of the Right one might have expected him to be in the fore-front of any campaign against Russia and her allies, but that was not the case. Although the Beaver abominated all the things for which communism stood, he was convinced that it was possible to negotiate with the Eastern Bloc and come to some sensible compromise. It was typical of the Beaverbrook optimism that he could not understand people who would let an 'ism' interfere with the smooth

Opposite *The post-war years brought not only victory but shortages. However, by 1949, things were starting to look a bit brighter.*

Gandhi, who had been execrated by the British Press, especially the Beaverbrook papers, was elevated to something resembling sainthood after his death.

running of their society. Surely everybody wanted more employment and higher wages? Surely these basic values were common to all nations?

This attitude was to take several hard knocks during the 1950s. The first of these was the defection of Burgess and Maclean. There had been previous spy scandals when the atomic scientists—Nunn May, Fuchs and Pontecorvo—had given details of their research to the Soviets, so there was some reluctance to make our security services look incompetent yet again. However, the news came through from the Paris office of the *Express* that their correspondent, Larry Solon, had heard a whisper that two Foreign Office officials called Burgess and Maclean might have defected. Some checking revealed that there were, indeed, two diplomats with those surnames and it was rapidly becoming obvious that the authorities were not keen to answer any questions about them. The *Express* took an enormous risk and published the story.

Christiansen afterwards recorded the gut-wrenching fear in which he spent the night after that story had gone to press. If it all turned out to be a mistake it would certainly have cost him his job and would have had the most serious consequences for his newspaper. Happily it was not long before confirmation started to come through, though it took many months before the whole story came out. The attempts by the government and the security services to hush the whole affair up

DAILY EXPRESS

No. 15,718 THURSDAY NOVEMBER 2 1950 CONTROLLING SHAREHOLDER LORD BEAVERBROOK Weather: Fog One Penny

GUN BATTLE Shots break up bid to kill Truman **THE WAR** Jets from China join Korea battle **PRICES** Liberals join protests on cost of living **SHAW** Just a shadow...cannot last much longer'

BID TO KILL TRUMAN

Gun battle on doorstep

The President looked down...A man sprawled, shot, on the steps below

Big Red attack in Korea

Jets from China join battle

3 SECRET SERVICE GUARDS SHOT

From VINCENT EVANS : Washington, Wednesday

TWO swarthy terrorists in pin-stripe suits tried to shoot their way into President Truman's home today in a bid to kill the President, who was taking a nap in his under-clothes in an upstairs room.

LIBERALS CHALLENGE ON COST OF LIVING

By GUY EDEN

A CHALLENGE to the Government on the cost of living was tabled by the Liberals last night.

NORTH KOREA, Thursday.
—Allied troops were attacked by strong Red forces on the north-west front last night. A U.S. spokesman said the situation is serious.
The enemy attacked at a U.S. task force, commanded by

4 a.m. LATEST

BATTALIONS—YES, DIVISIONS—NO ; SAYS MOCH

CENtral 8000

The war was over but the violence did not abate. After the murder of Gandhi came an attempt to kill President Truman; these were just the first in a long succession of peacetime murder attempts on prominent people.

were intense. So much so that there was quite a lot of genuine public outrage stirred up against the *Express*. For example, when the paper kept watch on Mrs Maclean after her husband's defection there was a great outcry about the way the 'yellow' Press was hounding the poor woman and her innocent children. The tumult only ceased when she herself defected and turned up in Moscow as, no doubt, she had intended to do all along.

Beaverbrook's hope for some sort of accommodation with the Warsaw Pact countries went through many vicissitudes during the '50s. When Krushchev and Bulganin visited Britain, the *Express*—with the notable exception of cartoonist Michael Cummings who saw no future for such negotiations—was full of hope. Then the invasion of Hungary dashed everyone's hopes. The U2 spy scandal in 1960 was another serious blow. Yet it was typical of Beaverbrook and the *Express* that optimism was always the keynote of their policies.

Another Beaverbrook hobby horse was the royal family. It is an issue which has dogged the *Express* for most of its life and it has made one of the most curious little snippets in the history of Fleet Street. The loyalty which the paper has always shown to the British Empire has drawn to the paper the type of reader who has very pronounced patriotic views. These views almost always go hand-in-glove with an intense admiration for the royal family. But here the paper has often parted company with its admirers. Not that the *Express* has ever been anti-monarchist, far from it, but it has never felt the need to mute any criticisms which it thought necessary. Beaverbrook, as has been discussed earlier, was quite immune to the British concept of royalty and, in addition to his natural disinclination to monarchy, he had a personal injury to nurse because of the attempt by the then King to block his peerage. Add to this the fact that he supported the 'wrong' side in the abdication debate and you already have a reasonable background of dislike and distrust.

This legacy has been handed down to us even now. Prince Philip is well known for having described the *Express*, during a visit to Latin America, as a 'bloody awful newspaper' (although his condemnation cannot have been total since he is also known to be a great admirer of Carl Giles' cartoons).

In the early '60s the whole matter actually came before Parliament. Sir Martin Linsay, Conservative MP for Solihull, introduced a motion of censure alleging that there was a campaign in the *Express* against the royal family. He claimed to have counted more than 70 adverse comments in just a few years. During a tour of America Sir Martin had been told by British consuls that 'the Queen's image was being tarnished'. He commented: 'The whole of this is a vindictive campaign for nothing else whatever but personal reasons of which I think everybody in this room knows. My answer to questions after my lectures was that this was the personal vendetta of one embittered man'.

Even today, long after the Beaver's departure, there are persistent rumours that the paper and the royals have little time for each other. One gentleman of 80, who had heard of the preparation of this book, walked many miles to hand in at the *Express* office a note saying that he hoped the author would not hesitate to draw attention to this matter. He felt that a picture which had appeared in the Hickey column which clearly showed Prince Charles' bald patch was especially reprehensible and demonstrated clearly that the paper was in dangerous hands.

Even the present chairman, Lord Matthews, has been the subject of disobliging comment in this context. *Private Eye* in particular has frequently alleged that there is little love felt by the Queen and her family for the Press Lord. The *Express* has always taken such rumours and allegations calmly. It insists that it has the warmest regard for the royals but that it will continue to refrain from mindless adulation when it believes there is a genuine cause for criticism.

*   *   *

In the mid-'50s the paper suddenly entered an era of rapid change. On July 21 1954 the following announcement appeared: 'Lord Beaverbrook has given a block of shares in the *Express* to the Beaverbrook Foundation, which has been established

Opposite *Under Christiansen the* Express *knew how to play a dramatic situation for all it was worth. This famous picture of the female relatives of George VI was to become one of the great classic news photographs of its time.*

DAILY EXPRESS

No. 16,113 Price 1½d.   TUESDAY FEBRUARY 12 1952   CONTROLLING SHAREHOLDER LORD BEAVERBROOK   Weather: Cold

The Week of Tribute...

PICTURE EDITION

As Big Ben struck twelve, six men and five women were waiting through the frosty night to file past the King's coffin today

THE THREE STAND ALONE

They mourn husband, father and son

Express Staff Reporter

THREE Queens of England—Queen Elizabeth II, the Queen Mother, and majestic Queen Mary—fought back their tears yesterday as they stood beside the bier of King George VI, lying in state in Westminster Hall.

Queen Elizabeth, mourning a father, stood a little in front at the head of the coffin. On her right, two paces behind, was her mother, mourning a husband. On the other side was Queen Mary, mourning a son.

THE EMOTION

Their heads were bowed. Long veils shrouded their faces. Their emotion was too great for them to join in the singing of "Lead With Me," as a short service drew to its close.

From the assemblage of Lords and Commons and dignitaries of the Realm, there went out a great crescendo wave of sympathy to the three sad Queens.

A few steps behind them, finding it hard to bear herself with fortitude, stood Princess Margaret, a frail, pale, pathetic little, unveiled figure of sorrow.

There too were the Duke and Duchess of Gloucester, the Princess Royal, the Duchess of Kent. The family was gathered.

That was the unforgettable picture in the 35 minutes of heartfelt drama which began when the gun-carriage bearing the royal coffin reached New Palace-yard.

THE SILENCE

It was at four o'clock that a great hush fell in the waiting hall. The Gentlemen Ushers in plumed hats, and the Yeomen of the Guard took up positions.

Down one side of the hall ranged the bishops in black and white and the peers in dark dress. On the other side were the members of Parliament, who had walked in procession, Government with Opposition, two by two.

So that Mr. Churchill had passed with Mr. Attlee, Mr. Morrison with Mr. Eden.

It was cold in the hall. The only sound was an occasional cough.

At four minutes past four there was a banging on the great ramparts oak doors. Two elderly Yeomen of the Guard slowly swung them open.

THE SALUTE

Outside the guard of honour could be heard moving in rhythmic precision to their salute. As the muffled Abbey bells trembled into silence, far-away military commands rang out staccato.

Eyes in the hall were turned towards the great doors. Out marched seven, one limping. They moved up each side of the hall with a splash of colour.

Among them was the Minister of Works, Mr. David Eccles, in plain mourning dress. He is Keeper of the Palace of Westminster, a post for which there is no state uniform.

These entered next the Dean of Westminster and Dr. Garbett, the Archbishop of York, taking the place of the Archbishop of Canterbury, who has been ill.

THE CROWN

Then, borne high on the shoulders of eight Guardsmen in long grey coats with white belts, came the coffin of King George VI. The Guardsmen stepped across the thick, dull brown carpet.

The quivered lights fell on the coffin of the King draped in the rich colours of the Royal Standard . . . on the Imperial Crown resting on its massive cushion, its jewels glowing with a burst of radiance with that sombre setting . . . on the wreath of snow-white flowers, the loving tribute of a wife, the Queen Mother.

Immediately behind was Queen Elizabeth, looking small and lonely in that huge hall, an effect heightened by her long

➤ PAGE TWO, COL. ONE

Heavily veiled, the three mourning Queens stand together as the coffin of the King is borne from its gun-carriage to the catafalque in Westminster Hall.... They joined the procession behind the coffin and as they turned to do so the Queen Mother stood back for the new Queen to precede her.

DAILY EXPRESS

No. 16,415   Price 1½d.   MONDAY FEBRUARY 2 1953   CONTROLLING SHAREHOLDER LORD BEAVERBROOK   Weather: Dry, bright; frost tonight

DISASTER WEEK-END: *North Sea floods smash through villages* — *Populations cleared from danger zones* — *Irish Sea gale kills 128 in sunk steamer*

THE DELUGE

152 known dead; 10,000 evacuated from one town

FLOOD DISASTER: PAGE OF PICTURES— BACK PAGE

THE QUEEN DRIVES TO DANGER ZONE

Express Staff Reporters

AT least 152 people were known yesterday to have lost their lives in Britain's worst flooding. During Saturday night huge seas tore down coastal defences in East and South-Eastern England, swept away homes, and left thousands as refugees.

● Many more people were unaccounted for last night. At Hunstanton, in Norfolk, 40 are believed drowned including many Americans; 20 are feared to have died at Snettisham, Norfolk; and 40 are feared dead on Canvey Island.

● All day yesterday troops, police, and firemen worked to rescue the marooned. More than 500 were rescued at Whitstable, in Kent. Last night volunteers were sandbagging the breached sea walls and river banks—to guard against a fresh night of horror.

For there were warnings of fresh gales in the sea areas adjoining the flooded coast.

● People who went to bed shocked by the loss of 128 lives in the Princess Victoria on Saturday awoke to find flood waters mounting in their own homes.

● The turbulent waters roared through country villages and seaside resorts, carrying away buildings.

● *From Kent up to Yorkshire there were areas of death and destruction, communities cut off and others evacuated—and emergency services organised.*

● Since the business of the rescuers was to rescue the living, the dead could not easily be counted. Last night this grim and incomplete table of lost lives was prepared :—

LINCS		KENT	
MABLETHORPE	1	BELVEDERE	1
INGOLDMELLS	1		
SALTFLEET	1	SUFFOLK	
SKEGNESS	2	FELIXSTOWE	1
		SOUTHWOLD	1
ESSEX			
CLACTON	4	NORFOLK	
SOUTHEND	6	HUNSTANTON	40
JAYWICK	4	GREAT YARMOUTH	4
GREAT WAKERING	7	KING'S LYNN	12
CANVEY ISLAND	40	HEACHAM	2
		SNETTISHAM	20
LONDON		SEA PALLING	1
		SALTHOUSE	1
BARNES S.W.	1	WIVETON	1
		CLEY	1

● Hour by hour the number of casualties increased. By late last night a total of 132 people—six of them dead on arrival—had been admitted to Southend Hospital, and 33 to Rochford Hospital.

● It was decided last night to evacuate all the 6,000 people of Mablethorpe and Sutton in Lincs, while 10,000 people of Canvey Island, Essex, were evacuated during the day.

● Benfleet High-street was trowded with mud-caked refugees on their way to reception centres.

● Three thousand people were homeless at Harwich, which is without gas or transport.

● In the naval dockyard at Sheerness the submarine Sirdar was sunk in the dock and the frigate Berkeley Castle capsized.

● The Littlebrook power station at Dartford is accessible only by boat—but still working; millions of pounds worth of plant at the Keno oil refinery on the Isle of Grain have been waterlogged; the Isle of Sheppey is cut off from the mainland, with Sheerness cut off from the rest of the island.

● The area-by-area drama is told in detail on Pages Two and Five; here, selected, is what happened, at Lowestoft, a cameo of the unforgettable night :—

At 8 p.m. a 25ft. tide, the highest of all time, hit the town and flooded nearly half of it. In the schoolroom attached to St. John's Church 48 children were having a party.

They were hurried into the church as waters rose quickly in the schoolroom. But the waters flooded the church—until they were feet deep in the nave. The children retreated to the chancel steps.

A pianist, Mr. E. Bennett, played nursery rhymes on the organ to keep up the children's spirits. Still the waters rose. Mr. Bennett smashed a window and shouted for help.

Three detectives arrived, stripped, and waded through the church, opening the doors. Then four boatmen moved their boats up the aisles and got out all 48 children—mostly dry.

● A shooting brake with Prince Philip driving and the Queen beside him went from Sandringham yesterday towards the flooded area of North-west Norfolk.

● Mr. Churchill is expected to make a statement on the floods this afternoon.

The ordeal of GREAT WAKERING

A mother clings to her baby 3 hours

JOHN LAMBERT phoned from the village of Great Wakering (pop. 2,750) in Essex, three miles up the coast from Southend :—

THE villagers gathered last night in their Norman church and prayed for 800 people stranded in an island of swirling brown water — and a chubby little boy of three who was lost.

On Saturday night in Great Wakering young people had danced in the church hall. One mother, Mrs. Ellen May Winch, of Rose Farm, lay watching her 21-year-old son Dennis.

On tiptoe

Dennis got back from the dance at 1.30 a.m. He turned in. "All right, Mum," he said. "I was just talking with the sister." Said Mrs. Winch, "I'll talk to you in the morning."

"All right," said Dennis. Then he shouted "Mum quick. Help. There's water pouring in."

With a great roar water swung on because of Rose Farm into the house. Mrs. Winch said, "We must get on the roof or we are lost." Painfully, Mr. Winch got on to the roof. Mrs. Winch and her son clambered up beside him. She clung there through and huddled on to wife and son in their nightclothes.

He said later : "I couldn't feel any part of my body. The wind was howling and the water began round and over. There was nothing I could do but wait."

For three hours we clung to that roof. We could not be relieved. All we could hear was the water roar and the groans of young children, and I was petrified through the night.

Prayers . . .

The Vicar announced : Home Farm. Young mothers clung to the roofs and to their children. Young Mrs. Nellie Whitehead and her husband Arthur Whitehead both lost their lives — but the baby got off safely. They clung to a chimney through the night.

For three hours Mrs. Whitehead held on. Then she fell into the torrent—but somehow her hand was saved. As dawn her husband tried to swim, was swept away into the darkness.

'Abide With Me'

Across the waters during the night came a hymn. It was sung by 76-year-old George Kirby and his 64-year-old wife Ethel. It was " Abide With Me." But the hymn and Mr. and Mrs. Kirby died as a near of water and they roared on.

— ◄ BACK PAGE. COL. ONE

HOLES IN THE ROOFS SHOW HOW LUCKY ONES ESCAPED

Four almost submerged Nissen huts at Great Wakering. In the roofs of three are holes battered by rescuers to free the trapped occupants.

FULL MOON A CAUSE

THE flooding seems to be due entirely to two straightforward causes (writes Chapman Pincher) :

ONE : Tremendous waves whipped up in the open sea by the gale.

TWO : The fact that it is full moon—the time when the tides are highest because of the double pull of both sun and moon.

RAIL SERVICES CUT

—And most electric trains will be cold

THOUSANDS of people will have to take a round-about route to work this morning because of flooded roads and railways.

Rail tracks near Lowestoft and Yarmouth were swept away. Services on the All Hallows branch beyond Sharfleet Street, Kent, and the Isle of Sheppey will be suspended.

EXTRA TRAINS

EASTERN Region arrangements for London-bound trains :—

Buses will run from Chelmsford and Leigh to Benfleet, and trains from Benfleet to Fenchurch-street.

Trains will run from Shoeburyness to Westcliff Central with extra trains from Southend Victoria to Shenfield and extra electric trains from Shenfield to Liverpool-street.

10,000 people taken off Canvey Island

WE EVEN STOPPED TO RESCUE A PIG

H. L. McNALLY tells of a run in a truck over deserted Canvey, of the shout "Anyone there?"—and the silence.

BY nightfall there were only some hundred people left on the flooded area of Canvey Island. So said Superintendent W. R. Pope who, with Chief Constable R. T. J. Peel, was in charge of the evacuation of 10,000 people.

They had mobilised the Army, the R.A.F., the police, the fire brigade, the ambulance and bus services, the Home Guard, the Civil Defence, the W.V.S., the Leigh-on-Sea fishermen with boats, the Red Cross, and worked from dawn until long into the night.

The disaster came to Canvey Island at 1.30 a.m., when the sea wall gave way at Tewkes Creek.

Within hours there were 30 other serious breaches ; and thousands of tons of water washed over the low-lying area.

Forced back

But neither boats nor heavy Army vehicles could reach them.

For all boats were devoted to saving the living.

At dawn thomas and fishermen in motorboats began rescuing people from roofs ; cheeks and bungalows, carrying them into—back through water 6ft. deep.

The rescued were taken area-beer by cars and handcarts at double-deck buses which arrived from all parts of Essex.

Hundreds of rowing-boats were rushed aft and smashed by the violence of the water.

The level of water rose during the stormy day and at afternoon high tide the flood made even more unmistake-bably by boat and lorry R.A.F. Duckw, which was pushed through 5ft. of water.

I rode on the top of one of these.

The homes were deserted here and there's a few people were leaving their furniture into boats with the water half-up their full.

Our truck stopped to rescue a pig. It took 11 firemen and two sailors to rope him and get him aboard.

Invalid last

When 64-year-old invalid Mr. Charles Waktin, who his wife was rescued from his sickbed, the waters mounted up the top of the saviours.

Several hours later the officer carried Mrs. King, but the couple returned off and shouted, ilous nothing to worry about.

NIGHT BID TO RESCUE 300

Rochford (Essex) men trying to take 300 stranded people off Foulness Island, Essex, during the night. The B.B.C. radioed an appeal : "Show lights in your windows."

3 a.m. LATEST

SHIP VICTIMS FOUND

Bodies of Master John Sinclair, deputy Prime Minister, Northern Ireland, Sir Walter Smiles, Unionist M.P. for North Down, and Captain James Ferguson, Newry, were among 32 bodies recovered on mainland inshore at Belfast last night.

CENtral 6000

as a British Empire Educational Trust. The newspapers have therefore passed out of his control'. Not again! As we saw back in 1929 the controlling interest in the *Express* was supposed to have been given to 'Young Max'. How then, a quarter of a century later, could Beaverbrook still have any interest to give away? This was another of his ruses to distance himself from his papers. Whoever legally owned the shares, there could be no doubt that whilst Beaverbrook continued to draw breath he controlled his papers.

A genuine change was to follow in 1956. At the height of the Suez Crisis, Arthur Christiansen had a heart attack. He had been staying at Beaverbrook's villa at Cap d'Ail and was immediately flown back to London for medical treatment. His own account of this event is brief, not to say bland; he merely states that it was the end of his career in journalism, that it gave him a chance to write his memoirs and that he later took up a new career in television. The truth is much more complex.

Chris had recovered from his illness and been invited by the Beaver to go and convalesce at his home in the Bahamas. The Beaver was himself staying there at the time and, at first, their relationship was as good as ever. But during the visit a copy of Francis Williams' book *Dangerous Estate* arrived. This was, and still is, one of the best histories of British journalism ever to be undertaken. Imagine, therefore, the anger of Beaverbrook when he read how Christiansen had 'stamped his personality on the *Daily Express* only a shade less indelibly than Beaverbrook himself'. This was not the first time that Chris had been given the credit which his boss jealously guarded for himself; back in the late '30s *Time* magazine had been rash enough to acclaim him as the man who had pushed the paper's circulation past the million mark. That storm had passed—the new one would not.

Chris was coldly ordered back to work—the story goes that a note was left at his place at the breakfast table. When he arrived back at the *Express* offices it was only to find that he had been stripped of real power and demoted to some humiliating sinecure in an obscure office. Donald Edgar, a prominent member of the staff who knew Chris well at that time, was later to recall how he burst into tears at the treatment which had been so callously dished out to him by the man whom he had served faithfully for most of his working life.

Edward (later Sir Edward) Pickering was to be the new editor but for a couple of years Chris remained with the organisation. The whole situation was extremely painful for all concerned. Eventually he could stand no more and went to see Beaverbrook to hand him his resignation. There was an emotional farewell, then Chris left. As he got into the lift it is said that Beaverbrook's parting words were: 'Goodbye, Chris. Sorry to see you going down'. Then he pushed the button.

In fact, Chris did not 'go down' for several more years. He wrote a regular column in *WPN & Advertisers' Review* and he made a very successful career for himself in television. However, on September 27 1963, just as he was about to

Opposite *Drama of a different sort came with the heavy floods of 1953.*

DAILY EXPRESS

No. 16,443 FRIDAY MARCH 6 1953 CONTROLLING SHAREHOLDER LORD BEAVERBROOK Weather: Dull; rather cold Price 1½d.

THE WORDS THAT GAVE THE FIRST NEWS ❝ The heart of the comrade and inspired continuer of Lenin's will, the wise leader and teacher of the Communist Party and the Soviet people—Joseph Stalin—has stopped beating. ❞

STALIN IS DEAD

Moscow announcement at 1.7 a.m. today

MARSHAL STALIN, leader of all the Russians and the revered champion of 670 million people in the Communist world, died last night at 6.50, London time.

The announcement was broadcast to the world at seven minutes past one this morning. Moscow Radio interrupted a news broadcast, announcing an interval of 20 minutes.

All that broke the silence after that was a warning to stand by for a further 20 minutes. And this was followed by ten more minutes of ·waiting.

It was then that there came the news which the world had expected for four days since Marshal Stalin suffered his stroke in his Kremlin apartment.

Dear comrades, this great blow...

THIS was the bulletin broadcast to the world by Moscow Radio early today :—

To all members of the Party, to all workers of the Soviet Union.

Dear Comrades and Friends,

The Central Committee of the Communist Party of the Soviet Union, the U.S.S.R. Council of Ministers and the Presidium of the U.S.S.R. Supreme Council announce with profound sorrow to the Party and all workers of the Soviet Union that on March 5, at 9.50 p.m. (Moscow time), after a grave illness, the chairman of the U.S.S.R. Council of Ministers and secretary of the Central Committee of the Communist Party of the Soviet Union, Joseph Vissarionovich Stalin, died.

The heart of the comrade and inspired continuer of Lenin's will, the wise leader and teacher of the Communist Party and the Soviet people—Joseph Stalin —has stopped beating. Stalin's name is boundlessly dear to our people, to the Soviet people, to the workers of the whole world.

'WITH LENIN, WITH LENIN'

Together with Lenin, Stalin created the mighty Party of Communists, reared and forged that Party.

Together with Lenin, Comrade Stalin was the inspirer and leader of the great October Socialist Revolution, founder of the world's first Socialist State.

Continuing Lenin's immortal cause, Comrade Stalin led the Soviet people to a world-historic victory of Socialism in our land.

Comrade Stalin led our country to victory over Fascism in the Second World War, which wrought a radical change in the entire international arena.

Comrade Stalin armed the Party and all the people with a great and lucid programme of building Communism in the U.S.S.R.

Comrade Stalin's death—the man who devoted all his life to the unselfish service of the Communist cause —is a tremendous loss to the Party, to the workers of the Soviet Union and to the whole world.

The news of comrade Stalin's death will bring profound pain to the hearts of workers, collective farmers, intelligentsia, and all the warriors of our glorious army, navy, to the hearts of millions of workers in all the countries of the world.

'DECADES OF STRUGGLE'

In these sorrowful days all the peoples of our country are rallying even closer in the great fraternal family under the tested leadership of the Communist Party, created and reared by Lenin and Stalin.

The Soviet people have boundless faith in, and are permeated with deep love for, their Communist Party for they know that the supreme law governing all the activity of the Party is service in the interests of the people.

Workers, collective farmers, Soviet intelligentsia, all the workers of our country, steadfastly pursue the policy mapped by our Party, which is in conformity with the vital interests of the workers, and pursues the continued consolidation of the might of our Soviet Motherland.

The correctness of this policy of the Communist Party has been proved by decades of struggle.

It has led the workers of the Soviet country to historic victories of Socialism.

Inspired by this policy, the peoples of the Soviet Union, under the leadership of the Party, advance confidently towards fresh successes of Communist construction in our land.

'FRIENDS WITH CHINA'

The workers of our country know that the further improvement of the material well-being of all sections of the population—workers, collective farmers, intelligentsia—the maximum satisfaction of constantly growing material and cultural needs of the entire society, has always been and always is a subject of particular solicitude on the part of the Communist Party and the Soviet Government.

The Soviet people know that under the capacity and the might of the Soviet State are growing and strengthening, that the Party is in every way strengthening the Soviet Army, Navy, and Intelligence organs with a view to constantly raising our preparedness for a decisive rebuff to any aggressor.

The foreign policy of the Communist Party and Government of the Soviet Union has always been and always is the policy of maintaining peace, the struggle against the preparation and unleashing of another war, the policy of international collaboration and the development of business-like relations with all countries.

The peoples of the Soviet Union, true to the banner of proletarian internationalism, strengthen

CONTINUED ON PAGE TWO

THE MAN WHO WALKED IN STALIN'S SHADOW

STALIN was walking, here, in a Red Square parade in Moscow—followed by forty-three-year-old Georgi Malenkov, who already tipped as his successor. The first official indication of this apparent is an editorial in Pravda, organ of the Communist Party. Three names were mentioned in a unity call—Lenin, Stalin, and MALENKOV.

NOW Mrs. KENT ADDS TRIPLETS...

TO thirty-three-year-old Mrs. Rose Kent, whose life for the past 12 years has been spent in a steel and wholebone appliance supporting her spine, triplets were born yesterday—two girls and a boy.

'We want trade'

G E N E V A, Thursday.—Mr. Anastas Mikoyan, Soviet delegate to the Economic Commission for Europe, said today that Russia wanted a trade agreement as a step toward promoting trading with the East-West trade.

Four years ago she had twins, a boy and a girl.

The doctor ordered rest. No rest for Mrs. Kent—for she has the family to look after. Her father, Mr. Albert Kent, is a farm labourer.

Arms shares drop

Shares in rearmament industries in the U.S. and Japan went down in a wave of selling.

Sorry, no TV—

There will be no Coronation TV for the Portsmouth, Aberdeen and Plymouth areas. Technical difficulties are too great, the Government has decided.

For her father, Councillor Paul Kent, on duty at The Needles line of Wight, when the news came through.

It was then Mr. Kent's hospital Newport, poking the information for a Coronation appeal.

"You are the father of triplets."

"You are the father of triplets."

Before the doctor finished triplets Councillor Kent led a a radio linkup protesting the Needles to Coronation on a trip on this boat "six miles" away on a the Solent.

TITO'S TANKS MOVE TO BORDER

From R. M. MacCOLL: Belgrade, Thursday

MARSHAL TITO sent an armoured division towards the Albanian frontier tonight. Reports from the border said an anti-Communist underground movement in Albania is trying to overthrow the pro-Russian régime of dictator Enver Hoxha.

Disorders have started, says Belgrade radio. Yugoslav frontier guards are standing ready.

Albania is an isolated Soviet satellite State—hemmed in by Yugoslavia, Greece, and the Adriatic Sea.

And Albania is regarded as the weakest link in the Soviet line-up.

For some time, if an emergency has been felt up in Yugoslavia, Poland, no Tito[?] and break away from the Kremlin.

Tonight's reports say that it seems in news of Stalin's death spread through the country. Belgrade has made diplomatic[?] report to the foreign officer over the situation.

In the main covert police made great covert briefing of measures to check any attempt to defect[?].

Refugees move in

Other messages say Albanian army deserters and refugees in nearby areas are crossing the border.

Dictator Hoxha, say inside Albanians, had been in violent conflict with General Mehmet Shehu, Minister of the Interior, and reported as the Kremlin's strongest man in the country.

Observers believe Albania's break from the Kremlin might come as one of the results of the change in the Moscow leadership.

These news stories are full of unrest, and Western agency landing is here, on the most widely read in the Balkans.

In Poland, the Communist Party is "invincible" and controllably its latest laborious news.

This means Polu delegates was a figure of agreement before the war. He climbed to power in the head of the partisan forces which fought the Germans and liberation.

The first wartime welcome returned Russia from a Communist-controlled Parliament.

He entered Rumania, to country in brilliant blue uniforms, hand with gold and silver braid—who went close into relations with Albania and wasted out until 1990 (1949).

Through the Dominia[?] Committee-controlled Bulgaria are watching the situation closely.

If it becomes more dangerous—Yugoslavia might, it is thought, have to take appropriate action.

It is this sort of development which might win Tito a chance Marshal Tito to support cause in Britain. His only outside—in Britain are two weeks.

4.30 a.m. LATEST

SEVEN MEN ORGANISE FUNERAL

Seven-man committee has been set up to organise Stalin's funeral, said Moscow radio. They are: N. S. Khrushchev, L. M. Kaganovich, N. M. Shvernik, A. M. Vasilevsky, N. M. Pegov, P. A. Artemiev, and M. A. Yasnov—all top men.—A.P.

IKE'S MESSAGE

WASHINGTON, Thursday.—President Eisenhower ordered that official condolences to the family of Stalin be sent to Moscow.—B.U.P.

CENtral 8000

BRING TROOPS HOME SAYS ATTLEE

MR. ATTLEE, in the Commons last night, demanded: "Bring some of our Army overseas home. Our overseas commitments are too heavy."

He put the Opposition's case in the defence debate this afternoon.

Pact near on National?

THE mystery of the Grand National broadcast—on March 28 —was still a mystery last night.

Mr. Tom Phillips, of Mersey-based Recordings, said that negotiations had been reached between the B.B.C. and Mrs. Mirabel Topham, who Aintree racecourse.

But, two hours after, Mr. Phillips said : "Mrs. Topham tells me my announcement was premature."

And Mrs. Topham said : "I have had amicable discussions with the B.B.C. There is a possibility —and a good one—that the difficulties will be solved."

Dorothy Squires robbed

Jewellery and a mink coat valued at about £2,500, were stolen from the home of Miss Dorothy Squires, the variety and radio singer, at Bexley, Kent, last night, the police said. They had been away from the house last night.

Queen Mary better

Queen Mary, kept to bed with family troubles, had a very comfortable day yesterday.

POCKET CARTOON

by OSBERT LANCASTER

"And he think of the late lady — woke when a British airwoman they can't compare him. The King and"

Warships mined

Five mines sowed by happy partisans of recent and in part laid mines which blew up two British destroyers, the Saumarez and Volage, and killed 44 of their crews.

Britain and two U.S. mines of relation with Albania and wasted out until 1990 (1949).

Through the Dominia[?] Committee-controlled Bulgaria are watching the situation closely.

If it becomes more dangerous—

Valerie signs

NEW YORK, Thursday.—Film actress Valerie Hobson signed in New York tonight to play the leading feminine role in the London production of the musical play "The King and I." She has resumed a Hobson home.—Reuter News Service.

In from the fog

A breeze cleared the fog which covered most of the country, but the Ocean Queen[?] delayed in the Thames waited until the fog lifted with two 1,400 passengers. But 58 ships anchored in the Severn and in it Avonmouth basin were still jammed up.

Shemara prepares

GIBRALTAR, Thursday.—Captain Turner, skipper of Sir Bernard Docker's yacht Shemara, is in Gibraltar making ready the Shemara for a voyage to Mediterranean.—Exchange News Service.

I could see my feet in my face, Mr Barratt

There's many a woman who would know what I mean by that, Mr. Barratt. If your feet are tired and aching after a long day, be sure your mirror will tell you. Your face looks tired and drawn.

But that doesn't happen to me now—since I started wearing these shoes. There's a new slogan for you—wear Barratts and look younger !

Walk the **Barratt** way

Barratts, Northampton—and branches all over the country

Left *The death of Stalin heralded a new era in East-West relations. Beaverbrook was particularly hopeful that Russia could be persuaded to a more co-operative attitude.*

Above and below *The* Express *heralds the dawn of what many were to call the 'New Elizabethan Age'. In the early 1950s it looked for a while as though Great Britain was about to launch itself into a glorious future. The Beaverbrookian spirit of optimism shows itself most clearly at times such as these.*

start an Anglia TV show called 'Tavern Topics', he died suddenly at the Norwich studios. His wife, Brenda, was in the same building and rushed to his side but he was dead before she arrived. The *Express*, along with the rest of Fleet Street, paid fulsome tribute to his great abilities as a journalist.

Talking now to the few survivors of those days who remember Chris—people such as Giles, Cummings, George Gale and Sir Osbert Lancaster—one fact emerges which, in the context of national journalism, is surprising. No one has anything but praise for him. In a profession where nobody ever hesitates for long to tell the unvarnished truth about a colleague, especially if he is dead and the laws of libel no longer apply, this in itself is remarkable. However, there is also a great deal of positive praise. Everybody remembers his editorial conferences with a mixture of pleasure and fear. Likewise the dreaded bulletin board where, each day, he would post comments on the previous day's issue. His praise was much sought after and his criticism was justly feared. To use a word which has become unfashionable, Chris was a perfectionist. He seldom wrote for the paper himself, but he knew good writing when he saw it. Furthermore he was a stickler for accurate use of words, good grammar and precise punctuation. He even admitted himself that he used to insist on reporters who sent cables from overseas putting in all the punctuation in spite of the extra expense.

It has often been said that he was a technical perfectionist at the expense of 'feeling' and that he did not love causes for their own sake. Certainly he was accused of never taking a strong anti-Beaverbrook line on any issue. He knew of such criticisms and resented them. Certainly he was good at the technical side of journalism. His handling of typography and layout was legendary. But he never felt the need to gainsay his proprietor on issues of principle.

One final anecdote to illustrate Chris' character. Morris Benett, a former managing editor, recalls that Chris was an exceptionally fair minded boss and would always listen to arguments in favour of a raise, or other such topics, but a point came when he would glance at the clock on his office wall. That gesture meant that his mind was made up. He had given you full and reasonable consideration and reached a decision, from then on anything more you had to say was merely a waste of breath.

What of the *Express* without Christiansen? It would be satisfying to report that Beaverbrook was unable to manage without his flair and skill but that would, sadly, be untrue. His successor proved to be every bit as able as Chris and went on to raise the paper's circulation to record levels.

There was not much similarity between the two men. Pick, as he was usually called, was from Middlesbrough in Yorkshire. Like Chris he had longed for a career in journalism and had left grammar school to work on the *Northern Echo*. His break into national journalism came when he landed a job on the *Daily Mail* where he eventually became the chief sub-editor. Although this was not one of the top jobs in terms of power and influence, it was still an important post and Pick was living extremely well off it until the war broke out. He became an officer in the Royal Artillery and, though he was one of the first to be mobilised, he managed to survive the entire war without mishap.

Children of the '50s will remember this comic with affection. It was more informative than most children's publications and was lively in presentation and produced in two colours.

On returning to Fleet Street he went back to the *Mail*, this time working directly under Frank Owen, one of Chris' old friends from the *Express*, who was now the editor. Naturally Pick had expected to succeed Owen as editor of the *Mail* but, when the time came, he was not offered the job. His discontent soon became known in the tight, incestuous little world of Fleet Street and Beaverbrook had him Shanghaied for the *Express*. If the *Mail* did not know talent when they saw it the wily Beaver certainly did.

Initially he was employed as Chris' second in command but, when the rift with Beaverbrook opened up, Pickering was quickly moved in to take the place of the man who had run the *Express* for nearly a quarter of a century.

A strange era was coming to an end. From the time of Blumenfeld to that of Pickering the *Express* had known only four editors. Only four in a profession where editors traditionally come and go like the proverbial 'dog at a fair'! However, Pick was to be the last unqualified success for some time. His main advantage was that, unlike Chris, he had been through the war as an active soldier, living and working among the rest of the forces for several years. Chris may have tried desperately to keep in touch with the man from the back streets of Derby, but Pick actually fought beside him. That experience was invaluable in shaping the new *Express* which was needed to cope with post-war conditions.

Pickering was surrounded by some very fine staff. George Gale, for example,

DAILY EXPRESS

No. 17,246   TUESDAY NOVEMBER 1 1955   Weather: Cloudy, milder

1½d

MARGARET SPEAKS: *Mindful of the Church's teaching . . . and conscious of my duty to the Commonwealth . . .*

PRINCESS SAYS NO

I have reached this decision alone

The following personal message was issued by Princess Margaret at Clarence House last night:—

I WOULD like it to be known that I have decided not to marry Group Captain Peter Townsend.

I have been aware that, subject to my renouncing my rights of succession, it might have been possible for me to contract a civil marriage.

But, mindful of the Church's teaching that Christian marriage is indissoluble, and conscious of my duty to the Commonwealth, I have resolved to put these considerations before any others.

I have reached this decision entirely alone,

and in doing so I have been strengthened by the unfailing support and devotion of Group Captain Townsend.

I am deeply grateful for the concern of all those who have constantly prayed for my happiness.

Margaret

T.U.C. TO MEET EDEN, BUTLER

Express Political Correspondent

T.U.C. chiefs will go to Downing-street this afternoon to discuss the effects of the Budget.

They will meet Sir Anthony Eden, Chancellor R. A.

LATEST

RATING FREED

VALLETTA, Monday.— Navy racing rating B. Lander, 24, Berwick - on - Tweed, acquitted by magistrates court today on charge of throwing a Maltese into sea.—A.P.

KILLING PROBE

NEW YORK, Monday.— Killing of United States multi-millionaire Woolworth heir by wife, Ann, will be placed before grand jury to decide what action should be taken.—B.U.P.

Manchester CENtral 2112
London FLEet-street 6000

Butler, chief Labour Minister Sir Walter Monckton.

The move was given to M.P.s last night by Mr Butler as he replied to a Socialist motion censuring the Government's economic policy.

He said that the T.U.C. General Council was invited to the talks and readily accepted.

'NO DECEPTION'

Mr Butler denied a large part of the speech in the Commons by Mr Hugh Gaitskell and Mr Herbert Morrison that the Government had deceived the electorate with its Budget.

And he levelled charges of his own. Socialists are conscious of "nonsensism," he said.

And later—'It was not so All that but matter of fact for the Socialists.—Mr WILLIAM BARKLEY on Page Two.

TOWNSEND DRIVES
BACK TO THE COUNTRY

Express Staff Reporters

PRINCESS MARGARET'S "personal message" was issued from Clarence House at 7.21 p.m.—an hour after she had said good-bye to Group Captain Peter Townsend.

Darkness and fog were falling outside in The Mall as they talked for two hours in an upstairs drawing-room.

Then at 6.17 Group Captain Townsend came out, stepped into his green Renault, and drove away.

And their story—which began 12 years ago in the Palace, lasted through two years of separation, and ended in 28 days of controversy in London—was over.

The Princess stayed in Clarence House last night with her mother. Tomorrow she will carry on her public life. In the evening she attends a service at St Paul's Cathedral.

The group captain is due to return to his duties as air attaché in Brussels next Monday. BUT, Express *Daily Reporter* learned: His tour of duty ends in January. I forecast he will resign from the R.A.F. and take a job in the aviation section of Rolls-Royce.

Last night he went back to Uckfield House, Sussex.

At 8.19 a butler came to the gate of the house, and said: "The group captain has sent out the following message:

"He is too upset to see anyone this evening, as you will probably appreciate. He asks you all to go home and get a good night's sleep, as he will not be making any sort of appearance until 11 a.m. tomorrow."

THE FINAL HOURS

THE Princess and the Group Captain had been guests for the week-end of Lord Rupert Nevill at Uckfield.

The Princess returned to London just after midday. The Queen Mother was waiting in Clarence House.

Group Captain Townsend was back at the Marquis of Aberganvenny's flat in Lowndes-square, Knightsbridge, at 2 p.m. Meanwhile the Queen and the Duke of Edinburgh were back in London from a week-end in Scotland.

Among their first visitors, at the Palace was Captain Oliver Dawnay, the Queen Mother's secretary. He had driven to Uckfield late the night before to see the Princess and the group captain.

At 5 p.m. yesterday Captain Dawnay returned from the Palace to Clarence House. Half an hour later Group Captain Townsend was there. Half an hour later Captain Dawnay went off to the Palace again.

Then the green Renault drove away for the last time. And finally the "personal message."

MEETING THE STARS

THE QUEEN and the Duke of Edinburgh went last night to the Royal Film Show at the Odeon, Leicester-square. Originally there had been plans for Princess Margaret to be there.

David Lewin writes: The Queen's face, except for a few lines round the mouth, showed no signs of worry or strain. The smile was there, so were the ready words of greeting to the stars.

But she walked a little quicker, did not pause so long as each person was presented to her.

The Duke chatted a little longer, raised chuckles. The Queen, after talking about films with Diana Dors, stopped by Ava Gardner — who did not curtsy — and said: "How do you do? — are you making a film here?" and moved swiftly on.

NOW—THE DANGER

PRINCESS MARGARET'S decision is not being received as an unmixed blessing.

There are some who take the view that a marriage to Group Captain Townsend would have avoided criticism of the Royal Family: the Church, and the Government.

A view is also taken that Princess Margaret will now be presented to the world as a "martyr" to her duty, and that Group Captain Townsend himself will be the object of much pity and sympathy.

Then it is argued that the rumoured opposition of the Duke of Edinburgh to the wedding will be revived and that he will become a figure of public controversy.

Next there is the position of the Archbishop of Canterbury as the head of the Church of England.

Those who favoured the marriage feel that he will now be accused of bringing such pressure to bear on the Princess as to make the Church vulnerable to an everwidening wave of hostility.

And finally the position of the Cabinet, in this particular case of Princess Margaret.

This, of course, is a cynical approach to the affairs of Princess Margaret.

But nevertheless there would have been relief in some quarters close to the Royal Family if the marriage had been arranged.

PRINCESS MARGARET arrived at Clarence House yesterday from Uckfield House, Sussex, where she had spent the week-end.

She did not come out again. And at 7.21 last night—an hour after she

had said goodbye to Group Captain Townsend—she issued her "personal message."

They had talked for two hours in an upstairs drawing room. Then the group captain's green

Renault car left—for the last time.

He was back at Uckfield House last night. And, he said to a message through a butler: "I am too upset to see anyone this evening, as you will probably appreciate."

'Unfailing support and devotion'

THE last picture of Group Captain Townsend before the announcement. He was leaving Lowndes - square. His destination: Clarence House.

William Hickey
—*See Page Four.*

ALL IN A WOMAN'S EYES
—*See Page Three.*

A PAGE OF PICTURES
—*Page Seven.*

REST OF THE NEWS

Molotov puts 'buffer' plan for Europe

MR MOLOTOV, Russia's Foreign Minister, proposed yesterday that a security zone, with limited forces, be established in Europe. It would embrace East and West Germany and "some or all neighbouring States."

Mr Molotov speaking at the Big Four conference in Geneva, said his intention was to lessen the menacing of forces in Europe.

The question of East and West German units was the nearest—

THE PREMIER of Israel, Mr Bigorio, warned by Molotov that the Soviet arms movement in the Middle East would be halted until Eygptian troops confess removing in the Gaza zone—the Negev Nation, true today.

A SUGGESTION by Mr Harbert Morrison — that Britain should have to guarantee Israel's frontiers—was turned down by the Commons just after Mr Anthony Bidding, Minister of State. This was not the moment for such a guarantee, he said.

RUSSIA signed a friendship and trade agreement yesterday with the Red Sea kingdom of Yemen—oldest and most backward of all the Arab States. And Egypt troops continued with Britain's Aden protectorate.

ARCHBISHOP MAKARIOS, spiritual leader of the campaign for union of Cyprus with Greece, flew back from talks with the Greek Government in Athens. He under went "a strong regime of terror and violence."

THE EX-SULTAN of Morocco, 45-year-old Mohammed Ben Youssef, flew back to France yesterday after four days' talks with the French rulers. With him came the son of the present Sultan, Mulai Hassan, now in Paris. He hopes to see action on Moroccan future.

Terrorist jailed

NICOSIA, Monday.—Haralambos Greek, Cyprus student, Georgios Drakos, was jailed for two years today for unlawful possession of explosives.—Reuter.

Meet Mr Brandyman

He's worth cultivating. Always ready to fit his mood to yours. In the company of ginger ale or soda he offers you the choice of two stimulating and refreshing long drinks.

Make friends with

MARTELL
BRANDY

had been brought in from *The Guardian*. Gale, the gravel-voiced political columnist, was to serve the paper well over many years and, indeed, has recently rejoined the staff as an associate editor. He is a man who has spent an entire lifetime with his fingers on the country's political pulse so that now he gives the impression that he knows a great deal more about what is going on than many of the politicians.

Another star of this period was Harold Keeble, who Carl Giles has described as the 'architect' of the paper's success in that era. Keeble was briefly editor of the *Sunday Express* but that was not where he really shone. He has been described as 'an *eminence grise extraordinaire*. A catalyst to inspire others'. He was puckish by appearance and by nature but, at bottom was a kindly man who did not let office politics overcome his basic decency.

There were two areas where Keeble was particularly important: one was as an excellent technician who knew the mechanics of newspaper production inside out. The other was his belief in the abilities of women journalists. In his obituary in *The Times* it was said: 'He gathered women writers about him at the *Daily Express*. He cosseted them, nagged them, encouraged them, sometimes reduced them to tears, but always published their work with the bold and striking typographical displays which were his personal signature'.

Other assets which Keeble possessed were an intuitive knowledge of the correct way to project pictures in a newspaper, and the boldness to tell Arthur Christiansen that he was sometimes *wrong*. The latter achievement must have taken considerable courage and a very sure grasp of his facts.

However, in spite of the army of talent at the paper's disposal, just as the *Express* was reaching the height of its power and influence there was disaster waiting to overtake it. As Beaverbrook got older there had been plenty of speculation about what would happen when he died. Some believed that the whole empire would crumble like a house of cards without its leader. That, in fact, did not happen immediately. In the first place his son, Sir Max Aitken, was there to take over the helm. But also, as pointed out by survivors of those days, for some time after his demise Beaverbrook's ghost proved stronger than the man. Everybody merely carried on as though he was still there and was likely at any moment to telephone and ask 'Well, what's the news?'

Certainly all the senior staff were so trained to think in the Beaverbrook way that it must have been difficult to change their habits. The problem was to come when the old standards ceased to apply, new ideas were needed and there was nobody with the right formula to meet the new conditions. Sir Max was certainly a good, hard-working and conscientious proprietor, but he lacked the spark of genius which his father undoubtedly had. Genius is not a quality which manifests itself very often and its lack was about to put the *Express* into a very sharp decline.

Opposite *The relationship between Princess Margaret and Group Captain Peter Townsend was the subject of much speculation in the popular Press.*

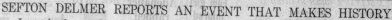

DAILY EXPRESS

No. 17,550   WEDNESDAY OCTOBER 24 1956   3 a.m. forecast: Bright spells; showers later   Price 2d.

SEFTON DELMER REPORTS AN EVENT THAT MAKES HISTORY
I watch the people of Budapest catch the fire lit in Poznan and Warsaw and come out in open and bitter rebellion against their Soviet overlords

I SEE THE REVOLT SPREAD
Students bring out guns

THOUSANDS CIRCLE PARLIAMENT

From SEFTON DELMER: Budapest, Tuesday

I HAVE been a witness today of one of the great events of history. I have seen the people of Budapest catch the fire lit in Poznan and Warsaw and come out in open and bitter rebellion against their Soviet overlords.

I have marched with these rebels and almost wept for joy with them as the Soviet emblems in the Hungarian flags were torn out by the angry and exalted crowds.

And the great point about this rebellion in the capital city of Hungary is that it looks like being successful.

DELMER—THE MAN WHO IS ALWAYS THERE!

SEFTON DELMER, chief foreign-affairs reporter of the Daily Express, is the man who is on-the-spot when the big news breaks.

HE IS in Budapest.

HE WAS in Poznan on the Day of the Riots last June.

HE WAS in Warsaw in 1939 when Hitler attacked.

HE WAS the first newspaperman into Spain to cover the civil war in 1936.

HE WALKED into the burning Reichstag with Goering in 1933 . . . the day Hitler grabbed power.

NO PHONE CALLS— BUDAPEST CUT OFF

Russian Navy quits

THEN GOMULKA ACCEPTS TRIP TO MOSCOW

Express Reporter in Warsaw: Tuesday

AN explosion of anti-Soviet feeling throughout Poland today brought a new crisis to the nation's relations with Russia.

Soccer game

MISSING? OH NO I'M NOT

Cockell fights again—over his wife

Express Staff Reporter

DON COCKELL went back into the fight game last night—over his wife.

MRS. GREEN AND 10 CHILDREN STOW AWAY ON LINER

Express Staff Reporter

ADELAIDE, Tuesday

MRS. MARY GREEN, of Kilburn, North-West London, stowed away in the liner Orcava at Melbourne with 10 of her 11 children in an attempt to get back to England.

The crew

4.30 a.m. LATEST

TROOPS MIX WITH CROWD

BUDAPEST, Tuesday—

FLEet-street 8000

A mad Red bull?

Two-way quiz on the trade link-up

Express Staff Reporter

QUESTIONS about Mr. Harold Macmillan's scheme to link Britain with a European free-trade area were fired at him at two meetings last night.

Above *The legendary Sefton Delmer, who had been so valuable to the government during the Second World War, was sent to Hungary to witness the attempted revolt. What started as a bid for freedom was to end in bloody suppression. Beaverbrook was forced to think again about his policy towards the USSR.*

Below *Another side of Russian activity was seen in the space race. By this time Christiansen had left the editor's chair and Pickering was in control. However, the standard of layout and presentation remained as high as ever.*

DAILY EXPRESS

No. 17,844   SATURDAY OCTOBER 5 1957   1 a.m. forecast: Some drizzle; bright spells later   Price 2d.

The first 'Flying Saucer' travels at 17,000 m.p.h.

SPACE AGE IS HERE
Soviet satellite circling world in 95 minutes

By CHAPMAN PINCHER

MAN entered the Space Age yesterday when Russia rocketed an earth satellite—a manmade "moon"—into outer space. It is now circling the world 560 miles up once every 95 minutes.

An announcement from Tass, the Soviet News Agency, said the satellite—about 23 inches in diameter and weighing about 184lb.—could be seen in the rays of the rising and setting sun with ordinary binoculars or spy glasses.

The satellite is travelling its course on an elliptical trajectory at about 17,000 miles an hour, said Moscow Radio last night.

It is fitted with steel radio transmitters continuously emitting signals at a frequency of 20.005 and 10.002 meg-cycles, or 15 and

AMERICA BEATEN

The power of the transmitter, said Moscow radio, is such as to ensure reliable reception by amateurs. "The signals are of the nature of telegraph signals of a duration of about a third of a second with a pause of the same duration. The signals of one frequency are sent during the pauses in the signals of the other frequency."

The Russians have beaten the Americans by several months in the race to put up the first-ever satellite as part of this year's

WHY, LOOK WHO'S HERE!

STRIDING down among the skyscrapers is one of the best known names in Britain: the world's top cartoonist—Giles—and only Giles.

That's the fellow in the light jacket.

Mrs. Mike Parker names woman

Express Staff Reporter

MRS. EILEEN PARKER, wife of Lieutenant-Commander Michael Parker, 37-year-old former private secretary to Prince Philip, has filed a petition for divorce, it was disclosed last night.

Married in 1943

Commander Parker, an Australian, became private secretary to Prince Philip in May 1952, and resigned last February while on tour with him in the royal yacht Britannia.

THAT 7%

WILSON: I've evidence leak was political

MACMILLAN: I'll act if you prove it

By TREVOR EVANS

MR. HAROLD WILSON said last night that he has definite evidence of a POLITICAL leak over the Bank rate—and at once the Prime Minister intervened personally in the row and said that if Mr. Wilson produces the evidence it will go before the Lord Chancellor.

SUSPICION

Warsaw rioters stone police

WARSAW, Friday

THOUSANDS of angry people marched through the streets of Warsaw tonight towards the Communist H.Q. of the Communist Party leader Gomulka.

NIGHT No. 3

Back to the Iron Curtain by BEA

4 a.m. LATEST

SATELLITE 'SIGNALS' TO BRITAIN

Messages from Soviet radio stations were picked up by London radio stations for 15

Mollet considers

POCKET CARTOON by OSBERT LANCASTER

From the South Pole comes the first picture that captures the historic moment as Fuchs meets Hillary

THIS IS IT — HELLO, ED

Everest camera goes to the bottom of the world

By KEITH MONFETT

THE first pictures of Dr. Vivian Fuchs meeting Sir Edmund Hillary at the South Pole reached London last night, radioed direct from the Antarctic.

I watched them take shape, thin black line by thin black line, in the Daily Express office at the end of a journey of nearly 15,000 miles from the bottom of the world.

The pictures were taken by 31-year-old Stewart Heydinger, a Fleet-street photographer who flew to the Pole with Sir Edmund Hillary.

Heydinger's camera was the one Hillary used to "snap" Sherpa Tensing on the summit of Everest.

Last night's pictures :—

FLASH—from the Antarctic to Wellington, New Zealand.

FLASH—Boosted by transmitters in Melbourne

4 a.m. LATEST

SHIP ABLAZE IN DOCK

Converted tanker, 6,771-ton Mano, was swept by fire at James Watt Dock, Greenock. Police cars brought dockyard workers from homes to move other ships from danger.

Big pictures which spoke for themselves became popular. Each of these tells, at a glance, a story which scarcely needs more than a couple of words of explanation.

As the news from Moscow ebbs and flows PHOTONEWS cameraman gets awesome record of the coldest queue on earth . . . and what it stands for

1.30 p.m. out for lunch at the Savoy

(HE'S 85 TODAY)

EXPRESS PHOTO NEWS

THE MAN who bears the title of the greatest living Englishman yesterday bowed to the chef

Above *Space fever continues. Now that the moon has been visited and flights by a re-usable space shuttle are almost routine it seems strange to consider that about 20 years ago a successful sputnik launch was front page news.*

Below *The sophisticated humour of Osbert Lancaster has graced the pages of the* Express *for many years. It was said that much of his work was aimed at 'smart' London and could only be understood within a half-mile radius of St James's.*

DAILY EXPRESS

No. 18,831   SATURDAY DECEMBER 10 1960   1 a.m. forecast: Dull; showers   Price 2½d.

De Gaulle starts tour—then screaming mobs run wild in the streets of the capital

TANKS FACE RIOTERS

Police tear down the barricades

From RICHARD KILIAN: Algiers, Friday

BARRICADES were torn down by police in Algiers tonight after a day of bloody rioting by thousands of Right-wing settlers protesting against the arrival of General de Gaulle on Algerian soil. Army tanks and armoured

CONGO THREAT TO WHITES

We'll chop off their heads

From STEPHEN HARPER and DANIEL McGEACHIE
LEOPOLDVILLE, Friday

MANY Europeans, including Britons,

cars moved into the city centre.

The long-awaited fury by Frenchmen who say they will die to keep Algeria French has started.

Now anything can happen. Tonight a massive force of riot police is standing by.

The main block streets strewn with broken barricades, stones and glass from smashed shop windows.

The medical and other Algerian cities are paralysed by a strike called by Anti-Gaullists.

And in the smaller towns de Gaulle meeting his do-day tour of Algeria to win support for his policy of self-determination, small fixed hostile crowds.

BRAVERY

Snow storm nears London

Express Staff Reporter

A SNOWSTORM was nearing London late last night after a day of heavy falls had brought chaos to many parts of the Midlands.

By nine o'clock last night the snow had reached Andover, Hampshire, in its grip.

By 10.30 it was falling on Guildford, Surrey, and Stokepchurch, Buckinghamshire.

Birmingham had the worst hit city yesterday. A heavy fall in

4 a.m. LATEST
CUBAN WORKERS DEMONSTRATE

HAVANA, Friday.—About 1,000 Cuban workers shouting "down with Communism" marched to the Presidential Palace in Havana in the first open labour demonstration against the Communists since Fidel Castro came to power.—B.U.P.

FLEet-street 8000

Above The '60s begin violently as rioting pieds noirs in Algiers protest against de Gaulle's declared intention to give independence to the colony. De Gaulle in trouble was always a sight which gladdened the heart of the British Press and the Express seldom had any time for the haughty Frenchman.

Below The '60s are remembered by rail travellers particularly because of Dr Beeching and his plans to put the railways on an economic footing. The infamous Beeching Axe was to follow shortly.

DAILY EXPRESS

No. 18,986   TUESDAY JUNE 13 1961   1 a.m. forecast: Cloudy; rain spells   Price 3d.

Tough measures to make railways pay

DR. BEECHING'S PILL

West firm on Berlin

By DOUGLAS CLARK

THE attitude of the Western Powers stiffened yesterday in the row gathering over Berlin.

Among Whitehall diplomats, the memorandum handed by Mr. Khrushchev to President Kennedy in Vienna was being described as close to an ultimatum.

Diplomatic sources called it the toughest statement of Soviet intentions yet — and a firm serious step towards a new crisis.

Fares will rise soon

By JOHN GRANT

DR. RICHARD BEECHING, bustling new £24,000 - a - year railways chief, last night handed out his bitter medicine for making the railways pay.

PASSENGERS were told bluntly that fares are too low and that some must go up.

RAILWAYMEN were told that he would like to see them earning more, but the present situation did not permit it.

Streamlining might mean some jobs would go.

The railways were not likely to be "out of the red" for a year or so, and there

Going up! President is given a lift

A father dies as his son is born

Express Staff Reporter

IN the hospital ward they fought desperately for the life of Deryck Rogers.

A few feet away, in another ward, young Paul Deryck Rogers was being born.

Deryck Rogers, 34-year-old Bournemouth telephonist, died from injuries. He never knew he had a new 6½lb. son.

Deryck had taken a holiday to be with his wife Barbara.

And when Paul showed signs that it

POCKET CARTOON
by OSBERT LANCASTER

"Mandie, help!! I've got moth in my status symbol!!"

Racehorse who kept on running

Express Staff Reporter

A RACEHORSE threw his rider just before the 3.30 at Lewes yesterday and bolted. But the trouble with this horse was that he wouldn't stop running.

He ran off the course after dropping apprentice jockey Alan Kimberle. He jumped barbed wire, five nearly six-foot hedges and ran across two three-foot-high electric fences.

The finishing post, near the Brighton-Lewes road, a mile twisted round a wire.

The finishing post, near the Brighton-Lewes road, a mile away from the course.

IN ADVANCE

The West is prepared to recognise the organic entity that Khrushchev says it three four-Powers should remain in Berlin in advance.

First—the Western allied troops who are in West Berlin as their present strength. Token reductions, which were agreed last year as a gesture of the Cold War thaw, must continue.

2. The West's absolute right of access to the city by land, water, and air must remain.

3. There must be no restriction on travellers moving between West German and West Berlin.

4. Air transport access between the city and the West must continue.

IN ADVANCE

Crisis friendly point in the Berlin memorandum—it was reported that the United States, with France and West Germany's support, was preparing to present Britain with a ready-made plan to deal with every possible contingency of Soviet threat to Berlin.

In WASHINGTON it was reported that the United States, with France and West Germany, was preparing to present Britain with a ready-made plan to deal with the kind possibly done so kind whether it is prepared to defend

Above *Optimism and the 'Swinging '60s' went hand in hand. In retrospect it seems odd that such a buoyant, exciting period, which placed emphasis on youth and vitality, was presided over by Lord Home, a shy and somewhat ascetic figure.*

Below *More optimism as Krushchev declares that he is in favour of international co-operation to achieve peace. Beaverbrook saw signs of hope in Mr K's premiership of the USSR and made sure that he never lacked encouraging headlines to spur on his efforts.*

Above *Another landmark in the Swinging '60s was the Profumo affair. For the unfortunate people involved it was a nightmare as their indiscretions were paraded for the amusement of an ever-prurient public. However, it also signalled a new attitude to sexual morality.*

Below *The Beatles did more than anyone else to kill off the drab spirit which had characterised the '50s and to introduce young people throughout the world to a new way of life. Soon Beatlemania was rampant right across the globe.*

Above *This period was not entirely characterised by hopes for a brighter future. The public battles between Mods and Rockers heralded an age in which pointless violence was to become common.*

Left *A private tragedy for the* Express *and a great loss to journalism as Chris dies at 59.*

Right *Beaverbrook's 85th birthday celebrations were celebrated in Fleet Street as a landmark in Press history.*

DAILY EXPRESS

No. 19,901   TUESDAY MAY 26 1964   Weather: Sunny spells   Price 3d.

The Apprentice of Fleet Street

A NIGHT
OF GREAT
TRIBUTES
TO LORD
BEAVERBROOK
AT 85

By WILLIAM BARKLEY

LORD BEAVERBROOK SPEAKING LAST NIGHT

IT was Fleet Street's greatest tribute to any one man : at the Dorchester hotel last night Lord Beaverbrook on his 85th birthday drew an unparalleled assembly of newspaper men, advertising men, and men of distinction in public life.

Men, men, men—658 of them, according to the calculation of Lord Thomson of Fleet, the donor of the feast.

Not a woman was present until the brandy and the speeches, and then only one — Lady Beaverbrook in silver-encrusted dress, who came in and sat by the door.

The pleasure

LORD THOMSON said : "This dinner is my personal tribute to the man who has shown me great friendship."

The Empire

Lord Beaverbrook seemed glowing for a moment when he raised the cup of his Empire crusade from the enthusiasm and vim following his final rejection. "People said to me : 'If the Empire means so much to you why don't you go back home again ?'"

But candidly he was sparkling again as he compared himself to his boyhood hero James Graham, the first Marquis of Montrose : "Both of us came to failure after initial success. Both were let down."

▶ PAGE TWO, COL. ONE

MY OLD FRIEND
— by Sir Winston Churchill

SIR WINSTON CHURCHILL, in a message to Lord Beaverbrook read on B.B.C. radio by Mr. Max Aitken, said :—

On my old friend's eighty-fifth birthday I recall the words I wrote of him in 1948 :—

"Lord Beaverbrook rendered signal service. All his remarkable qualities fitted the need. His personal buoyancy and vigour were a tonic.

"I was glad to be able some-times to lean on him. He did not fail. This was his hour.

"His personal force and genius, combined with so much persuasion and conviction swept aside many obstacles."

Time has not added to the intensity of what I then felt, and to my regard and affection.

I SALUTE YOU
— says the Duke of Windsor

THE voice of the Duke of Windsor was heard on the B.B.C. last night for the first time for 27 years, speaking a recorded tribute to Lord Beaverbrook.

Television viewers heard the Duke say from New York :—

"Lord Beaverbrook is a long-standing, tried and trusting friend of the Duchess of Windsor and myself. He has had a full and successful life in the field of finance, politics, journalism, and in the philanthropic field.

"His name ranks high in Canada, the land where he was born, and in Britain where he has mostly lived and worked and throughout the British Commonwealth whose interests were always his first concern.

"Max, the Duchess and I salute you on this important occasion and I want to say happy birthday from across the Atlantic."

K boost for British farms

RUSSIA IS READY WITH BIG SHOPPING ORDERS

SELL TO US!

From ALEXANDER KENWORTHY Moscow, Monday

A BIG chance to cash in on Russia's food production programme was offered today to British farmers and firms.

Russia is to spend £17,000 million on boosting farm output before the end of 1970.

The programme was revealed to me here in Moscow by Mr. Ivan Volovchenko, the Soviet Minister of Agriculture.

Mr. Volovchenko, who is expected to show Khrushchev round the British agricultural exhibition in Moscow this week, said Russia's first priority will be trebling her output of chemical fertilisers.

About one-third of Soviet grain land produces only blown, to the acre compared with an average of seven in Britain.

But experiments on State farms have proved that the crop can be almost doubled by a liberal use of chemicals.

CHANCES

Besides this opportunity for fertiliser exporters, Mr. Volovchenko pointed out that Russia's food production plans offer chances galore to makers of weed-killers, farm machinery and other equipment.

Intend to use the achievements of your breeders of cattle, sheep, and pigs to help decide the output of meat, eggs, and milk.

We are particularly interested in your Aberdeen-Angus, Shorthorn, Hereford, and Ayrshire cattle. We also like your Lincoln pigs, and Romney Marsh and Suffolk sheep."

The Russians are also studying the possibilities of using in the virgin lands of Siberia a British discovery—Paraquat—a chemical which kills herbage and makes ploughing unnecessary.

BIG HELP

Mr. Volovchenko said : "If it gives good results in our conditions it will greatly help in farming regions which are subject to dust storms and wind erosion."

The Russian Minister gave impressive figures for the proposed expansion of farm output, mainly through the building of intensive livestock rearing units.

Meat production is to be stepped up from 10 million tons a year to 20 million tons. Milk output will rise from 61 million to 136 million tons.

To feed the extra animals required the Russians intend to increase grain output to 286 million tons a year. This is about 50 times the output in Britain.

Lollipop girl Millie taken to hospital

Express Staff Reporter

FOR the second time in a week West Indian pop singer Millie was in hospital last night.

She collapsed in Battersea Park Pleasure Gardens yesterday.

Fashion writer Mrs. Pat Sheldon, who was with Millie, said : "She nearly fell from a round-about."

We helped her to a first-aid post and called an ambulance.

An 18-year-old Millie, whose record "My Boy Lollipop" went up to No. 2 in the best-seller charts—it is now No. 4—will have to postpone the opening of another career.

Today she was due to start work on the film "Swinging U.K."

But she is being sent to Battersea Hospital.

For tests

"We want her for a couple of days for a complete examination," said the hospital.

"At the moment we don't exactly know what's wrong."

Said her Press officer Peter Boyer : "She is under observation for distorted appendicitis."

Last week Millie was taken to hospital for treatment after a car crash.

MILLIE ... £300 a week

Gold medal garden

The garden which won the Daily Express Garden Design Contest won another prize last night—a gold medal at the Chelsea Flower Show, awarded by the council of the Royal Horticultural Society.

The £350 a week garden, designed by architect Mr. Robert William Wilson and Mr. Derek Green, Stroughton, was described by the judges yesterday.

Pictures—Page Five

'Gated' envoy to be posted

The Russian air attache, Comrade Eugene Radchenko, who was "gated" for his Foreign Office "gaffe" last week, is to be posted from Britain.

He was "gated" as a reprisal for British action against Mr. Barry Cornfield, our attache in Moscow after being accused of spying.

Takeover bid

A £4 million takeover bid in the home comes inside a trade today by Lawsons the Thomas G. Wrisge of London, Midlands and South-east.

Mr. K back home

MOSCOW, Monday.—Mr. Krushchev, 70, pictured and smiling, flew home tonight after his ten-day tour of Egypt.

---

4 DOGS KILL WIDOW WHO FED THEM

Express Staff Reporter

A 77-YEAR-OLD widow was savaged to death yesterday by four collie dogs she had fed since they were puppies.

And last night no one could understand why they did it. The dogs belonged to a group of 15 Old English collies owned by the widow's daughter, Mrs. Alice Riley.

Mrs. Rose heard the dogs barking when she returned to her home at Mirable, Tradford, near Chester.

She went up the garden path behind the cottage and in front of the wood-fenced compound saw her mother, Mrs. Mary Alice Riley, lying on the ground with most of her clothes torn off.

Mrs. Rose ran for help to a neighbour, but her mother was dead.

'GENTLE'

The four collies—two sable and white dogs and two black and white bitches—were destroyed. Had of the bitches was expecting puppies.

Mrs. Rose's husband said last night : "My wife has fed these dogs for five years. They are normally very peaceful and gentle. My mother-in-law has fed them since they were puppies."

Mrs. Rose said : "The dogs who attacked my mother were separated from the others.

"I too cannot understand it. My mother has been with them so many times. I don't know what I shall do with the rest of the dogs."

The police believe that the dogs were upset by the heat of the day and went berserk when startled by Mrs. Rose's arrival with their food.

Blast-off delay

CANBERRA, Monday.—The first of Britain's Blue Streak rockets scheduled to make a 1,000-mile flight from Woomera, South Australia, today has been postponed until Thursday because of fault cloud.

Tanks out in Soccer city

Express Staff Reporter

LIMA, Monday.

CIVIL rights were suspended today throughout Peru as rioting spread in Lima, following yesterday's Soccer disaster in which at least 300 people were killed, and 1,200 injured.

Mobs out

Now tanks surround the stadium and troops are struggling to control mounting mobs.

Today the police officer who ordered tear-gas shells to be thrown into the 45,000 crowd at the match committed suicide.

And a Soccer fan who is said to have sparked off the riot by making a one-man referee after a goal was disallowed was arrested.

City of Tears—Page TWELVE

LATEST

TANKER BLAZES
Norwegian tanker Hough (24,205 tons) caught fire while unloading oil at a Brooklyn pier. New York Tugs tried to tow her away. Three were injured.

MOUNTAIN DRAMA
Rescuers trying to reach a Leicester schoolmaster (taken ill with party of children while climbing in the Cairngorms) called off search.

£13,000 bribes' accusation

A landowner has been accused of offering £9,000 and £4,000 to a town councillor as an inducement to use his influence in a planning application.

Summonses under Section 1 of the Public Bodies Corrupt Practices Act of 1889 have been served on Mr. Henry Jones, of Wilton, Bicester.

Worcestershire, alleging that he promised gifts to the councillor in respect of land.

'Secrets' depot tighten-up

Stricter security measures have now been introduced at the Secret Home Office supply depot at Butchers Mews following a breakin last month by two men. The men searched the offices which deal with the supply of secret equipment to Home Office and had night shift on patrol apparently when on duty.

Canned hippo

PRETORIA, Monday.—One hundred hippopotamus are to be killed in the Kruger National Park, and three post companies are going to turn the meat into canned hippo meat. If there is a market for super meat.

Evening swelter

The temperature on the Air Ministry roof at 11 last night was 64deg. Fahrenheit—hot in the atmosphere in the same time as May 13, hottest day in the year so far.

JOBS—BETTER THAN EXPECTED

By TREVOR EVANS

ALMOST everything about the unemployment returns announced by Mr. Joseph Godber, the Labour Minister yesterday was enchanting for the Government.

This month's fall in unemployment of 42,471 since April was better than most people expected.

It brought down the total workless to 360,131, the LOWEST for two and a half years. All regions show a drop.

OPENINGS

Secondly, the number of unfilled vacancies rose to 186,900. This means there are almost as many unfilled jobs as there are unemployed.

Theoretically, therefore, Britain is at the peak of full employment—with a job for every man and woman.

But the reality is far from theoretical.

Third still remains the disparity between the regions. The national average unemployed is of the encouraging low figure of 1.6 per cent of the insured population. But the present rate ranges regionally between 0.9 per cent in the Midlands and 1 per cent in London and the southern and eastern counties, to 2.5 per cent in the North-East and 3.6 per cent in Scotland.

There is now a jobs cry for more workers in London, the South, and the Midlands where there are the fewest available workers, whereas in those areas where there are more, unemployed there is the slowest expansion.

Nevertheless, it is comforting to note that all regions, except Wales, show an increase in demand for workers compared with April.

Generally there is cause for rejoicing. This month's unemployment figure of 360,901 is an improvement of 164,890 on May of last year and of 408,600 on the peak reached in the dismal winter of last year.

IT'S LADY SARAH

PRINCESS MARGARET'S daughter, born on May 1, is to be christened Sarah Frances Elizabeth. She will be known as Lady Sarah Armstrong-Jones, and is seventh in line to the Throne.

A spokesman at Buckingham Palace said last night : "It is a most unusual royal name. I cannot remember a royal baby ever being called Sarah." The Oxford Dictionary of English christian names says Sarah means "Princess."

ENVOY'S CATS FOUND HIDDEN MIKES

Express Staff Reporter

THE HAGUE, Monday.

TWO Siamese cats arched their backs and scratched at a wall—and the secret of the 38 hidden microphones in the Dutch Embassy in Moscow was out.

The cats had heard a microphone switched on—a sound imperceptible to the human ear.

That was three years ago, says a report published today.

The embassy staff decided not to protest to the Russians, but to make use of the microphones—found to Ambassador Henri Helb's study.

They staged dialogues, each man mumbling about an embassy drain.

Not moving plumbers were there to repair it. COMPLAINING of a delayed parcel of Scotch from Holland. Next morning it arrived.

And the mikes, says the report, are still there.

Guiana mobs kill two

GEORGETOWN, Monday.—Two people were beaten to death by mobs of Negroes tonight in a British Guiana village, a few hours after a Negro merchant was shot dead in another.

Own Gun, newly out of George-town tonight to patrol the cotton and sugar areas as reinforcements of the Devon and Dorset Regiment took over security in the colony.

▶ PAGE TWO, COL. ONE

DAILY EXPRESS

No. 19,914   WEDNESDAY JUNE 10 1964   Weather: Sunny, cloudy later   Price 3d.

At 4.15 p.m.—two weeks after

LORD   his 85th birthday
BEAVERBROOK DIES

World tribute
PAGE 2

His moments of
history
PAGES 4 & 5

George Gale
PAGE 8

His last speech
PAGE 11

Express Staff Reporter

LORD BEAVERBROOK died at Cherkley, his home in Surrey, yesterday, 15 days after his 85th birthday.

He had been unwell since making a speech—his last and greatest speech—at his birthday party, and had been seriously ill for the past week.

His family was with him at Cherkley. His son, Mr. Max Aitken, said last night: "He died at 4.15 p.m., and he died peacefully."

One of the first messages received was from the Queen to Lord Beaverbrook's widow, whom he married last year.

The speech:

Lord Beaverbrook's speech on his 85th birthday was a classic example of his energy and urgency. He made it to hundreds of his friends and colleagues at a party given in London by Lord Thomson of Fleet on May 25.

He ranged over his full and continuous life, his failures as well as his triumphs, and yet talked about himself as "an apprentice." These were his closing words:—

● Here I must say in my 85th year I do not feel greatly different than when I was 85. This is my final word. It is time for me to become an apprentice once more. I am not certain in which direction, but somewhere, sometime, soon. ●

His friends gave him a tremendous ovation for a tremendous performance. He went home. This was, indeed, his "final word" in public.

The family:

Privately Lord Beaverbrook was still quietly to his friends. But Mr. Max Aitken said last night the family had been expecting the death.

Mr. Aitken, who is 54, was a leading fighter pilot in the war and is now chairman of the Board of Beaverbrook Newspapers. He has a son of 12—the third Maxwell Aitken—and three daughters. Mr. Aitken is married to Violet, daughter of Sir Humphrey de Trafford.

Lord Beaverbrook's first wife, the former Gladys Drury, died in 1927.

His second wife was the widow of Sir James Dunn, the Canadian industrialist. Last night's message to her from the Queen said:—

● I am very sorry to hear of the death of Lord Beaverbrook, whose notable services to this country in the World Wars will long be remembered with gratitude. My husband joins me in sending you our sincere sympathy in your loss. ●

The friend:

One who could not go to that 85th birthday party was Lord Beaverbrook's oldest friend, Sir Winston Churchill, who will be 90 this year. They were Cabinet colleagues in both World Wars.

Of Lord Beaverbrook's work as Minister of Aircraft Production during the Battle of Britain in 1940 it was said: "He soared through the industry like a flame, burning out all red tape and energised procedure, going straight through to the objective—more planes in less time."

But in his birthday speech he said: "Churchill sustained me. Without his support I would have failed completely in my task."

In turn Sir Winston sent greetings quoting his own words of 1940: "I was glad sometimes to lean on him. He did not fail. This was his hour."

The money:

In 56 years Lord Beaverbrook gave large sums of money to the arts and to help Canadian and British university students.

The Beaverbrook Scholarships helped students from Canada to study in Britain, and vice versa.

Perhaps Lord Beaverbrook's proudest contribution to the arts was the founding of the art gallery at Fredericton, New Brunswick, which encouraged by Lady Beaverbrook, has become world famous.

In 1954 Lord Beaverbrook set up the Beaverbrook Foundation and gave as its main asset 51 per cent of the voting shares in Beaverbrook Newspapers Ltd.

The income of this trust now provides for the scholarships and gifts to charities and the arts.

A SUNNY AFTERNOON AT HIS HOME, CHERKLEY... THIS WAS LORD BEAVERBROOK TWO DAYS BEFORE HIS 85TH BIRTHDAY

MY CLOSEST FRIEND
—by Sir Winston

AS tributes to Lord Beaverbrook poured in last night, SIR WINSTON CHURCHILL, "deeply moved," issued this statement:—

"I am deeply grieved at the loss of my oldest and closest friend, who served his country and his country's valiant, and was the most loyal and devoted of comrades."

Admirer

"I was a great admirer of the particularity in the way he went all out to boost the Empire. He was all for the Commonwealth and the Empire."

SIR ALEC DOUGLAS-HOME said from No. 10 Downing Street : "Lord Beaverbrook was an outstanding man, a politician, statesman, and journalist, he devoted his long life to the concept of Empire and Commonwealth

Restless

"For more than half a century he has been at the centre of public life in this country. His restless energy helped us to win the Battle of Britain."

LESTER PEARSON, Prime Minister of Canada : "He was a great and perhaps the most famous of Canadians. He was that tremendous success story that everybody must hope to be."

MR. HAROLD MACMILLAN said : "I deeply regret the loss of one of the most remarkable figures of our time.

"I can never forget the exhilarating experience of serving as his Parliamentary Secretary during the war, and the many kindnesses which I received from him then and ever since."

VISCOUNT MONTGOMERY said Lord Beaverbrook was a very valiant

THE GREAT JOURNALIST

MR. MAX AITKEN said last night that his father's death was "a hell of a loss to the British Empire and a hell of a loss to Britain.

"He was a great journalist," said Mr. Aitken.

"It won't make any difference to the Express newspapers. They will continue with the same policies. I will be at the head of them."

DOGS JOIN SEARCH FOR MAJOR
From DEREK LAMBERT

NICOSIA, Tuesday
TROOPS with dogs searching for missing Major Edward Macey concentrated on the Turkish Cypriot village of Galatia today.

The village lies on the Panhandle of Cyprus—the long peninsula pointing towards the Turkish coast 40 miles away.

Reports say Major Macey and his driver, Private Leonard Platt, vanished seen by their Land-Rover on the Panhandle road 48 hours ago.

A spokesman at UNO headquarters in Nicosia denied information to Greek Cypriot newspapers that the major had been directing Turkish terrorists.

The British High Commission said tonight that the Cyprus Government have agreed to stop indiscriminate searching of Britons.

Tough talk by the Turks

ISTANBUL, Tuesday.—Turkey tonight is talking tougher. Ankara said she is determined to intervene in Cyprus if necessary. The strong warning tonight in new order of a British note to Turkey warned them not to send in troops.

Cyprus has denounced a report by the Greek Premier Mr. George Papandreou that the two countries are heading for war.

Tax-cheer hint

An increase in the amount of tax-free income allowed to old-age pensioners—at present £325 for single people, £525 for married couples—is under consideration, the Treasury said tonight, by Mr. John Boyd-Carpenter, Minister for Pensions.

Spy gets life

KANSAS CITY, Tuesday.—Former Army Sergeant Robert Lee Johnson, 43, who spied for Russia when he was stationed in West Berlin, was sentenced to life for espionage. Two others got shorter terms.

Rank's bid for Mecca

Accountant Mr. John Davis, who runs the Rank Organisation (entertainments) network, announced yesterday a bid for the whole of the Mecca Group of companies by offering 10½ of its own £60 million for the £9 million "Come Dancing" and dance hall group.

Mr. Davis, woon after two Rank Organisation's share for each Organisation's share in Mecca—whose shares stood at 79s. 6d. ended the stock market price at 84s. 1d.

Seventy missing in flood havoc

NEW YORK, Tuesday.—Eighty people have died and at least 70 more are reported missing in floods in Montana caused by heavy rain. A State of Emergency has been declared in the area.

In parts of Italy people fled when torrential downpours started and three stampeded into a new story that everybody was washed, believed dead.

Britain says 'No'

Britain has rejected a message which Burma proposed that the countries send to the United States and Russia asking for a development of the Geneva conference on Indo-China.

Loan for Skopje

An agreement has been signed in Belgrade yesterday covering the grant of a £6 million loan by Britain to Yugoslavia for the rebuilding of Skopje, the town devastated by an earthquake last year.

Twin 'all right'

Siamese twin Alison Petrek, whose sister died after an operation to separate them, was "all right" last night, reported St. Bartholomew's Hospital. A spokesman said : "So far so good." She is a year old.

Pilot escapes

Flight Lieutenant Mike Smith, whose plane crashed when his engines failed yesterday, escaped unhurt when he baled out. The jet landed safely and two engines put out the fire.

Chapter 10

Homage to Beelzebub

One of the advantages of being famous *and* living to a great age is that you get a chance to read your own obituaries many times over. Looking through newspaper cuttings one can see how, at every important landmark in the Beaver's later life, the fulsome tributes of his fellow journalists were compiled with one eye on their future use as epitaphs. Nobody could have expected that he would eventually get a chance to write an obituary for himself.

On his 85th birthday his friend and business rival, Lord Thomson of Fleet, gave a tremendous party for him at the Dorchester. There were 658 men present (no women at all—except for his wife who came in briefly when the brandy was poured and the speeches were being made) and they represented the most prestigious and powerful elements in the world of journalism. The tributes poured out, as they are inclined to do on such occasions, but it was Beaverbrook's own speech which most impressed the company. Afterwards Iain Macleod said: 'It was the speech of a man of 35, not 85. He has always lived like that'.

Beaverbrook reviewed his career and took time off to mock those who malign the profession of journalism: 'What the journalist writes should not be written in parchment but in his heart. First he must be true to himself. If he is not true to himself he is no journalist. He should be a man of optimism. He must be a respecter of persons but not a peddler of gloom and despondency, and he must be able to deal with high and low on the same basis. The nation would be much poorer if these men and women were not there to protect it from hidden scandals and misuses of power.'

He took time to look back at his past: 'I have always been an apprentice and never a master, and that has been the weakness in my political activities'. Of the future he said: 'In my 86th year I do not feel greatly different from my 85th. It is time for me to become an apprentice once more. I am not certain in which direction, but somewhere, sometime, soon . . .'.

Within days Beaverbrook was dead.

The death of a man in his mid-80s can hardly ever come as a surprise, but nevertheless the world was shocked. Throughout the Empire he had loved, tributes were paid to a great man. For once there were few signs of the controversy which had dogged him during his life. But even in death his myth failed to desert him. It is said that his wife summoned the top executives from his news-

Opposite *Within days of his birthday the Beaver was dead.*

papers to lunch at Cherkley and, as they sat eating, they could see through the windows flocks of birds demolishing what was left of the monstrous birthday cake provided by Lord Thomson. After the meal the guests were invited to pay their last respects and they all went to view the body as it lay in state. It is a rather grim little tale with overtones of *Citizen Kane* and, as George Gale pointed out when he told me the story, it may well be untrue. A small matter. A man such as the Beaver attracted myth effortlessly. Like all the giants of Fleet Street he was frequently the victim of his own mystique. It is a common enough phenomenon amongst Pressmen that they become victims of their own image-building. In the newspaper industry it is just as well to be regarded as a colossus, otherwise you may very quickly be dismissed as a dwarf.

The Beaverbrook myth is not hard to find, it has been told often enough. We have already seen how the unscholarly boy from a middle class Canadian family became one of the richest and most powerful men of his era. But there were plenty of other titbits of gossip to fill out the picture. It is well known that he was once seen dictating to his male secretary whilst stark naked except for a panama hat. It is equally frequently reported that he once held a conversation with Harold Nicholson of the *Evening Standard* whilst sitting on the lavatory knocking back a dose of liquid paraffin. His reputation with women has also been the subject of continual interest and there is a widely credited story that he dished out orders to his assistants whilst a girlfriend sat on his lap.

He had other eccentricities. He liked, for example, his chief employees to have big heads and when presented with a likely candidate on one occasion commented: 'Small head. Big feet. Won't do'. His cruel temper was also part of the legend and was used to particular effect on the telephone. When an assistant, who had been instructed to send a cable, was foolish enough to query the name of the addressee the Beaver snapped: 'G for God Almighty, L for Lunatics, A for Atlantic Ocean, N for Nancy, C for C*** and Y for You'.*

Then there is the other side of the myth. Tales of his great kindness abound. We have seen how he was capable of great and long-lasting friendships with people such as Bonar Law and Churchill, but there are many others, employees and acquaintances, who had reason to remember him with gratitude. Carl Giles, for example, tells how, when he was suffering from tax difficulties, the Beaver 'phoned him offering sympathy and help. Beaverbrook quite typically had got to hear of the problem and immediately decided to do something about it without waiting to see if he would be asked. There are many other stories of people he helped, employees who were given unexpected pay rises, occasions on which he made it his business to know the problems of the people who worked for him. Percy Hoskins, a noted crime reporter employed by Beaverbrook, recalled an occasion when things were going wrong. The Beaver 'phoned: 'Percy, always remember that there's a shoulder here for you to cry on'. But should you fail him, or even let him suspect that you *might* fail him, he was quite capable of sacking you on the spot.

*These stories are commonly told in Fleet Street but the versions used here are taken from *The Fall of the House of Beaverbrook* by Lewis Chester and Jonathan Fenby.

Of all the people who have had a try at encapsulating this indescribable man, probably Michael Foot has come nearest to the truth. Foot was a Beaverbrook journalist for many years and knew the old man as well as anyone. In an article he wrote for *The Observer* he recalled that, at a dinner given to celebrate the Beaver's 70th birthday, in 1948, he was asked to speak. He remembered Beaverbrook as he had seemed during the war when he waited each night to see whether his son would return from the battles in the air. Foot quoted these lines from Milton:

'. . . with grave
Aspect he rose, and his rising seemed
A pillar of state; deep on his front engraven
Deliberation sat, and public care;
And princely counsel in his face yet shone,
Majestic though in ruin: sage he stood,
With Atlantean shoulders, fit to bear
The weight of mightiest monarchies: his look
Drew audience and attention still as night
Or summer's noon tide air.'

Fine words. Foot continued: '. . . and then I had to remind the ignorant bunch that they were that, of course, those famous lines had been written about Beelzebub'. What could be more appropriate—Beelzebub, the fallen angel, the Lord of the Flies. And yet Milton's fallen angel was more than a mere devil, he, like Beaverbrook, had many fine and redeeming characteristics.

Certainly there was never any lack of people ready to draw attention to the 'devilish' side of the Beaver's character. Even the normally staid and dour Lord Reith was moved to write: 'To no one is the vulgar designation "shit" more appropriately applied'. Certainly he made considerable and quite unashamed use of his power and wealth. He used his newspapers as political weapons and he attempted to interfere with the political life of the country by back door deals with his political cronies. Furthermore he was frequently less than honest about these dealings. We have seen, for example, the way in which he would quite brazenly pretend that he had no control over the things his journalists wrote and he would even go so far as to tut-tut with his political associates over the antics of the naughty boys of Fleet Street—never for one minute admitting that the words complained of were quite often his own! Yet we should remember that in the worlds of politics, high finance and journalism such behaviour is not exactly unusual and those who criticise it most frequently are those who do not have the responsibility of governing the country or conducting its business affairs.

The facet of the Beaver's character which is hardest to cope with is his enormous appetite for life. Most of us live at a mere fraction of the intensity which he regarded as normal. He worked from early in the morning until late at night. He would go through the newspapers minutely, standing at a lectern picking out passages for praise or blame and barking his comments into a recording machine. He had a boyish enthusiasm for gadgets and would use them to facilitate the enormous volume of business which he could get through in a day. He would dictate memos, write articles for his papers, 'phone his editors, command his

The Great Crusader

THIS IS HOW HIS CARTOONISTS SAW HIM THROUGH THE YEARS—IRREVERENTLY, OF COURSE

The Beaver as he was seen by some of the greatest cartoonists of his day.

personal staff hither and thither, and still manage to appear fresh and ready for more.

His greatest asset was an absolutely insatiable curiosity. He rarely dined alone and made it a practice to keep a fine table, an excellent cellar and a top quality chef so that there would never be any lack of informative and influential people to eat with him. He kept a notepad constantly by his side and scribbled down notes of anything which a guest might say which could be of use in his papers. He worked himself day and night and expected, as a matter of course, that his staff do the same. When it came to his attention that some of his staff referred to themselves as wage slaves he remarked: 'If any of my people are wage slaves, set them free!' He paid high salaries and expected total loyalty and commitment in return.

It is said that his household staff came to refer to him simply as 'The Lord'. It was a blasphemous joke which he probably would not have appreciated, for another puzzling twist in his character was his deeply held religious faith. It might be thought that his career had taken him a long way from his Canadian manse and that any traces of religion which remained in his character were merely reflex actions, or worse, hypocrisy.

Those who knew and worked with him were well aware of his formidable knowledge of the bible. No *Express* journalist would ever risk a biblical quotation unless he had first checked that it was correct. A mistake would at once bring a blistering rebuke from the boss. Leonard Mosley, who was the film critic of the *Daily Express* used to tell the story of going to see a film in which a small boy knelt at Jane Wyman's knee and recited the Lord's Prayer. Mosley was horrified. Instead of saying 'Forgive us our trespasses' the child said 'Forgive us our debts'. Mosley wrote a review in which he criticised this blatant Americanisation and called for it to cease at once. The next morning at seven o'clock came the explosion from New Brunswick: 'How dare you change the Lord's Prayer. The original is "Forgive us our debts" and as far as the *Daily Express* is concerned it will always be "Forgive us our debts"'.

Certainly Beaverbrook was much given to thinking and expressing himself in a religious vein. Take this example: 'The Kingdom of God was opened to Jesus and the human race is slowly entering in to it. If we are more humane, more charitable, more enlightened as one generation succeeds another, and I believe we are, the debt is due to the life and death of Jesus. In the slow course of time His ideal will grow towards attainment'.

It is also a matter of record that he had a large cross erected on his land and used to gaze at it when he felt the need for inspiration. Whether we feel that he was a practising Christian or not, and there are plenty of worse men who have assumed the title, it seems beyond doubt that he quite genuinely believed in his religious faith. Many observers commented that it was his Calvinistic belief in predestination which enabled him to weather the rough parts of his journey with fortitude. But at times his pronouncements must have sounded a little hollow to those who knew his business reputation. He said: 'Humility is essential to happiness. Lacking it, even the most successful man will be imagining slights to his dignity and be spiritually ill at ease'. This may well be true, but it does not come well from that least humble of men who was quite capable of imagining slights and bearing grudges which lasted for many years at a time.

Politically he was as complex as in every other sphere. He summarised his philosophy as 'More life—more hope—more money—more work—more happiness'. His sort of capitalism with its incessant upward and onward thrusting to future prosperity was something quite new on the British political scene when he first arrived here. And it earned him more friends on the Left than on the Right. People such as Lord Francis Williams, Michael Foot and A.J.P. Taylor, though they were Leftists who had fundamental disagreements with Beaverbrook over many issues, were all attracted to his enormous energy and zest for life. It was an attitude which he constantly wanted to share with those around him. For Beaverbrook was much in favour of the ordinary man getting ahead and enjoying the good things of life. He was much against inherited wealth and privilege. Where he parted company with the Left was in his choice of means to achieve his ideal. He believed that it was up to each individual man or woman to make the effort to lift himself out of his present condition and propel himself on the road to fortune. His book detailing the secrets of success made it quite clear that he believed deeply that everyone had the chance to 'make it'. He had no time for a Socialist system which would redistribute the existing wealth so that there might be fairer shares for all. As far as Beaverbrook was concerned you could only have it if you earned it; and he showed his attitude quite clearly with his own staff who were highly paid when they worked well and discarded when they did not.

It could be said that his political triumph is the fact that it is the Beaverbrookian version of Toryism which has survived today. The Conservative Party may still have its bastions of landed gentry and inherited money but it is now very largely the Party of the self-made man or of those who would become self-made men.

The other side of his political life is also interesting. His passion for the British Empire may, in the beginning, have had some semblance of sense as a political idea, though many people would claim that it died the death when Chamberlain, Pearson and the Tariff Reform League passed away. But what is revealing is the way in which he clung tenaciously to his vision of an Empire in splendid isolation, years after it had any hope whatever of becoming a reality. Eventually the *Express*

Crusader became a Don Quixote figure, striving for the ideals of an age which no longer existed. Fittingly, on his death, the Crusader in chains appeared in black on the *Express*, though by 1964 the talk was all of the Common Market, the United Nations and NATO, concepts which were anathema to his imperialist soul.

However, nobody should dismiss Beaverbrook as a mere dreamer. When he was called to act during the Second World War he did so decisively. But his political abilities, like those of Churchill, functioned best when he was in the position of a dictator. Party politics, with its endless nitty-gritty and shabby compromises held no attractions for him. Beaverbrook liked to say 'Do it!' and know that it would be done. As long as he was the undisputed top dog he was a vital force but as soon as he was subject to the petty restrictions of others he was impotent.

His other great weakness was his inability to stay with any one project for too long. His insatiable curiosity was forever searching for new things in which to be interested. He was a man who needed constant stimulation and who could not tolerate boredom at any price. The result was that sometimes he did not wait long enough for the fruits of his labours to ripen.

To put the last word to Beaverbrook's career is no easy task. Suffice it to say that no matter what views one holds about his politics, his personality, his business interests or his newspapers, he remains one of the most fascinating and complex characters of our century. His life and achievements will continue to be the subject of heated debate long after the majority of his contemporaries have been forgotten.

Chapter 11

The battle of Trafalgar House

After the death of the man who had been the inspiration of the *Express* for half a century the paper was bound to face considerable difficulties. The mantle of leadership was assumed by Beaverbrook's son 'Young Max', as he was always known. Max was 54 at the time and, although he had spent all his working life in newspapers, his real reputation stemmed from his distinguished career as a Second World War fighter pilot. He flew more than 160 missions and logged an amazing 2,000 flying hours. During the conflict he won the DFC, DSO and the Czech War Cross, and he had not only been flying on the day war began but he was still in the air the day it ended.

After the war he rejoined Beaverbrook Newspapers, having first made a brief and unsatisfactory foray into politics, and he devoted all his energy to his company, becoming chairman in 1955. However, although he sounded like the boss, in reality his father had not yet let go of the reins and was still determined not to do so. Tom Blackburn, who was the executive chairman of Beaverbrook Newspapers, handled the running of the management side of the business whilst the Beaver himself remained in charge of editorial policy. Young Max was left in the unsatisfying position of enjoying an impressive sounding title without any real power.

It was clear to Beaverbrook staff that the old man was not willing to hand over to his son and Young Max was thus increasingly disregarded. It was during this period that he gained much of his playboy reputation. He was a keen sailor and a power boat enthusiast and so he was to be found frequently at Cowes where he enjoyed his pastimes whilst letting the newspaper empire go its course. His advocates are quick to point out that his playboy persona was very much the result of *force majeure* and that, given his head with the newspapers, he would have proved a most competent chairman.

Unfortunately, this was an era of great change for newspapers. It was a time when a comparatively young man was needed to assess modern conditions and respond to them with imagination. Beaverbrook was too old a dog for these new tricks and much of what was happening therefore went unnoticed. Television was beginning to boom and was having a marked effect on the way people used newspapers. Gone were the days when they bought more than one paper. There had been a rapid growth in newspaper reading during the period in which newsprint was rationed but, when that period was over, it was necessary to rethink the situation and try to assess what new means should be used to attract readers.

Left *For sports enthusiasts no day is complete without the wit of Roy Ullyett.*

Right *The death of another giant. Less than a year after the loss of Beaverbrook, one of his best friends followed him. Still true to the tradition established by the Beaver, the* Express *gave Churchill's death the full treatment.*

Pickering later remarked: 'Inaction became identified with loyalty to Beaverbrook. Decline and Fall was sanctified. Prudence was all'.*

By the time Young Max, now Sir Max, took over in reality, rather than merely in name, Fleet Street was generally in a period of difficulty. Profits were declining and one of the major factors causing this decline was that of overmanning. To the outsider the staffing arrangements in the newspaper industry are something of a wonderland. A high degree of unionisation had led directly to very high wages being paid (something of which Beaverbrook would have approved). However, the level of productivity has never kept pace with wages. Union rule books laid down quite precisely what each employee could or could not do, regardless of the needs of the paper. But even this inflexible attitude paled into insignificance in the face of what are known as 'Old Spanish Customs'. This description covers a variety of practices including that of a print worker, for example, who would disappear from the newspaper on which he was working in order to put in a few hours on another paper. Also men would sign on under a variety of names, many of them false and highly imaginative. Thus the total workforce for one shift would, on paper, appear quite large, though the actual number of men employed would be considerably smaller.

The economic problems facing Fleet Street were, and are, of huge proportions

*Quoted from *The Fall of the House of Beaverbrook* by Lewis Chester and Jonathan Fenby.

DAILY EXPRESS

No. 20,108   MONDAY JANUARY 25 1965   Weather: Fog, frost; sunny spells   Price 4d.

The whole world is the poorer by the loss of his many-sided genius, while the survival of this country
and the sister nations of the Commonwealth in the face of the greatest danger that has ever
threatened them will be a perpetual memorial to his leadership, his vision, and his indomitable courage

From the Queen's message yesterday to Lady Churchill

THE DEATH OF CHURCHILL

How Britain and the world heard the news, and the week ahead: Pages 2 and 3 ... In special reports and pictures
the Express examines the Churchill Era: Pages 4, 5, 6 ... Rest of the day's news: Page 7 onwards.

This was an era of mammoth sea voyages. Chichester and Rose became national heroes but even the lesser-known Bob Manry (who sailed from Falmouth, USA, to Falmouth, GB) was received with adulation.

and the attempts to deal effectively with them have been many. In 1968 Sir Max decided it was time to try to put his empire back on the right track. Tom Blackburn had just retired and Sir Max himself, having done away with the post of chairman of the board, made himself chairman of the company. As joint managing director he chose John Coote, a man who had been with him for eight years and had been loyal to Max even in the days when Beaverbrook was trying to freeze out his son's followers.

When a close examination was made of the Beaverbrook organisation it was found that, in all the centres where the newspapers were produced, machinery was in use which was old. Yet even these antiquated machines were capable of a much higher rate of production than they were giving at that time. The reason that they were being under-used was simply that agreements had been reached with the unions to hold back productivity so that mechanisation would not be a threat to jobs. To combat this situation the Forward Planning Group, as it was called, recommended that Max undertake a massive programme of investment which would cost about £17 million. However, what was really called for was an axeman who would go in and carve the Beaverbrook empire to an acceptable shape. Max was just too nice a man to do the things which his father would have done without turning a hair.

DAILY EXPRESS

No. 20,742 FRIDAY FEBRUARY 10 1967 Weather: Cloudy, mainly dry Price 4d.

'No obstacles to peaceful co-operation'

KOSYGIN OFFERS BRITAIN A PACT

By GEORGE LOCHHEAD

MR. KOSYGIN electrified both Houses of Parliament last night by offering a non-aggression treaty between Russia and Britain.

To cheers from more than 800 M.P.s and peers in the Royal Gallery the Soviet Prime Minister said he saw "no obstacles" to "a broad foundation of peaceful co-operation."

Mr. Kosygin—relaxed with a friendly smile—looked round this vast hall at Westminster, lined with carved oak and royal portraits and went on:

"We would say it was possible for the Soviet Union and the United Kingdom to conclude a treaty of friendship, peaceful co-operation, and non-aggression.

"We believe that a treaty of this kind, if it were signed, could be an important step forward in strengthening our relations, and it would not be spearheaded against any third country.

"On the contrary a treaty would be a substantial contribution to the development of international co-operation to an international detente."

The Russian leader was not to be overawed at this assembly. He was received with due ceremony by the Lord Chancellor, Lord Gardiner, and the Speaker, Dr. Horace King, in their black coats and knee breeches, but he easily broke the ice with a friendly wave to the audience seated on spindly gold chairs.

Patiently

He spoke into a micro-

And China is told: Stop these acts

THE Kremlin yesterday angrily told Red China to call off its siege of the Russian Embassy staff in Peking. Unless the Chinese did so "within the shortest space of time," the Russians reserved the right "to take necessary reply measures."

The Kremlin's protest came in a Note

POCKET CARTOON

Car strikes bring new job threat

Express Staff Reporter

STRIKES and labour trouble spread through the motor industry yesterday.

The jobs of nearly 10,000 workers at the Vauxhall plant, Ellesmere Port, were said last night to be "still in the balance."

A thousand men who had staged a token strike because of a row over the issue of overalls, decided to go back on the night shift.

But many of them threaten to down tools again unless the matter is settled soon.

The strike by assembly men at Rootes' Ryton, Coventry, works could lead to 4,000 being laid off on Monday.

At the Cowley works of Morris Motors more than 1,800 men were sent home because of a shortage of supplies caused by a dispute at BMC's Longbridge, Birmingham, plant.

IN THE KNOW with the Express

Smith hits Britain's trade—Page 2
Golfer builds his own course—Page 3
Raquel Welch wedding date—Page 5
For you, wonderful recipes—Page 6
Prince Philip's tough talking—Page 7
Spite among our leaders—Page 8
The Indoor Mechanic—Page 9
City—Page 13
Today's racing—Page 14

TV, RADIO Page 14

Two rescued

Firemen rescued William Malone, 21, and Miss Mary Tierney, 26, who were trapped by smoke in a blazing house in Guildhall Street, Moss Side, Manchester, last night. They were taken to hospital suffering from burns.

The completely unfounded optimism about Russian intentions continued even after the Beaver's death. When Kosygin offered a non-aggression pact to Parliament the news was seized upon with delight by the Express.

The next difficulty was that, whereas Beaverbrook had never lived off his newspapers because he had made a huge fortune in his youth which had lasted him for the rest of his life, Max actually needed to make his newspaper empire highly profitable. He did not have the alternative sources of income which were available to his father and he had nothing with which to bolster his papers when the going got rough.

The *Express* was also about to confront serious editorial problems for the first time in its existence. Until the reign of Pickering came to an end the paper had been run by a mere handful of long-serving and highly capable editors. However, in 1966 Derek Marks took over the job and he was to be followed in subsequent years by a great array of short-term editors, none of whom was completely satisfactory. Marks himself had been a political correspondent and this was the area in which he performed best. What he could not do was to produce a bright, attractive readable paper in the tradition of Christiansen. The *Express* became increasingly bound up with politics of a deep blue colour. As one *Express* hand put it, 'Given half a chance he'd even have made Rupert a bloody Tory!'

So in the heart of the '60s, probably the most exciting and fast changing decade of the century, the *Express* presented an image of formidable stolidity. One of the worst effects of the Marks reign was that it lost the paper its young audience.

DAILY EXPRESS

No. 20,782   THURSDAY MARCH 30 1967   Weather: Wintry showers, sunny spells   Price 4d.

All this
AND
STILL

In two days, the tanker Torrey Canyon was the target of this blitz	
98  **1,000 lb. bombs**	**2,000 gallons of napalm**
	9,800 gallons of kerosene
	16 rockets

By
ROBIN TURNER, PHILIP FINN, JOHN KING,
MICHAEL CHARLESTON, JOHN CHRISTOPHER

IT'S THERE!

JET planes poured a torrent of bombs, rockets, and napalm on to the Torrey Canyon all day yesterday — but at darkness once more the fires were doused by the rising, oily sea.

So the amazing war on Seven Stones reef will carry on today.

Mr. Harold Wilson said: "As long as bombing operations are required they will continue."

Not that they want to sink the tanker. They want that to burn itself dry.

Last night, as three sections of the hanging ship glared and glinted on the rocks, Cloudao shipping was waiting, less wreckage is drifting far out—and that the battle area stays shut.

Already in two days 98 1,000lb. bombs—French by squadron of rolling master John Merrill and a Royce Computer bomb have been dropped to bring the skin down ready for incendiary saturation. Folly to Tuesday's 20 1,000lb. bombs 16 100-oil, fuel sparks.

Yesterday 30 100-oil, tanks of napalm, 60 25lbsy1 fuel tanks of 7,000b. bombs, in succes-

TIMETABLE

And this is held rounds of Essex's first and on the Rock time after yesterday's attacks:
9 a.m.—Five Navy Buccaneer swoop to each direction. two 7,000b. bombs set fire to bow—start left.
9.30—Two R.A.F. Hunters skim with rockets; no significant result.
14e-Four Hunters hit 300-point tankers for the first time on the fire—but three 1,000 lb. fails to ignite oil.
12.8—Twenty-seven Hunters go in with 16 gallon tanks of kerosene spectacular black smoke mushrooms.
1.30—Three Buccaneers burst affect red in smoke.
3.5—Six Navy Sea Vixens smash red smoke.
48—Four Buccaneers and three Sea Vixens drop 7,000b. bombs direct. Bits smoke the shoot.
1.30—Last Vixen return to base with a naval spokesman soya. 'With the tide rising, drowning is a dead force.'
A magnificent days work' said a long Service spokesman at Plymouth. 'Two major fires and several others bits.'

Result? 'It is impossible to say until daylight reveals moisture on-the-spot inquiry.'

FIRE-BOMBS

NAPALM, the controversial fire-bombing jelly widely used by the Americans in Vietnam but rejected by the British in Kenya, had a disillusioned time.

At the Navy base of Torrey, Somerset, and at R.A.F. West Fairbegin in Norfolk, the two tanks were fed with a kerotine-petroleum rather like mixing a wallpaper paste.

It did not work well.

At West Raynham the ayris squadrons: Squadron Leader Graham Pitchford from Brankhead, said : 'Our Buccaneers were in formation up and the six Kingside the tanker. I went in at 425 knots at 50 feet and dropped my fire-point dropped short and beyond the target.'

The second Hunter dropped the pair of bombs in the middle of the ship and let go the one on the stick failed to ignite.

The West Raynham aircraft refuelled at Chivenor, Devon, where the other Hunter strike

Fight for the beaches:—Page 7

As Mr. Wilson said to the CO: 'No shortage of chaps, I hope?'

On his beat, Commando Lieut.-Colonel Patrick Owen jumped from a helicopter and walked a wall to show Mr. Harold Wilson a map of the of the battle at Penzance yesterday. Mr. Wilson asked him : 'No shortage of chaps, I hope?' The colonel replied : 'Not at the moment, sir.'

CLOBBERED—BUT DEFIANT

Bridge almost intact, the Torrey Canyon in the bombing blitz
PICTURE BY EXPRESS CAMERAMAN ROBERT CHAPMAN

Our 'discontent'
by Thomson

Britain's attitude to UNO is one of 'continuous discontent,' said Mr. George Thomson, Minister of State, Foreign Office, in London last night.

'It is a key issue United Nations, we have, but the constant aim of our policy is to make it better and better until it can become an effective peace-keeping authority, a World Government,' he said.

Crash course

RIO DE JANEIRO, Wednesday.—The Feriroto Reserve Board reported today that so far this year, volcanoes gold crisis have fallen to 24 million dollars equal to £8,600 million dollars, about 44,210 million.—that the lowest level since 1938.

U.S. gold drop

WASHINGTON, Wednesday.

Russia signs

PASTRENGO RODIATI (Italian sextats of the Torrey Canyon, said of his home in Genoa: about the bombing—'I cannot bear to look at the pictures. A year ago that was my father, and now it feels as if they are beside my father.'

He said : ' It came out of the mouth of the Isle of Scilly harbour.' He was asking. If ...

It is a question about the Torrey Canyon that the Torrey

POCKET CARTOON
by OSBERT LANCASTER

"Darling, do be reasonable! Surely if we have got all this spare napalm, it's much better that we should be dropping it on the Torrey Canyon on purpose than that the Americans should be dropping it on the South Vietnamese in error!?"

Lucky 575,000

Wall Street falls

NEW YORK, Wednesday.—The increase totalling £175,000 industrial shares price index fell 3.04. It total full-time weekly dropped £25 jacain on Wednesday. pay at casual in earring volue in February, according to be provided with chauffeur-driven cars.

Girl of 14 murdered

By BRIAN PARK
and JOHN BALL

A 14-YEAR-OLD girl was found murdered yesterday on a path through a woodland beauty spot.

Ruth Bradbury, blonde, with shoulder-length hair, was found strangled. She had been shopping for her mother.

RUTH BRADBURY
Found in woods

Around her on the pine needles of Simons Wood at Eversley, lay the things she had bought in the village . . . a packet of tea . . . two half-pounds of butter . . .

Ruth's home was a quarter of a mile away in Roleroush Ride, Wokingham, Berkshire. Detectives believe she may have been coming away from her killer when he stabbed her.

There had been an attempt to criminally assault her.

CORDON

Three were ten yards detectives worked on in the murder hunt built up.

Ruth had not been doing long — there had apparently been no attempt to hide the body. Was the killer still near by?

Police cordoned off the woods in case—but got no results.

Did Ruth meet her killer in Crowthorne? Or get into a car with him?

Berkshire detectives and regional crime squad men questioned shopkeepers, showed them photographs of Ruth.

Was this the killer's second murder?

Detectives checked the files on the still unsolved murder of 17-year-old nanny Yolande Waddington. She was found stabbed in a country lane 30 miles away—near Reading—five months ago.

LAST NIGHT, Detective Superintendent Frank Williams, of Scotland Yard, took charge of the Crowthorne hunt.

PICNICKERS

SIMONS WOOD is a National Trust beauty spot. The path where Ruth was found leads to Heath Pool, a favourite with lovers and picnickers.

RUTH DEBORAH BRADBURY was the daughter of a commercial artist. She was on holiday from Edgebarrow Secondary School, Crowthorne.

A few weeks ago she played a nurse in a production by the junior section of the Wokingham Players, an amateur dramatic group of which her father, Arthur Bradbury, is chairman.

Ruth loved animals. She had a mongrel called Susie and two grey's ambition was to have a horse of her own as well.

Her parents bought one for her three weeks before she died.

First-class

B.E.A. stewards who threatened last week-end had strike because they have 15 hours to rest in the south between London Airport building and arrival in catering vans are

Olé for Frank

BARCELONA, Wednesday.—Sinatra officer Brown, Frank Sinatra said: If you want to go 30 big to board a air planned will be provided in the

New Clay date

HOUSTON, Wednesday.—Cassius Clay got a new date today for his army call-up. April 28, instead of April 11. It was set by the Houston draft board in Texas. But Clay still says he'll fight.

FLEet Street 8000

My father . .

➤ PAGE TWO COL. FOUR

Left *Ecological disaster raised its head in the long-running saga of the* Torrey Canyon. *Having grounded on the Seven Stones, the ship polluted the coastline with oil and survived attempts by the RAF to blow it up.*

Above *The political figure who dominated most of the 1960s was Harold Wilson, here seen doing battle with the* Express *over 'D-notices', the 'voluntary' system by which the British Press is advised by the government to censor itself over issues of national security.*

Traditionally the readers had been youthful and so had the staff; the atmosphere of youth and hope had been an important part of the *Express* image. However, that was now lost in a welter of political tedium. The best of the young journalists no longer wanted to work on the *Express* when other papers, particularly some of the 'heavies', were doing exciting things and breaking new ground. The staff evolved into a preserve of middle-aged men with middle-aged outlooks.

However, not all was gloom. In 1968 Jocelyn Stevens joined the company. In the best traditions of Fleet Street he was a legend in his own lifetime. His personal mythology clung to him as closely as that of any Press high-flier. He was young and rich, his grandfather—Sir Edward Hulton the newspaper owner—had left him £750,000. He had been given the advantages of education at Eton and Cambridge and he had been seen in the company of members of the royal family, especially Princess Alexandra and Princess Margaret. His marriage to Jane Sheffield, who was later to be one of Princess Margaret's ladies in waiting, was a

DAILY EXPRESS

No. 20,853   WEDNESDAY JUNE 21 1967   Weather: Chance of showers   Price 4d.

TERROR IN ADEN: 18 BRITONS DIE

2 a.m. fly-home families tell of airport ordeal

From JOHN DRAKE: Aden, Wednesday morning

THIS IS WHY
Donald Seaman: Page 2

BROWN TO MAKE SUMMIT PLEA TO KOSYGIN

From RENE MacCOLL
NEW YORK, Tuesday

BRITAIN'S Foreign Secretary George Brown has a date with Russian Premier Alexei Kosygin.

Timing is not yet fixed —but it will be as soon as possible.

Mr. Brown arrived in New York today to take part in the United Nations Organisation debate on the Middle East.

Seeking better terms dually for Arab and Israeli, he will go to see Mr. Kosygin and Foreign Prime Minister Mr. Andrei Gromyko.

The Foreign Secretary's visit announced by the United Nations will be followed by a British move to bring the Americans and the Soviets closer together and to fortify the United Nations between President Johnson and Mr. Kosygin, which still hang in the balance.

MEDIATOR

Mr. Brown sees U Thant, UNO Secretary-General, and stand by Britain view that an intermediary's assistance could be called on in the Middle East at once.

Mr. Brown will be the first speaker at tomorrow's Special Assembly session. He will be followed immediately by the Egyptian delegate.

His officials declared was it to make the mediation motion of restoring while to a UNO according to a British spokesman, and the British aim generally is to get the whole Middle East question moved back into the Security Council.

Tonight the U.S. Secretary of State, Dean Rusk, stated at Mr. Brown's hotel for a discussion. Even to under the suggestion of power politics was whether when Britain now disengage wished out of the General Assembly when Israel declared herself against Arab charges of aggression.

The nip of the matter is that Mr. Kosygin will not go to
► PAGE TWO COL. FOUR

Clay gets five years

HOUSTON, Tuesday—Deposed world heavyweight champion Cassius Clay was sentenced to five years jail and a $10,000 fine here today after an all-white jury had found him guilty of refusing to be enlisted into the U.S. Army.

Clay's lawyers immediately said they would appeal, and Clay was released on bail pending the hearing in a Texas court. He remains out of the ring for the period.

Crawley, M.P. to quit

Tory M.P. Mr Aidan Crawley has announced yesterday that he is to resign his West Derbyshire seat to become chairman of the new London TV consortium.

At the General Election he had a majority of 4,061 over his Labour opponent.

Merger talks

A.B.C. Television and Rediffusion Television had yesterday disclosed last night that they are to hold talks about forming a joint company to run week-day programmes in London. A capital share of the King's Own Royal Border Regiment went in to restore order.

B.E.A. warning

B.E.A. will not make a social flight this summer, its chairman, Sir Anthony Milward warns today in the B.E.A. magazine. He blames the Government measures and B.E.A.'s rigid financial structure for the omission.

SEVENTEEN British soldiers and a British civilian were shot dead in Aden yesterday.

It was the grimmest day of the long emergency and bullets are still flying early this morning.

Part of the South Arabian Federal Army mutinied and fired on British troops.

This is the army in which millions of pounds in care and was promised by Foreign Secretary George Brown only 36 hours earlier.

In the middle of the fighting—with bullets whining when the runners—an airliner took off safely for London with 86 people aboard, many of them women with babies.

The mutinous troops were supported by some of Aden's Arab police. In clashes with the British, and eight British soldiers were mown down in an Arab machine-gunner switched on the roof of a Federal armoured car.

I can report that at least three British officers and others and at least two were killed in the Crater area of Aden.

By midnight 18 people had died. A British military hospital was shot down. Arab terrorists with police help brought up a back-machine barracks and shelled the building in the Crater barracks.

Loudspeakers blaring from Aden mosques called on the population to take up arms against the British and their allies in the South Arabian Federal Government. A general strike was declared.

The mutiny started with riots at a Federal Army camp known as Lake Linar in the Shev's Othman area of Aden. The troops was quelled by Federal Army officers.

But as the riots lasted Champion Lines in the Cheradmiral district more troops joined the mutiny and started shooting. At the request of the Federal Government, a complete of the King's Own Royal Border Regiment went in to restore order.

A spokesman for the Federal terrorist organisation said British paratroops were fighting in the Crater area.

South Arabian forces patrolling the Government commercial at the Federal capital of Al Ittihad, 20 miles from Aden, reinforced to deal with the mutineers there.

ADVANCE

One of these officers was a company commander of the Royal Northumberland Fusiliers. Another was company commander of an advanced party of the Argyll and Sutherland Highlanders — the regiment which is to take over from the Northumberlands who are due back in Britain within a few days.

Close to midnight I spoke by telephone to Police Superintendent Mahmud Hunter in Crater, who by then had crept behind British soldiers there.

PICTURE BY COLIN MAHER

Back from Aden early today: Mrs. June Congdon (front) and her daughter Loretta

JAIL DASH

An eye-witness said armed men, some with machine guns, broke open Aden's main jail and released all the 500 prisoners.

A spokesman of the Federal High Commission in Aden said eight of the soldiers killed belonged to the Royal Northumberland Fusiliers and others to the Kings Own Royal Anglian and the King's Own Royal Border Regiment.

LONDON: Briefly after Britain troop have been freed early today, the Ministry indicated members with crystal-leaves in arms, order officers clothing their holders burdened with difficulties.

Their R.O.A.C. plane was seven hours late leaving Aden because of the fighting.

Mr Tony Auckland, a schoolmaster, came home with his wife and family.

He said: "Bullets were whining across the runway. I think some of the fire and the military were near here. The soldiers were hit but we were told the rebels planned to attack the airport."

Mrs. Elizabeth Cook, aged 27, and her son, Mark, aged three, were among arrivals. She said: "I never went to attend anything. But I'm frightened."

"My world near the airport."

A radio officer came out of the airport immigration as said: "Everyone was running, and I was in it. But please that I mention got home—I've got to go back"

Motion on D-notices

By WILFRID SENDALL

THE Government late last night tabled its motion for the debate in the Commons tomorrow on the D-notice affair.

There were complaining last night that last unnecessary delay in producing this motion.

It asks the Commons to "approve" the Government White Paper which disputed our findings of the Radcliffe Committee—which the committee cleared the Daily Express to Mr. Wilson that the newspaper had breached the voluntary D-notice convention.

The Radcliffe report itself is merely "noted."

Then the motion invites the Commons to endorse the Government's acceptance of all the recommendations in that report leaving out the Radcliffe system and of producing adequate protection for the nation's secrets, while safeguarding the freedom and independence of the Press.

Today the Tories will table a sharply-worded amendment to the Government's motion.

It will draw attention to the fact that Mr Wilson undertook to be guided by the Radcliffe Committee when he set it up—and then rejected its findings.

Last night a Commons question on the Defence Affair tabled by Mr. Arthur Lewis, Labour M.P. for West Ham North, was answered by the Prime Minister.

Mr Lewis asked what action the Government propose to take against the Daily Express or to refrain of Mr. Chapman Pincher and whether his action will include prosecution.

Mr Elwyn Jones told Mr Lewis in a written reply that no proceedings of any kind against the Daily Express nor the editor or Mr Chapman Pincher "are contemplated."

BEAT-OIL-BAN PLAN

By PHILIP DITTON

RUSSIAN oil may be imported by Britain if the Arabs maintain their embargo on supplies.

The Government is considering such a move—and a decision in favour would be a major change to import policy.

Mr. Marsh, the Power Minister said yesterday:

"We could steal the effect on the cost of living would probably like to steal an estimated one for the world. Its indicated at the moment."

The Board of Trade has imposed several requests for an almost import permits for Russian oil.

And the Power Ministry also has the question "under examination."

Petrol prices have been discussed informally at the Power Ministers and the oil companies. But they have been no formal request for an increase.

The Government, fearing the effect on the cost of living, would probably like to steal an estimated one for the world. Its indicated at the moment.

In the City communities to hire tankers to bring oil from the Persian Gulf and Venezuela is likely to push charter fees to their highest rate since the 1956 Suez war.

You can't stop Olivier working says his wife

By JOHN CRUESEMANN

JOAN PLOWRIGHT talked last night about the illness of her husband Sir Laurence Olivier.

"He insists on working like mad," she said. "That is the kind of life he likes, and there is no point in stopping him.

"But we hate all made a part of the National Theatre to keep him in hospital for at least a week or two."

Sir Laurence, 60-year-old director of the National Theatre, is having treatment at St. Thomas's Hospital, London, for cancer of the prostate gland—with a few discharged, but a slight bout of pneumonia.

Joan Plowright, looking cool and composed in a pale pink summer frock, told me: "It is now obvious he must rest up a bit. We can do our bit by carrying on as an organisation."

How long has he been suffering? "He has had this discomfort for about three months," his wife said. "but it was only in the last week's investigation under anaesthetic that they diagnosed the cancer.

"As soon as he realised it he said 'Of course it's serious—alarming, but once you learn to live with it, it ceases to be alarming."

Treatment

The treatment? Joan Plowright said: "For the present, because he has pneumonia, he is making St. Thomas's his home.

"Normally he would go into hospital two or three times a week for intensive treatment lasting an hour, followed by a period of rest.

"We know it can keep the disease under control.

"Last night the doctors told him that he will feel a bit tired at first. That is why he is laid up just now, overcome things. But he had to find out for himself.

"This treatment is something quite new. When he was told about it he said: 'I'd like to be a guinea pig.' And after the first course he grinned and said: 'I feel that was not just seven and patience worth.'"

When the treatment is complete? "He will take a holiday, and be in good form to undertake the National Theatre's Canadian tour in the autumn.

Will he never stop working? "He never mentioned the word 'retirement'," said his wife. "Oh, he is quite aware that after a certain time he will have to reduce his scope—the pressure is too great. But not yet."

Heenan 'concern'

The condition of 85-year-old Cardinal Amigo, Roman Catholic Archbishop of Westminster, is causing concern, a member of his staff said last night.

He has visited the Bermondsey home Bishop Patrick Casey, Vicar-general for the archdiocese.

Insurance to go up

Higher National Insurance contributions will be levied to pay for pensions if a Bill becomes law in early-age pensions that seek pay by a short Commons. Details will be given in a Bill to be published today.

Slim issues

Food-Minister Lord Hilton, who is has concerned all supplementary for several weeks on medical advice.

Yard 'birds'

Scotland Yard is to protect blue helicopters from the Army for a two-week experiment in aid patrols.

French say: We can't afford swing-wing

By CHAPMAN PINCHER

THE £250 million Anglo-French project to build a swing-wing plane has virtually collapsed. France has made it clear that she is unable to go on with it.

The news came in an unexpected Note to Mr. Denis Healey, the Defence Minister, from M. Pierre Messmer, his French opposite number.

The uncompromising wording of the message—that insufficient funds for the French share of the costs will be available in the forseeable future—shocked Mr. Healey.

For him the news is a political disaster.

The plane was to have been the mainspring of Britain's defence in the 1970s.

IN THE KNOW
with the Express

Yacht fiddle	Page 3
Nickey at Ascot	Page 3
Wilson and de Gaulle	Page 4
The cousin on the	
Harkie Mille	Page 5
Chairman critic	Page 6
£,000 in salt cellar	Page 6
Nickel Dressy	City, Page 16
Today's racing	
	Pages 13 and 15

TV, RADIO Page 5

More railmen join strike

A further 200 British Railways workers—lorry drivers at Kensington goods station in London—voted last night to join the unofficial strike against the operation of the Conservative rail freight terminal at Stratford, London.

4,000 out today—Page 7

LATEST

SHIP ON FIRE IN THAMES ESTUARY

Danish coaster 990t Trude, 124 tons on fire in Victoria bank of the Thames Estuary. Swedish lifeboat launched and the tug and two tugs from Medway called to help.

Nurses' pay claim for Prices Board

A pay claim by 100,000 nurses and midwives is to be reverred to the Prices Board. An increase of up to 8s per cent, varied by £1 to 6s cent but not half their work.

FLEet Street 8000

huge social occasion much drooled over in the gossip columns. At the age of 25 he bought himself *Queen* magazine for £250,000 and, with the help of a few friends and acquaintances, started to turn it into a roaring success. The secret of *Queen* was that it appeared to send up the smart set but in such a way as to appeal to them. Stevens was reported to have said that his magazine was aimed at the 'fresh upper crust—crumbs held together by a lot of dough'.

If the formula was a success, so was the image of the editor in chief. Stevens directed his magazine with demonic energy and his tempestuous style of staff management became legendary. The anecdote from this period which was to pursue him throughout the rest of his Fleet Street career concerned a young fashion editor who, when made to resign by Stevens, went back to her office and started to throw the furniture out of the window. Immediately Jocelyn did the only thing a gentleman could do in the circumstances—he turned to and helped her. His much-quoted comment was: 'Until you've seen a four drawer filing cabinet hit the road after falling three floors, you haven't seen anything'.

The Stevens' love of drama, not to say melodrama, was a useful way to create an image in a business where images are important. But it did not detract from the fact that the carpet-chewing furniture thrower was also a shrewd operator who knew what was what in journalism. Eventually he attracted Beaverbrook's attention and was offered a job. At first he refused—there was a long-standing feud between his own family and the Aitkens because it was believed that Beaverbrook had cheated Sir Edward Hulton shortly before his death. Fortunately Sir Max then stepped in and started to use Stevens' services as a consultant. Whilst he would not contemplate working for the Beaver direct he managed to salve his conscience in the case of Max, whom he liked. Eventually, in 1968, Jocelyn Stevens was persuaded to rid himself of *Queen* and to start work full time as Sir Max's assistant. He soon proved his sound grasp of newspaper management and, the following year, he was asked to become managing director of the *Evening Standard*. In spite of the current difficulties which beset the newspaper, Stevens' reign proved to be a beneficial one and he was moved to the *Express*, also as managing director, in 1972.

By the time Stevens arrived at the *Daily Express* Derek Marks had departed and his place had been taken by Ian McColl. However, circulation was continuing to fall and Stevens felt that a bold new initiative was required to pull the paper back together again. He embarked on a project known as DX80 which was to revitalise the *Express* and put it back amongst the Fleet Street front-runners. After the disastrous period in which Marks had tried to politicise the paper, McColl had made an attempt to head down market. He could not have failed to be impressed by the huge success which the *Sun* was enjoying at the time and he felt that there was room for the *Express* to dabble in the same type of journalism. It was not a view which found much favour with the readers and DX80 was supposed to save

Opposite *This was the era of the rapidly shrinking Empire. As one area after another was granted independence, the British Army was often given the unpleasant job of controlling the local populace as they jockeyed for power in the nascent state.*

DAILY EXPRESS

No. 20,954   TUESDAY OCTOBER 17 1967   Weather: Cloudy, showers   Price 4d.

Aberfan, 3 am

A YEAR AGO TO DISASTER

200 HOMES EVACUATED

By JOHN CHRISTOPHER
Aberfan, Tuesday 3 a.m.

OVER 400 people were evacuated from 200 houses in Aberfan early today when the river running through the village threatened to engulf them.

Extra staff were put on duty on the coal tip which a year ago—October 21—slid down and killed 116 children and 28 adults.

But an engineer said: "The tips are quite safe. There is nothing to fear."

People who lost homes and children by the 1966 disaster were hit again this morning when their surrounding houses were flooded.

But the main damage was being done at the other end of the village, in Tuff Street and Crescent Street.

The River Taff, swollen by 24 hours' torrential rain and led by water from newly engineered culverts, was threatening to smash several hundred homes.

Water reached 4ft. to 5ft. deep round the little houses, trapping families on the upper floors.

Merthyr's Chief Constable, Mr. N. Harris and J. Griffiths, ordered evacuation in case the river burst its banks completely.

BUSES

A fleet of buses operated a shuttle service from the flooded streets to Abbnair standing on higher ground. Ambulances helped with the sick and aged. But many people, cut off in the rainy darkness, still refused to leave. "We will sit it out till morning," they said.

Civil Defence, W.V.S., and other welfare services served soup, bread and tea at a school in Merthyr Vale. Another school at Troedyrhiw was stacked with blankets and bedding.

Mr. Griffiths said: "This is a major operation. I fear what would happen if the river burst through. It could bring great danger."

Chief officials of Merthyr Corporation, including the medical officer of health, the education officer, the town clerk and the fire chief, were all called in with their men to help the public.

WADING

Mr. Griffiths said: "Some of my chaps have been wading chest-high in the water to plead with the people to leave their homes. Some will not heed our advice, but most are now moving."

They motored in: was feared that some in the new council houses will have to be evacuated.

Householders complained bitterly that they thought all flooding would have been stopped by the extensive drainage work done since the disaster.

Mr. Leslie Davies, who was foreman on top of the tip the day the avalanche wiped out the village school, said: "This is the worst flooding I have ever seen."

Electricity danger as cables fall

POLICE closed off an area around Bowna, near Rothesay, Kent, late last night after high voltage cables were blown down by the gale.

Short-circuiting fire, woken cables in the scorina rain.

Firemen standing by were advised to police no to leave their vehicles because of the electricity.

Macclefir Heard tram-lines were to be off the current, then began repairs.

Police board 'mutiny' tanker

British police boarded the Italian tanker Vittorino yesterday after her master radioed that there had been a mutiny aboard.

One man was arrested and police escorted him ashore too the bold after the tanker had sailed into Plymouth to Marathe.

The quiet Den

Last night's report from The Den, when Millwall beat Norte League 3—1. No fighting. No scrub-a-scrup by the referee Match / Back Page

HEATH: WE FACE COUNTRY AS A TEAM

By ARTHUR BUTLER

MR. EDWARD HEATH, quizzed about his opinion poll setbacks, said last night that he had not considered giving up the Tory Party leadership.

Millions of TV viewers saw him tell questioners on the B.B.C. Panorama programme:

"We face the country as a team and we're proud of it."

He declared: "I'm used to criticism. I've had it all my political life. Of course I've not considered giving up."

He said: "Popularity isn't everything. What matters is doing what you believe to be right."

Asked whether the criticism undermining his confidence, Mr. Heath replied: "No, it does not. Surely the important thing about criticism is to learn from it."

Asked echoing the words of former Secretary Mr. George Brown he said: "I believe in being myself. In fact if I was cautioned to the word 'image.' That implies that a politician must be something which he isn't. This is false."

Disclaimer

He went on: "This is not a presidential election in this country. I don't think it is going to be one. I don't think anyone is going to make it one."

On the Tory plan to reduce state union tax, Mr. Heath was asked whether it would make the Liverpool dockers and the Barnsley pickets in the City of London exempt if there was no damage to the country.

He said: "Yes," and he added: "I quite the great majority of these officials are people who want peace. I don't want to see this affecting inroad to other country, the trade union. I would be this hope: has ever."

Under the Tory proposal, every worker would get a copy of the contract setting out the terms of his employment which he would be expected to observe.

Windblown Julie ducks out from her own premiere

PICTURE BY JOHN DENNING

By COLIN MACKENZIE

WINDSWEPT actress Julie Christie, in the midst of minis, made a dash from the royal premiere of her latest film last night.

The first was entirely unofficial—she and her her-friend escort Don Bessant, slipped out through the ladies lavatory only five minutes after the film began.

The second (above) was much more public. After sneaking BACK into the Odeon, Maciste Arts, five minutes before the film was to end, Julie and Mr. Bessant, an art teacher, ran the gauntlet of the first-night crowds—and a mischievous wind—to the foyer.

And among last night's charity premiere guests —Princess Margaret.

But Miss Christie said afterwards: "We walked out five minutes after it had begun. I don't think Princess Margaret noticed us going. She was far too busy."

She remained: "Don and I went to the home of some friends and just sat around drinking. We came back before the end. I've seen the film about five times already. That would seem quite enough times for me!"

PHOTONEWS and film review—Page Five

Ultimatum for rail guards

By JOHN GRANT

A SHOWDOWN on the railways looked unavoidable last night after Railways Board chiefs gave an ultimatum to their 14,600 guards to work normally from midnight tomorrow or be stood off.

Today Minister of Labour Mr. Ray Gunter is expected to call the National Union of Railwaymen and board representatives for talks, but peace hopes are negligible.

Ostensibly the row is over the union's official rejection of a report turning down demands for a bonus for all guards in exchange for some of them doing the second man's duties formerly done by firemen.

In fact, there is little doubt that the Railways Board, thoroughly exasperated by a long record of union brinkmanship, is now ready for a fight in which it believes it has Government and public support.

It can point to the results of the independent inquiry by Professor Donald Robertson, who was appointed by Mr. Gunter to judge the case.

He found entirely in the board's favour. But the N.U.R. executive retained its ban on guards doing second man's duties and spurned the final findings despite the advice of its own general secretary, Mr. Sidney Greene.

Terms

Last night the board's industrial relations member, Mr. Len Neal, announced that all railwaymen who refuse such duties will from midnight tomorrow be sent home for a day without pay.

Mr. Greene will put the board's decision—given in a letter delivered by hand at his Euston offices—to the 24-strong N.U.R. executive probably today.

Whatever the executive decides to do—and some members are likely to urge stronger action, like a total national stoppage by guards —the rank-and-file railwaymen who took unpopular action before the Robertson inquiry are expected to repeat it when men are told to go home.

This, in turn, is likely to provoke the board into ordering indefinite suspension of unofficial stoppages. That would inevitably spread the strike further.

Crisis

Mr. Neal confirmed that within 10 days there could be trouble with the coal mines because of the shortage of wagons to transport coal to power stations and gas works. He suggested some this might be closed.

The overall position could rapidly deteriorate if there was a spell of fog or ice.

Mr. Neal disclosed that the board will appeal to the railwaymen over the heads of the union leaders not to operate the ban.

"The board," he said, "has a duty to the public, the Government and the staff, but above all a duty to manage."

"Railwaymen have a tremendous loyalty to their trades unions and also to the public. It depends which triumphs."

"But," said Mr. Neal, "now we have come to the end of the road. There may be short-term difficulties, but in the long term I do not think that weakness and vacillation pays."

Deck strikes tip up cargoes abroad—Page 7

Barbican battle, then 24 arrests

Express Staff Reporter

TWENTY-FOUR men will appear at London's Guildhall Court today following yesterday's battle near the Barbican building site. Charges range from police assault to insulting behaviour.

One policeman was taken to hospital to have stitches in his lip and the back of his head, and another man had a fractured wrist after 200 police men and some 440 site workmen fought in the street.

Meanwhile, secret steps were being taken last night to protect the 36 men who went to work at the Barbican yesterday.

Get off!

They followed a complaint from one of the men — married with a family—that if he valued the safety of his wife and children he should "get off the contract."

Told of the threat last night strike leader Lou Lewis said:—

"I'll kick any scab around this town but we are not going to put pressure on wives and kids."

Full story and picture Page 7.

LATEST

POLICE PROBE GUN INCIDENT

Police went to a house in Court Road, Addlestone, Surrey, after a report that someone had threatened someone with gun. Police took away a gun and ammunition. Later a man was helping with inquiries.

TV, RADIO Page 12

PHONE (STD CODE 01) 353 8000

IN THE KNOW with the Express

WHAT OXFORD ISN'T ALLOWED TO READ

The banned Oxford: The real figure in September for all motor vehicles registered increased 13,669 against 20,709 in the same period in 1966.

Salvation Army and the Beatles : Page 4

L-car passenger price direct cost : Page 3

New cars : Page 13

M & S sales boom : City, Page 13

Car sales increase

The number of private cars registered for the first time in September was 81,219 compared with £4,397 in the same month last year. It was an estimated last night.

Drug defeat

The Cambridge Union last night rejected a debate motion that "this generation has no chance of saving itself." In an unseemly infringement on the freedom of the individual. The vote: 140 votes for, 334 against.

a deteriorating situation. Lewis Chester and Jonathan Fenby wrote:

'Now DX80 was to try to push the paper up-market again, aiming at a younger, more intelligent and more affluent readership. Some of the journalists who were to write and edit the paper were incredulous about the possibility of another switch in direction. At a presentation in a West End restaurant, they were shown a film of the kind of paper they were now meant to produce. Some of them pelted the screen with bread rolls and sugar lumps'.

By 1973 the financial situation of the Express group was very serious indeed. Lloyd's Bank told Sir Max that, as far as they were concerned, the company would get no further credit. The first effect of this dire situation was that Sir Max replaced John Coote with Jocelyn Stevens as deputy chairman of Beaverbrook Newspapers and managing director responsible for the group's newspapers. Coote was shifted over to deal with properties, newsprint and subsidiary companies.

Now that Stevens was indisputably in the top job and had rid himself of his chief rival he was also responsible for trying to extricate his company from the worst of its troubles. It was a task few would envy. At that time the price of newsprint was rocketing. By 1974 the company was paying £21 million for its newsprint and that was £8.8 million more than during the previous year.

Economy measures were called for and, as a first step, it was decided—reluctantly—to close down the works where the Scottish edition of the *Daily Express* was printed and to move production to Manchester. 1,800 jobs would be lost and, what was much worse, it was not to be enough to improve the situation. Prices were increasing irresistibly and there was a limited amount that anyone could do to save the Beaverbrook empire.

Editorially another change was made. Alastair Burnet, well known from television and a success when he worked on *The Economist*, was brought in as a way of giving weight to the up-market image which had started with DX80. He was not given much chance to succeed. Chester and Fenby again:

'Burnet's influence, whilst apparent from time to time, did not permeate the paper as a whole. Like other editors before him, he had to deal with an entrenched conservatism, a set pattern of news judgements dictated by ''the back bench''—a corps of senior sub-editors and lay-out men who could keep the paper much as they liked whoever was editor, particularly if the editor was not able to dominate them in technical terms. Whatever directives the editor of a daily newspaper issues, his power is very limited unless he can actually execute them himself'.

In 1976 Roy Wright took over as editor. As a gritty northerner who had worked in newspapers since boyhood and had been long employed by the Beaverbrook organisation, he was seen by some as a reincarnation of Christiansen. However,

Opposite *Two names forever associated with the 1960s, Aberfan and Julie Christie. The mixture of the serious and the frivolous is not accidental, it is a secret which is at the very heart of good, readable journalism.*

Now that Mick Jagger and the Rolling Stones are the grand old men of rock music it seems strange to reflect on the times when they were being held on drugs charges and no mother would have considered 'letting her daughter marry one'.

the situation was now so serious that it seemed unlikely that any new editor, no matter how talented, could save the organisation single-handed.

Stevens and Peter Hetherington, the group's financial adviser, were looking around for outside help and decided to approach Victor Matthews, a man who was well known to the organisation since he used to work for a company called Trollope and Colls who carried out building work for Beaverbrook. However, although Matthews investigated Beaverbrook's finances he did not make any move to get involved financially with the ailing newspaper empire. At that stage he was not given reason to believe that his help was being sought seriously.

When it came to serious alternatives the one which stared everyone in the face, and which they could not bring themselves to accept, was a merger between Beaverbrook Newspapers and Associated Newspapers, the group owned by Lord Rothermere and best known for its ownership of the *Daily Mail* and *Evening News*. The relationship between the two mighty organisations had always been a rather strained one. They were deadly business rivals since each owned a newspaper which strove to dominate the middle ground of daily journalism. On the other hand, there had, at least in the upper echelons, been a good deal of friendly contact as well. It will be remembered from an earlier chapter that, when Beaverbrook wanted advice about setting up as a newspaper publisher, it was to Northcliffe and Rothermere, the two founders of the Harmsworth empire, that he went.

There had previously been attempts at a merger. At one point it was decided to

After the shooting of President Kennedy the second great political assassination of the decade was that of Dr Martin Luther King. Political shootings, like hijacking and terrorism, were to become a regular occurrence.

try to marry Young Max off to one of the Harmsworth girls thus creating a single dynasty. That had been in the 1930s and the plan was a failure simply because Max had had his eye on someone else.

It was decided to revive the merger idea at a more serious level and, consequently, Duke Hussey, Associated's managing director and John Coote, Beaverbrook's man, started having confidential meetings to try to work out some kind of formula. The idea was a simple one. The *Daily Express* and the *Daily Mail* would join forces to produce a single monopoly morning paper. Similarly the *Evening Standard* and the *Evening News* would join forces. The exception to the merger would be the *Sunday Express* which, as a profitable enterprise, the Beaverbrook group wanted to maintain.

This first attempt at a merger fell through at the last minute because Sir Max just could not bring himself to an alliance with the organisation which had been his rival for so many years. It turned out that Vere Harmsworth felt exactly the same way; he too could see the financial sense of the move but was emotionally unable to complete the transaction. One of the main opponents of the deal within the Beaverbrook organisation had been Jocelyn Stevens. By January 1977 Stevens was chief executive and joint deputy chairman and he was joined by Peter Hetherington who was also joint deputy chairman.

After the defeat of the first take-over plan the in-fighting by no means ceased, indeed it redoubled. As well as the original combatants, people such as Sir James

DAILY EXPRESS

No. 21,218   FRIDAY AUGUST 23 1968   Weather: Sunny; dry   Price 5d.

OUT! OUT! OUT! ROAR THE CZECHS

Denis Blewett
An Express man in action : Page 8

reports from inside Prague

THURSDAY NIGHT

Britons dive for cover as guns blast square

TWO Britons had narrow escapes when a fierce burst of firing by Soviet tanks swept part of Prague's Wenceslas Place today.

They were taking a stroll before going to bed when a Czech sniper began firing on parked tanks.

Two tanks swung round and faced the bank from which the shooting was coming. For three minutes they poured shells into the upper floors.

Mr. Alan Lord, aged 25, of Bankside Lane, Bacup, Lancashire, said : "I threw myself into a doorway. Some Russian soldiers tried to get into the bank. After the tanks stopped firing the...

DUBCEK
A new mystery

THE battle of Prague continued tonight on two levels— bloodily between tanks and people in the streets, and defiantly between the Russian invaders and fugitive Czech leaders using the wavelengths of "freedom radio" stations.

AN ULTIMATUM from the Czech Communist Party congress was reported to have ordered a general strike from noon tomorrow unless the Russians negotiate. AN ULTIMATUM from the Russians threatened to take over the country completely unless a pro-Moscow regime is set up.

The confusion and danger of the situation was illustrated tonight in the heart of the capital before the new curfew came down.

Ten thousand people squeezed into Wenceslas Place were warned by radio to clear the streets by 8 a.m. or "there will be 150 Russian tanks there within minutes."

Emil Zatopek, the Olympic hero who is now a major in the Czech Army, repeated the appeal through a loudspeaker.

"We are trying to negotiate with the Soviet troops for their withdrawal," he blared. "If you stay here it will be regarded as provocation. The troops have open...

TOUGH LINE AT UNO FACES VETO

Express Staff Reporter
NEW YORK, Thursday.

SEVEN nations headed by Britain, the U.S. and France, today demanded that the Security Council condemn Russia, and...

ON PAGE 2

What makes a Quisling?

Woman who leads Czechs

Russia rages at Dubcek

Moscow is told We'll strike if you stay

2 a.m.

Radio hams tell of 'Dubcek killed' message

Express Staff Reporter

A RADIO "ham" in England reported early today that he had picked up a message from Czechoslovakia saying:—

"Our President Dubcek was killed one hour ago."

Mr. John Morris, a science master in Cannock, Staffordshire, said the message was transmitted on the 20-metre band to America at 12.45 a.m.

Mr. Dubcek, of course, is now the President of Czechoslovakia. But as first secretary of the Communist...

IN THE KNOW with the Express

I'm in a pickle

THE EXPRESS COOK SAYS

It's exotic and gorgeous
Turn to Page 6

Also inside

Bogota's troubled welcome to the Pope : Page 2
Triumph of the 11-plus "flops" : Page 4
A road warning from Sarah : Page 7
Child justice: alarming facts : Page 8
The firm with 130 bosses : Page 9
Women priests: bishops' delay : Page 10

SELLERS TO DEFEND ACTION BY BRITT

LATEST

CRUSADER

"Mr. Coote says that bloody lot can come down for a start"

Sir Max : Our Future

Crusader
The monthly staff Journal of Beaverbrook Newspapers
JUNE 1969   No. 1

WE have a world-wide communications network for getting the news into our newspapers, but no regular means of spreading news of what is going on among the 10,000 people in our own organisation—for example, in the many clubs and societies which offer opportunities for the enjoyment of their leisure hours.

Inter-office football and cricket matches, golf meetings, angling tournaments, gardening competitions, motor rallies, go on all the time, almost unnoticed.

People are promoted, retire, get married or die, with few outside their immediate circle knowing about it.

These alone would be reason enough to justify the expense and effort of producing a house journal for an organisation of our size.

But there are other, more urgent reasons.

The national newspaper market has never been more competitive than it is today.

We intend to ensure that our newspapers survive, and indeed enhance the dominant position which they have achieved over the years.

This means we must have the best and most up-to-date equipment, which we can only afford if every year we maintain a realistic margin between income and expenditure.

Although we have spent over £12 million on building and replanting in recent years, we shall have to find and invest as much as this again if we are to remain competitive over the next decade.

We are also planning a very costly pension scheme.

To carry out a development programme of this kind requires detailed overall planning of the Group's activities—in order that our efforts may be co-ordinated—and it cannot be achieved overnight. It will take several years.

Above all, it will require the enthusiastic and uninterrupted co-operation of everyone on the payroll.

It is my intention that we shall use Crusader to keep all of you informed about these plans for the future as they evolve and to seek your assistance in achieving their accomplishment.

We have already suffered too much this year due to poor communications on both sides of our industry.

Crusader is only one step towards rectifying this situation.

I wish the Editor (Arthur Brenard) and his many correspondents every success.

Max Aitken

Above *Another sort of terrorism. The spring of 1968 had seen the birth of 'communism with a human face' in Czechoslovakia. However, the Russians were not prepared to tolerate such deviation for long and soon the tanks rumbled into Prague.*

Left *Nearing the end of the '60s and trouble was already in the offing. However, in the staff newspaper Sir Max Aitken and Carl Giles put on a brave face.*

Right *As the Americans arrive on the moon the sub-editor throws caution to the winds and celebrates with a massive type face.*

65.1 *69*

DAILY EXPRESS

No. 21,499   MONDAY JULY 21 1969   Weather: Sunny spells; very warm   Price 5d.

2am: 'We'll walk now'

MAN IS ON THE MOON

NEIL ARMSTRONG   EDWIN ALDRIN

DATELINE:
Sea of
Tranquillity

TWO hours after landing on the moon last night Neil Armstrong and Edwin Aldrin decided that they would step on to the lunar surface at 2 o'clock this morning.

Mission Control in Houston, Texas, signalled: "O.K.—we are ready to support you on that."

The moon walk was brought forward by 5 hours 12 minutes mainly because Armstrong and Aldrin were in tremendous form.

But there was also some concern about possible trouble from pressure in the fuel pipes of the descent engine.

The spacecraft had touched down on the moon at exactly 9.18 last night. Armstrong called the earth: "The Eagle has landed." First reports to Mission Control in Houston said it was a perfect landing.

Armstrong, the mission commander, said:

ROBIN ESDEN, ROSS MARK AND RICHARD MILLAR REPORTING FROM HOUSTON, TEXAS

"We are in a crater the size of a football pitch. It looks beautiful from here . . . the Sea of Tranquillity base."

Then Aldrin came through with a report of what they saw on the moon as they looked from the spacecraft's windows: "It looks like a collection of every variety of shape, angularity, granularity . . . a collection of just about every kind of rock.

"Colour depends on what angle you're looking at . . . rocks and boulders seem as though they're going to have some interesting colours."

Armstrong said he could see a hill about a mile ahead . . ." and literally thousands of little craters."

But there were also craters varying in estimated width from five to 70ft. across, ridges, and angular blocks of rock probably 2ft. across . . . "and very large boulders."

Armstrong came through again: "The colour of the surface is grey, very white, and then chalky grey as I look further out. It's considerably darker grey as I look towards the sun."

Some rocks, apparently broken open by the blast from the descent engine showed a darker grey inside. Armstrong said they could be basalt.

a rock which in earthly form has been transformed by volcanic activity.

Ground control told the astronauts they had landed a little north or south of their planned landing site, in the Sea of Tranquillity, but that they were within the east and west limits. They were four miles from the planned landing point.

Armstrong told Houston that in the tense last minutes the job of landing Eagle in the rough surroundings had kept them so busy . . . Aldrin cut in "We did not know exactly where we were."

Armstrong again: "I HAD to take over manual control to fly it over the rock area." Mission Control in Houston reported: "It looked beautiful to us."

Officials at Houston gave the time taken on the flight from earth to the moon as 102 hours, 45 minutes and 42 seconds. With the landing confirmed, a controller said: "We're breathing again. But we've got a bunch of guys here at Houston about to turn blue."

Ground Control said the landing took place 41 seconds earlier than scheduled. They told the two men that all systems of their craft "look pretty good" after the touch-down.

But there were two problems. Some fuel had been trapped in the pipe line feeding the descent rocket engine. Ground Control "did not think it critical." And their clock had jammed. It was repaired later.

Within limit

Reports on the way in which Eagle had landed said it was resting at an angle of 4 degs. That is well within the limit set for a safe take-off to rejoin Michael Collins in the command module after Armstrong and Aldrin complete their moon walk today.

In the touch-down, the last few miles, the signals flashing to earth from Eagle indicated smooth progress.

Aldrin, who piloted Eagle most of the way, called Houston and said: "Looks real good." And the flight directors replied: "Yes, everything is looking good to us."

With seven minutes to go to landing Mission Control called Armstrong and told him: "Continue your powered descent." Eagle signalled back: "We have the moon right outside our window."

Armstrong reported that they experienced no trouble in descending from a weightless condition in space to the one-sixth gravity of the moon—where they will weigh only one-sixth of what they do on earth.

Michael Collins orbiting 60 miles up in the command craft asked Houston to tell Eagle to switch to a transmitting antenna that would enable him to hear Armstrong and Aldrin talk "as I will miss all the action."

Armstrong called to him: "Just keep that orbiting base ready for us to rejoin you in time."

Then Armstrong gave man's first description of earth as seen from the surface of the moon: "It's big and bright and beautiful."

The astronauts tested the temperature and the pressure inside their craft. At Mission Control awaited over reports of these checks, the new American base in the lunar Sea of Tranquillity was completely tranquil.

Armstrong again reported: "I can't see any

Continued on Page 2

APOLLO 11 MOON LANDING SITE

MAP BY JOHN BOOLE

And the Russian robot is just 10 miles up

RUSSIA'S mystery unmanned spaceship Luna 15 switched orbit last night and swung in to just 10 miles above the lunar surface—much closer to the point where the American touched down.

But there was still no indication that it was going to land, or what its real mission is.

A Tass announcement said no more than that the spacecraft is continuing "scientific exploration of near-moon space."

At JODRELL BANK, where Luna's activities are being monitored, director Sir Bernard Lovell commented—

"It could still land or explore moon space—including a clear reconnaissance of the American landing site."

Sir Bernard speaking on TV last night, said the Luna mission seemed "indefinitely" compared with Apollo 11.

Goldsmith, Rupert Murdoch and Tiny Rowland all started to take an active interest in the affairs of Beaverbrook Newspapers. Sir Max remained adamant that he did not want to sell out to any of the likely bidders. He felt wary of Goldsmith, whose formidable reputation in the world of finance has made him a familiar figure even to those with no interest in such matters. On the other hand there was a feeling that Murdoch, owner of the *Sun* and *News of the World*, would merely turn the *Express* into another tits-and-bums newspaper were he to get his hands on it.

A new attempt at an alliance with Associated Newspapers was contemplated. This time the emphasis was on a merger of the two London papers, the *Evening Standard* and the *Evening News*. Again not everybody could see the advantages of such an arrangement, in particular Charles Wintour, the dour head of the *Standard* for many years, felt that it would be criminal to sacrifice it in a merger with what he regarded as an inferior paper.

The wrangling over the evening papers was interminable. For many involved in the industry whose jobs would depend on the outcome of these tortuous negotiations the suspense must have been beyond belief. Furthermore, just when everybody thought they knew who all the main contenders were, a new one stepped into the ring.

Victor Matthews seemed a very different figure from the mainly upper-crust financiers who had been involved in the struggle so far. He was born in Islington in 1919 and had grown up surrounded by difficulties and financial hardship. After service in the Navy he had taken a job with Trollope and Colls and had worked for them until 1960. He then acquired his own firm, Bridge Walker, and turned it in only a few years into a considerable success. Eventually he merged his business with that of Nigel Broakes and worked with him under the chairmanship of Lord Crowther. Broakes and Matthews were joint managing directors. When Crowther resigned, Broakes became chairman and Matthews sole managing director. The business partnership of Broakes and Matthews became the talking point of the financial world during this period.

These two turned their attention to the *Express* and set about trying to acquire it. They were now in direct competition with Rupert Murdoch and were not tipped to win against a man whose experience in journalism gave him the edge over rivals who had no connection with newspaper ownership.

Meanwhile things had not been standing still on the editorial front. The *Express* had become a tabloid in an attempt to acquire a new image and attract new readers. Since the *Mail* had already made such a move it merely served to emphasise the rivalry between the two papers.

Eventually, after further fraught negotiations, the issue was decided in favour of Trafalgar House. It was an historical occasion because it marked the end of the Aitken domination of a large slice of Fleet Street. It did not, however, mean that all the problems which beset the industry would be solved overnight. In due course a merger was arranged between the *Evening Standard* and the *Evening News* which left the *Standard* as the survivor whilst the historic *News* disappeared from London's streets.

President Nasser of Egypt, once the bogey-man of the Press during the days of the Suez Crisis, died a sadly discredited figure. After having been humbled by Israel, he no longer looked like the great Arab leader he had always wanted to be. Ironically he was replaced by Sadat, an unknown General whose qualities outshone those of his predecessor in every way.

Under Matthews the succession of editors continued. Derek Jameson, the ebullient cockney who had earned himself the Fleet Street soubriquet of 'Sid Yobbo', was replaced by the much quieter and more restrained Arthur Firth, and he in turn was replaced by the current editor, Christopher Ward. However, these changes were not the only ones to rock the paper during a stormy passage in its history. Express Newspapers was also eventually to lose the man who had been its leading light for several years.

The fall of Jocelyn Stevens, when it came at last, was as dramatic as one would have expected. The first the outside world heard was on the lunchtime radio news bulletin on November 24 1981. However, thereafter reports were brief and uninformative. I 'phoned the *Express* to try to get the 'inside story'. There was still an air of shock in the place and nobody seemed able to produce any details, or even any good guesses as to what was going on.

Next day the *Express* itself carried a report not much bigger than a commemor-ative postage stamp which baldly stated that Mr Stevens would be leaving the organisation 'with immediate effect'. Over the next few days this was followed by personal statements from Lord Matthews concerning the state of Express News-papers. The gist of his messages was that the company was in good shape, that rumours of financial difficulties were quite untrue and that there would not, repeat *not*, be a merger with Associated Newspapers. Not a word about Jocelyn Stevens.

DAILY EXPRESS

THE VOICE OF BRITAIN

No. 22,166   FRIDAY SEPTEMBER 24 1971   Weather: Showers; bright intervals   Price 3p

MPs DEFY 'NO VOTE' CALL

By WILFRID SENDALL, GEORGE LOCHHEAD

LABOUR backbenchers forced a division last night at the end of the two-day Commons debate on Ulster. Voting was 203 to 74—a Government majority of 129.

The Labour M.P.s' move was intended as a protest against internment in principle.

It was made despite a plea by Mr. Harold Wilson. Not merely earlier that a vote could be misinterpreted in view of the Summit between Mr. Edward Heath, Mr. Jack Lynch of the Irish Republic, and Mr. Brian Faulkner of Ulster next week.

That plea was backed in the debate itself by Mr. James Callaghan, Shadow Home Secretary, who said that although the Opposition thought the Government ought to be reassured, it did not want to register a vote which might be considered as an encouragement of disagreement by extremists on either side.

The result was stronger than expected. Sixty-eight Labour M.P.s, including the two tellers, defied the Shadow Cabinet's advice. Three Liberal M.P.s, including Mr. Jeremy Thorpe, the party leader, three Opposition M.P.s from Ulster, one Tory, and one independent made up the total.

The bulk of Labour M.P.s abstained.

They, Mr. John Brian Robinson, not on had thought to vote against the Government. He was a victim of the Tunor. who urged him to abstain made them likely to see.

The division was on the technical motion that the House should adjourn. The Government voted against their own decision—notionally. Any Labour M.P. who wanted to make a protest needed to create an adjournment to take place.

'DESPAIR'

In winding up the debate the Prime Minister emphasised that the danger of anarchism in Northern Ireland...[*illegible*]...drove one to despair. But he insisted that he was seeking ourselves to be daunted by the insensate task of working through these rounds of violence in a solution that led to despair.

Mr. Heath insisted that the appeal was to the interned men must retain the first impetuous in his personal turn of may.

He urged in the idea of an all-party deputation to visit the internment camp and said that enough facilities were made to verify that relatives of internees were not being detained.

The last few sentences of the Prime Minister's speech were spoken amid a deliberate barrage of heckling from the Opposition benches.

"The papers are back and we're not playing 'I Spy' this morning."

Back—smiling!

Now you can READ all about it...starting with Giles

IT'S ALL GO WITH THE EXPRESS

❝ The newspaper is—and will remain—the principal recorder of the human story. These last paperless days have proved that abundantly ❞

OPINION See Page 8

Rhodesia—Summit decision expected today: Page 2

Schools where children learn nothing: Page 7

Revenge of jilted lover: Page 9

Clachers...Safety warning: Page 10

BACK... your favourites

HICKEY Page 3

MARY COLLINS Page 4

ACTION LINE Page 4

GEORGE BEST Back Page

LATEST

LABOUR HOLD WIDNES

V-sign Harvey gets all-clear

By JILL KING

THERE was no mistaking the gesture that show jumper Harvey Smith made to Douglas Bunn yesterday after being cleared in that 'V-sign' controversy.

It was a handshake.

The friendly approach came within minutes of the British Show Jumping Association deciding that Smith was innocent of an "offensive" gesture after winning the Jumping Derby for the second year running at Hickstead, the course Mr. Bunn owns in Sussex.

Harvey Smith last night

Rolls shock as director quits

By KEITH THOMPSON

MR. HUGH CONWAY has quit as top "technical" director in the new Rolls-Royce board-room set-up.

He tended the raw nine-man board headed by Lord Cole, with financial authority 'doctor' Mr. Ian Morrow as No. 2.

Last night it was thought Mr. Conway had felt because he felt there was considerable overlapping between his job and that of managing director Mr. Morrow.

Blast kills 2

A man and a woman died in an explosion in Belfast's Lower Falls area last night. An ambulance trying to reach the casualties was held back for almost 20 minutes by broken-up streets.

Click, click —400 pick up a —bonus

FOUR HUNDRED racketeers hit a £48,000 jackpot yesterday when a computer sent out their monthly pay-cheques.

Not e u i t y was the 10 per cent pay rise unexpected — it was also backdated for six months.

And because of the oddity involved in understanding the £48,000 electronic brain, halting bonuses Ealing Council decided not to argue with the computer's decision.

Alas . . .

One of the helpmeets of West Petroleum who picked up an extra £155 after tax said:

"They'll have to call the computer fiddle after this. It's as good as winning the Pools."

Deal ends dispute

By DECLAN CUNNINGHAM
Express Industrial Reporter

NATIONAL newspapers were being produced in London and Manchester last night for the first time this week—though there was some early tension and the Newspaper Publishers Association warned that if production of any paper was disrupted all would close down again.

It was reported that several other branches of the National Graphical Association were meeting.

A statement from the N.P.A. said: "Agreement was visually reach affecting the dispute in Salford."

TV-RADIO: PAGE 12

PHONE STD CODE 01
353 8000
TELEX 21661

James Wootten,
EDITOR OF PLANNED SAVINGS, says:—

Famine talks

Foreign Ministers this May brought moves to aid the stricken population of East Bengal which threatens famine. General U Thant in New York today, on the famine crisis in East Pakistan.

Train death

An unidentified woman was killed on Monday West line, near Preston, when she fell from a fast London train.

Wall Street down

The Dow Jones index on Wall Street closed 3.67 points down, at 89.98 after trading to 141 million shares.

➤ PAGE TWO, COL. FIVE

JUST FANCY THAT

FRED GOWER, aged 63, refused to leave his goatskin coat at the flat because it was too far from his house. Now the council at Tongham, Harvey, has agreed to rehouse Fred only yards from the Anchor public house.

Rising jobless storm

By BARRIE DEVNEY

UNION leaders and employers were convinced last night that next more than a million workers will be without a job by winter.

Even Employment Secretary Mr. Robert Carr conceded yesterday that the unemployment is very serious.

Another agency that the department produced figures showing that there are now full unemployment in the United Kingdom.

And there are fewer vacancies than last December.

Mr. Carr said that next year more than a million workers will be without a job by winter.

But he promised "it is the Government's determination to give priority to reducing unemployment. It will take some time before producing results but, I feel it may produce results."

Both wings of industry agreed that the figures were a matter for grave concern.

Mr. Campbell Adamson, director-general of the Confederation of British Industry, said: "The Government must act quickly to show its determination to improve the situation."

The huge, intricate under machine a 20,000 chip — a growing of the average tho six jobs lost each day.

"If this Government will not provide for jobs then the people will rise to give a Government which will."

Mr. Jack Jones, leader of the Transport and General Workers' Union, described the Budget as showing that Britain must do "one million unemployed."

Left The shape of things to come. As labour disputes rack the newspaper industry, Giles manages to find the funny side. And Harvey Smith has his own way of expressing his opinions.

Right Pictures are the mainstay of any popular newspaper. This one, by Ernie McLintock, was so revealing that it was eventually used as evidence in the trial of the razor-wielding youth at Glasgow High Court.

Below A sinister side of the modern age—the ceaseless war in the Middle East.

EXPRESS

Weather: Sunny spells — Price 3p — THE VOICE OF BRITAIN

Exhibit A yesterday: This Express picture

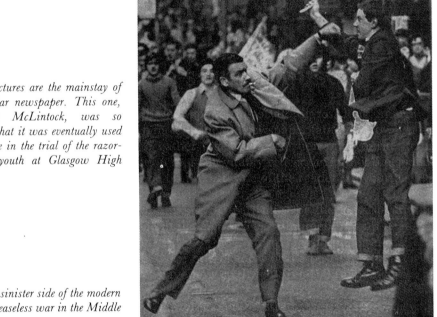

One woman's taste of war

'Each discarded tank a tomb to at least four of some mothers' sons'

Sandy Fawkes GOLAN HEIGHTS Friday

THE TANKS came rolling up the road with unseemly haste and I followed suit into an irrigation tunnel under it.

I had come to look at the aftermath of battle and got caught right in the middle of an Israeli counter-attack against the Iraq-Syrian and Jordanian infantry.

I had already noted the columns of black smoke half a mile up the road, heard the guns echoing off the mountainside like doors slamming down the Corridors of Power.

I had already seen the size of the holes gaping in the sides of the blackened tanks, tilting like grotesque tipsy giants.

In the wake of the Israeli tanks came the half-tracks, a kind of armoured open landau on tracks, lorries loaded with troops and jeeps carrying the Red Cross at the front.

The troops waved and whistled. I knew them then.

Life and death in the farmyard

HE DIED with his new boots on, defending a Syrian strongpoint which had been a peasant's farm. A brave man who fought to the death without ever questioning why a farmyard was so important. Now the Israelis hold it, the fighting has moved on, and the farmyard is of no importance after all. Except to the original inhabitants.

When the Sundays started to hit the streets the story came out. Obviously tongues had been busy wagging in El Vino's in Fleet Street for more than one paper produced what it claimed was an exact account of the events leading up to Stevens' departure. The *Sunday Times*, which has always been a good source on the internecine warfare of Fleet Street, told how *Express* employees learnt the news. Apparently Stevens had gone to the catering manageress and asked if she could lay on a leaving party for 100 people. 'Who's leaving?' she asked. 'Me,' he said. She burst into tears.

Her reaction was reported to be widespread, for Stevens had been, to use an overworked expression, a charismatic figure. His energy and sheer force of personality had impressed everyone, including the industry's hardbitten union representatives. As one *Express* man put it: 'They knew Jocelyn wouldn't stand for any of their bullshit and they didn't stand for any of his'.

The account of the last painful disagreements between Jocelyn Stevens and Lord Matthews also appeared in the *Sunday Times* in great detail. Apparently three weeks earlier Stevens had been summoned to Matthews' office and told, 'We've decided to divest ourselves of you'. This, he must have thought, was it— the sack. But no, all Matthews meant was that he was proposing to get rid of Express Newspapers. The plan to do this was a closely guarded secret and had been code-named 'The Float'. The newspaper side of the business would not, on its own, have been a sufficiently attractive proposition to stimulate interest and therefore it had been decided to include the profitable publishing subsidiary, Morgan-Grampian, to sweeten the deal.

However, there was a problem. Stevens viewed the prospects for Express Newspapers during 1982 with much less optimism than did Trafalgar House. He was not overkeen on the idea of The Float anyway and, it is rumoured, he refused to accept a more optimistic view of the future which would have given the scheme a chance of success. Thus Stevens was sacked and replaced by Mike Murphy as deputy chairman. Ironically it was said that Murphy had himself just resigned and was on his way to become deputy managing director of News Group who publish the *Sun* and the *News of the World*. However, by late 1982 these predictions had not come true and Murphy was still occupying the seat of power at Express Newspapers. Furthermore, The Float had not come into effect either and the Trafalgar House organisation was still sticking stoutly to its public position that the newspaper empire could and would be profitable.

What of Lord Matthews? As this history closes he is the man in whose hands rest the destiny of the *Express*. There is no doubt that, whatever the financial considerations, he relishes the idea of being in control of a major national news-paper. His chairman, Nigel Broackes, has written: 'It was in May 1977, at lunch at the Ritz, that I persuaded Victor that we could, and should, buy the Beaver-

Opposite *Hundreds die in a massive air crash. The* Express *could make the most of its broadsheet format with stories like this. Note the powerful use of photographs and headlines to grab attention. The amount of actual text is quite small in comparison.*

DAILY EXPRESS

No. 22,921   Monday March 4 1974   Weather: Bright intervals   Price 4p

FOREST OF HORROR

World's worst air crash: 160 Britons among 345 dead as jet explodes

The Turkish Airline DC-10, code name "Ankara"

Michael Brown, Colin Pratt, Frank Howitt, William Hamsher PARIS Sunday

A TRAIL of devastation, a mile long and 50 yards wide, is the epitaph to the world's worst air disaster tonight.

It lies 25 miles outside Paris, where 345 people, including about 160 Britons, died when their giant DC-10 holiday jet plunged into a pine forest soon after noon today.

A pall of smoke from the brief fire still hung over the scene as hundreds of rescuers searched for survivors. But there was none.

The almost fully loaded jet, code name "Ankara," belonging to Turkish Airline, was on its way to London from Istanbul via Paris.

Disintegrated

Among those aboard were 216 passengers, mainly Rugby supporters over for the international, who joined the plane at Orly Airport at the last moment.

They were stranded by the strike at Heathrow Airport which affected British Airways flights. Other Britons aboard included 81 Thomson Holiday clients who got on at Istanbul, and 21 tourists booked through Leicester travel agency Page and Moy.

But the passenger list showed 50 names which could be those of Britons who boarded at Istanbul.

It was the disaster the world had feared—because three times CF-6 turbofans, similar to those powering the ill-fated plane, have disintegrated during flights of other DC-10s.

Another theory is being examined for today's crash— sabotage. "It is possible the plane could have picked up a bomb at one of its stopping points," said a French Government spokesman.

For there are reports of an explosion before the DC-10 began its death plunge.

Said a rescue officer: "Villagers and woodcutters in the forest here said there was an explosion when the aircraft was still flying and some of them claimed that seeing small eight bodies drop in the ground.

The first hint of the disaster came when survivors saw light planes zig-zagging over the forest.

Then the pilot of a light plane radioed an urgent warning that he had just seen an airliner pass his plane's smoke pouring from the tail.

On a hillside where the forest Stragglesfield an eye witness, Catherine Jacquemot, saw the plane sinking ever lower, its wings wobbling from side to side. She caught a glimpse of the form in the cockpit.

Then, there was the start tearing and crashing for... pine and I had a fall of dust.

An official believes the pilot tried to make a forced landing.

Strapped in

From the site the forest looked like a long, grave plant, and one of the British team of investigators on the scene.

The 10-crewmen, a co-holiday airbus keeping distance, intoned into a scythe that it left at Orly.

Scientists the pilot published he held it straight and flew to down, in harrow value, the DC10's wing chopping 100ft trees as it ploughed forward.

The passengers were still strapped in. They had been flung over their bodies and had covered some 40 miles from Orly.

As the plane dived deeper into the forest its three bits still flashing, the Wings of which and then only the fuselage was driven by and he part forward in the wreck.

The scene had a terrible cylinderical. Rescuers had been but the drama of or strap counted near bodies we did not again.

The other section was the strap of the passengers on the cockpit and all has not been drawn into several feet deeper.

On a small sight is an airline pilot's a unheated air.

Beside it was a crumpled dictionary.

A gendarme retrieved a book called "Three Vincent Damage held, economist director, London born Mrs. M. Sim.

French attempts to rescue

Page A, Column 4

Is this why?

THIS is an artist's impression of how the plane may have crashed.

One of the theories investigators probing the disaster will consider is the break-up of one of the DC10's three jet engines.

For General Electric's CF6 turbofans—made in Great Britain—used for powering the Turkish Airliner, have disintegrated three times previously during flights of other DC10s.

Eye-witnesses say the Turkish jet appeared to be flying normally one moment and the next, plummeting into the forest, hacking trees down like a scythe.

The possibility of a malfunction was backed by an Orly Airport official last night, who said there was no explosion.

There had been no warning of anything wrong from the cockpit.

"We do not know what caused the explosion but we believe it was some sort of malfunction rather than a bomb," said the official.

Sabotage has also been ruled out because Turkey has been the target of guerrillas in the past.

Crash analysis: Page 4

Eye witnesses saw aircraft suddenly nosedived—was this because an engine broke up, as has happened before?

Engine pod casing

Turbo fan— did it pierce the casing?

Town mourns its Rugby dead

A TOWN went into mourning last night as wives and husbands, parents and friends awaited the final toll of the local Rugby club's 636-to-lead weekend trip to Paris.

For 18 members of a 26-strong group from the Bury St. Edmund's Rugby Club died together in the DC-10 disaster.

The tragedy touched off levels of misery in the Suffolk market town, where Rugby is revered with all the fervour of a Welsh mining community.

Most of the dead were married men in their 30s, with families and young children.

Many had young families. All had relatives in the town and surrounding villages.

The tragedy left more than 30 children fatherless.

'Friendly'

They had arranged to play a friendly game with a team from the famous Racing Club de Paris. But the match never took place because their return flight was threatened by a strike at Heathrow, so they switched to the Turkish DC-10 from Paris.

Confirmed dead last night were Brian Arthur Cross Barcer, Mark Jones, aged 36, of Bury St. Edmunds: their club chairman, Brian Ellis, aged 39; Robert King, a local Lynn, Graham Lever, aged shand 34, of Methian; Jacques Mullins, aged 33; Monk Rymhand of Great Lowestoft.

Robert Borman of Bungay, Peter Withers of Haverhill; Ives Titmuss of Chevington; Mike Whitehead of Ixworth; Tom Marriage of Bury.

Other members of the group who died were also from the area. Those who came from Haverhill, and lived in Bury St. Edmunds.

THIS is a 29-year-old Esther Collin, from Cookham, Surrey, who died in the crash on her way house from a short holiday in Istanbul. She was due to get married next week. Relatives weep
—Page 4

Firemen search for more bodies

PAGE FOUR: The agonising wait
PAGE FIVE: Photonews on disaster
PAGE SIX: Hijack goes up in flames

Target Page 2 ● Letters Page 3 ● Weather Page 6 ● World News Page 5 ● William Hickey Page 7 ● Large Crossword Page 9
TV, Radio Page 10 ● Money Page 13 ● Sport Pages 15, 16, 17 and Back Page ● Small Crossword Back Page ● Jobs Pages 7, 11, 14

DAILY EXPRESS

No. 23,056   Friday August 9 1974   Weather: Sunny spells; showers   Price 4p

EXIT NIXON

2am 'I resign' speech clears the way for Ford

Ross Mark WASHINGTON Thursday

RICHARD NIXON went on TV tonight and told the American people he was resigning as President —the climax to the most astonishing scandal in the country's history.

The decision, painfully reached after months of crushing pressure and threats of trial, means that 61-year-old Vice-President Gerald Ford will be sworn in tomorrow evening as 38th President of the United States.

The pictures here tell the story. Mr. Nixon (on left) looks a shadowy departing figure at the White House, his exit hanging loosely on him. Mr. Ford (on right) is seen, also at the White House, being briefed by Secretary of State Henry Kissinger for his future role.

The American people had to endure yet another day of suspense and rumour before Mr. Nixon himself let them know his final decision as President.

He first told his wife Pat and daughters Tricia and Julie the night before. He also had a long talk with Mr. Kissinger to whom he felt his formal letter of resignation must be delivered.

The resignation will take effect from 8 a.m. local time tomorrow—1 p.m. in London—according to an Administration spokesman. And his acceptance of Mr. Ford as the successor, powers and duties of the office will follow automatically.

The man who has sat it out as

Above and opposite *By the early to middle 1970s a comfortable, but rather dated, formula had been evolved. The bold headline and large front page picture were not sufficient to grab attention any more. The announcement that Britain was to join the EEC also put paid to the paper's anti-Europe campaign.*

brook Newspaper group'. He continued: 'I must admit that, at the forefront of my mind was the desire to see Victor once again engrossed with a challenge'.

Matthews has shown every sign of enjoying his new role. The in-fighting with union negotiators and political figures is just the sort of thing guaranteed to bring out his enthusiasm. There is also an element of Beaverbrook about him. For, although Matthews insists that his papers are business interests and are not used for propaganda as they were in the Beaver's day, he has personal qualities which remind one strongly of the old maestro. Both are thought of as tough, aggressive characters who have come up the hard way and pushed aside many an obstacle on the way to the top. Both suffered at times from that peculiarly British snobbery which damns people for their origins despite their achievements. And both succeeded so profoundly that their detractors could not do much but admit defeat.

Pearson, Beaverbrook and Matthews—three tough, determined men who, in 80 years, have changed the *Express* in some ways beyond recognition but in others hardly at all.

The battle of Trafalgar House

YES—Britain decides with landslide majority

TED HEATH'S MESSAGE YESTERDAY:

❝ *The British people have now shown conclusively that they accept and endorse the historic decision taken by Parliament under my premiership to join the European Community. Once again they have shown their true sense of vision and destiny. We must now play a major and constructive role in the development of the European Community.* ❞

How Cummings sees it: Turn to Page 10

HOW YOU VOTED

ENGLAND (47 regions)		
Yes 14,918,009 (68·7%)	No 6,812,052 (31·3%)	
WALES (8 regions)		
Yes 855,135 (64·8%)	No 472,071 (35·2%)	
SCOTLAND (12 regions)		
Yes 1,332,186 (58·4)	No 948,039 (41·6%)	
NORTHERN IRELAND		
Yes 259,251 (52·1%)	No 237,911 (47·9%)	

With all 68 results in
Total Yes Vote 17,378,581 (67·2%)
Total No Vote 8,470,073 (32·8%)

EUROPEANS!

By Walter Terry and David Buchan

BRITAIN'S Yes to Europe rang round the world last night louder, clearer, and more unanimous than any decision in peacetime history.

With all 68 regional results declared in the Referendum the overall figures were :—

YES ......17,378,581 (67·2%)
NO ....8,470,073 (32·9%)

Everywhere except in the Shetlands and the Western Isles—a long way from London, never mind Brussels—the margin was a massive two-to-one from a 65% turnout of the electorate.

And nowhere could the anti-Marketeers say they were robbed. The poll was consistent, with Labour supporters coming out in strength for the E.E.C. Even Ulster—tough territory—stayed home on the Market side.

It was a thrashing for the Left which had pitched as much hope and energy into the "anti" struggle. And it was a smashing victory for the Europeans of all parties.

The first political question is what happens to

That certain smile unites old rivals

CONFRONTATION was the headline word when Ted Heath and Vic Feather used to meet.

The economy, industrial relations, prices and incomes ... all were fought over fiercely by the then Prime Minister and T.U.C. chief.

TOGETHERNESS is the headline word now with Ted a backbencher and Vic a lord and both...

Moor wife's farewell to her murdered family

Mrs. Moran's wreath for her daughter

BRAVE AND ALONE

By Peggie Robinson

FOR even the bravest of women it was too much to bear, the loss of husband, child, and parents in that nightmare of murder, and at the funeral yesterday Mrs. Gill Moran broke down.

"I was amazed at her courage," said Canon Stanley Branson. "She stood up very well until nearly the end. I tried to comfort her."

To all but 100 friends and relatives Derbyshire police closed the grounds of Chesterfield crematorium, not far from Pottery Cottage, Eastmoor, where William Hughes killed his hostages.

In the chapel on the hill, flowers covered the four coffins at the altar.

From Mrs. Moran for her 40-year-old husband Richard there were red roses and white carnations with the message "All my love, Gill." For her 16-year-old daughter, pink roses and spring daffodils with the card : "To Sarah, all my love darling, Mummy." More roses for Mrs. Moran's parents, elderly Arthur and Amy Minton.

The scars

Starting on Monday:

The new Express, a new experience

THERE'S a great new Daily Express coming your way on Monday. Smaller in page size; bigger in every other way.

Today's paper is the last in its present format—after 75 years. But everything you have come to expect from your traditional Express will continue in the tabloid shape, with more, much more, besides.

You'll find a four-page instalment of the long-awaited AUTHENTIC account of the secret life of Howard Hughes who controlled a fortune greater than Getty's yet died of self-neglect.

This compelling series begins tomorrow in the Sunday Express. It continues in the new Daily Express all next week—an utterly absorbing account which shows the truth about Hughes to be even more bizarre than the far-fetched legends that were built around him.

What else will you find in the new Daily Express?

The best news and picture service, of course. And the great sports pages. And the famous features such as Giles, Jean Rook, Hickey and fashion.

You will also find a new dimension. The Express is going to participate more in YOUR life.

The first move in this direction comes on Monday. A new feature, Living Together, examines the problems of men, women and children when their lives come into contact. Sometimes explosively.

Other new features will appear later. Like the new Crusader column and extras to help you with money problems and enlarge your leisure activities

DAILY EXPRESS

HOWARD HUGHES — THE NEW EXPRESS GETS THE STORY THEY ALL WANTED

PANTHER IN MURDER QUIZ

Haven't we done well

DAILY EXPRESS

HOWARD HUGHES — THE NEW EXPRESS GETS THE STORY THEY ALL WANTED

PANTHER IN MURDER QUIZ

The girl who'll try anything

At the beginning of 1977 the Express underwent the most dramatic change in its history when it became a tabloid. Here we see two editions of the new newspaper. The emphasis was on traditionally popular subjects packed with drama and human interest.

The early tabloid issues went for pure sensationalism. In this edition it was claimed that, using documents which were freely available, the Express *had designed an atomic bomb.*

DAILY EXPRESS

No. 23,913   Tuesday May 17 1977   Weather: Showery   5p

Express makes a nuclear device to expose the danger of terror

THE REAL ATOM PERIL

THE HOME MADE A-BOMB
Special inquiry

By Michael Evans

AS a warning to the Government a Daily Express investigation reveals today that terrorists could make a do-it-yourself atomic bomb.

We have designed and built such a nuclear device, portable, using declassified documents and materials which are freely available.

Missing, of course, was the final ingredient — plutonium. But we have followed the plutonium trail in Britain and found that a terrorist hijack would be possible.

The official response to previous warnings has often been: "It's non-sense—the technology required is far too sophisticated."

The fear

But yesterday Professor Jo Rotblat, a former atomic weapons scientist, when shown a picture of our device, with a breakdown of design and construction, admitted:

" If I was a member of the Government and was shown by a group of terrorists what you have shown me, I would not like to gamble with the lives of thousands of people."

He added: "I would also be terrified."

Last month President Carter announced a ban on the recycling of plutonium in the United States, enhancing a world-wide fear that countries could face nuclear blackmail by terrorists with home-made bombs.

Such a danger was voiced here last year in the Flowers Report, but so far the British Government has made no detailed response — although nuclear decisions on nuclear policy are expected this year.

The Daily Express device was designed and constructed by our team working alone with declassified documents obtained from the United

PLUTONIUM will be stockpiled from reprocessing nuclear waste at Windscale, Cumbria, to give 35 tonnes over 10 years, the Government has revealed. That is enough for 2,000 "home-made" bombs.

States which—though written 30 years ago — included all the necessary mathematical equations and structure plans.

Our scientist researched and created the fusion mechanism in little over a month, using ordinary workshop techniques.

He did not use high explosive or fissile material, which would have been against the law.

While no nuclear weapon can be accurately assessed without a test, the device if truly charged was designed to explode with a force of one to three kilotons (one kiloton—1,000 tons of TNT).

Our device has now been dismantled and destroyed. But the danger it demonstrated remains.

Tomorrow the Express will tell how it was constructed.

Power for peace—or terror: Is this the road to nuclear hijack? See Centre Pages

Agent extraordinary!

IRA victim: Captain Robert Nairac, in full Grenadier Guards uniform. Troops were searching for his body last night. Undercover man's last mission: Page 3

Lord Matthews introduces himself to his readers. The paper had cost Trafalgar House £13,690,000.

ROCK'S JAMES DEAN PAGE SEVEN

DAILY EXPRESS

No. 23,952   Friday July 1 1977   Weather: Changeable   8p

Trafalgar House buys Beaverbrook

YOUR EXPRESS: A NEW HORIZON

A message to readers
by VICTOR MATTHEWS

THE financial strength of the £500 million Trafalgar House group was put last night behind Beaverbrook Newspapers, publishers of the Daily Express, Sunday Express, and Evening Standard.

A £13,690,000 takeover bid by Trafalgar, which takes in property, civil engineering, shipping and hotels has been accepted by the main Aitken

Express City Editor Roy Assersohn

and the Beaverbrook Foundation.

Trafalgar will invest heavily in Beaverbrook, and all three newspapers will continue to be published.

Mr Victor Matthews, deputy chairman and managing director of Trafalgar, will be appointed executive chairman of Beaverbrook and its four titles. He is also likely to be the presiding officer of the Evening Standard.

Sir Max Aitken, for Sir James Goldsmith, who brought the Trafalgar and Aitken parties together for Beaverbrook, said he could not accept the position "We will keep Sir Max Aitken

Getting younger by the day

NEWSPAPERS of the Daily Express was £2 in the first six months of this year.

name and all three newspapers will stay alive.

I have a very personal commitment to keeping the three newspapers, and I would hope to see this group achieve a very strong financial future in the new Beaverbrook.

The Trafalgar offer, which is subject only to approval from the City's Panel on Takeovers and Mergers, brings to an end months of speculation over the future of Beaverbrook.

Who has carried on the family business, head of the Canadian food group and Sir Rupert Clarke, will be

Page 2 Column 3

Pocket Cartoon
By Osbert Lancaster

COMING UP SOON! THE GREAT MOTOR FAIR: CENTRE PAGES

"Didn't they say that about The Mousetrap?"

Chapter 12

Sixty years in the same trousers

It is difficult during the course of a newspaper history to digress long enough to discuss some of the features which have made the newspaper famous. However, it is the intention in this chapter to gather together a selection of favourite items from the *Express*. Any such collection must inevitably reflect the author's personal choice and much material has to be omitted. If one of the reader's favourites has been left out, the author can only apologise.

Of all the regular features in the paper, Rupert must be the longest-running and most popular. A recent article in the *Sunday Times* summed him up neatly— 'Rupert: 60 years in the same trousers'. For the uniform of red jumper and yellow checked scarf and trousers has become one of the world's best-known sartorial creations. Books of his adventures have now sold well over 100 million copies in countries throughout the world.

The strip was created by Mary Tourtel, a book illustrator who was also the wife of a sub-editor. It was to be the *Express'* answer to the *Mail*'s Teddy Tail, a cartoon mouse. However, Rupert long ago outstripped all the competition and became one of the world's most successful cartoons—he even predates the legendary Micky Mouse by many years.

Although Rupert has now been going for over 60 years he remains strictly unchanged. He is permanently about seven years old and he lives with his parents in Nutwood. His clothes are also unchanging; it is a house rule, which is never broken, that his trousers should have six, and only six, horizontal stripes. Originally the Mary Tourtel stories had much in common with the legends of the brothers Grimm, though they were watered down to such an extent that there could be no mention of magic, fairies or evil characters who might frighten the children.

Eventually Mary's eyesight began to fail and, in 1935, she ceased to draw the cartoon. She died in 1948 at the age of 74. However, her place had already been taken by the unlikely figure of Alfred Bestall, a batchelor in his 40s. He was the son of a clergyman, had served during the First World War and had thereafter worked as an illustrator on *Punch*.

Bestall set about introducing some subtle changes which were to improve the character immeasurably for a new generation of fans. In the first place, the original Rupert had been very much like a real bear. Bestall altered him so that he became more of a boy. He also introduced some colourful new characters. Among these was the fascinating Chinese conjuror, with his son and his beautiful young

LITTLE BEAR'S ADVENTURES.

RUPERT IN TROUBLE AGAIN :: By . . . MARY TOURTEL.

No. 27.—The Way of Escape.

The Raven through the Witch's yard
Guides Rupert till they see
A door set in an old stone wall.
"Undo the bolts," cries he.

"Once outside we shall be all right:
Be sure to close the door.
No one will notice if it's left
Exactly as before."

Cartoons have always had a special place in the Express. *Apart from the political drawings of people like Michael Cummings and the one-off cartoons of Giles, there have been a large number of excellent serials. Rupert is certainly a classic among these and can be seen here both as he was originally drawn by Mary Tourtel and as he looks today. Other long running series include 'Colonel Up and Mr Down' and the never-changing domestic sit-com of 'The Gambols'. Among recent additions have been the highly successful 'Tramps' and the hilarious but unfortunately short-lived 'Albert Herbert Hawkins (the Naughtiest Boy in the World)'.*

Colonel Up and Mr Down

by Walter

ALBERT HERBERT HAWKINS (The Naughtiest Boy in the World) **BY FRANK DICKENS**

I DON'T GET IT.........

LAY A **QUIET** TOY DOWN IT STAYS PUT....

PUT A **NOISY** TOY DOWN IT JUST DISAPPEARS......

155 Dickens

TRAMPS
by Iain Reid
drawn by **Fiddy**

APPARENTLY HITACHI PAYS LIVERPOOL FOOTBALL CLUB A FORTUNE SIMPLY FOR CARRYING THE NAME OF THE COMPANY ON THEIR FOOTBALL SHIRTS!

REALLY?

HOW MANY 'T'S' IN HITACHI?

1409

The **GAMBOLS** *by Barry Appleby*

YOU BOUGHT **THAT** FROM A MAN AT THE DOOR?

AND HE TOLD YOU THAT MRS JONES DOWN THE ROAD HAD BOUGHT ONE?

YES

AND YOU WANT TO KEEP UP WITH THE JONESES?

'....ER

WELL— THERE ISN'T A MRS JONES LIVING IN THIS ROAD

DIRECTORY STREET BY STREET

© 1981 Daily + Barry Appleby 1956

daughter, Tiger Lily. This move neatly circumvented the bar on the use of magic, although in later years Bestall came to regret the ease with which his character could escape from awkward situations by the use of magic rather than by his intelligence and ingenuity.

Bestall believed very strongly that Rupert should 'behave as parents want him to'. This led to careful scripting so that, in the words of his most recent creator, James Henderson, he is, 'careful without being namby-pamby, polite but not obsequious, truthful but never priggish and brave without being reckless. He gets caught up in adventures but never initiates them'. A pretty tall order.

There are one or two other ground rules for Rupert. In the first place he may never take his clothes off. This is nothing to do with Beaverbrookian prudery, it is a purely practical matter. He has a bear's head but human hands. How on Earth do these match up in the middle? It is a question best left unanswered, although those who remember the infamous School Kids' Issue of *Oz* will know that, in an obscene parody of the cartoon, Rupert was shown indulging in some untypical activities with an old lady; it was an occasion that fans are keen to forget.

Bestall kept drawing the strip until well into his 80s and even when he no longer worked on the daily cartoon he continued to contribute to the annuals which are still as popular with children as they ever were. James Henderson then took over as editor of the strip, though the entire production became a team effort and no longer the work of one man. The Bestall rules were retained, for example, Rupert must appear in *every* frame of the cartoon, even if you can only see one ear; and any machine shown, no matter how unlikely it may look, must at least look as though it could work. Some updating was also required. Although Mr Bear was still permitted to puff on his pipe occasionally, cigarettes were *out*. Also golliwogs and other racially suspect characters were eliminated.

There is absolutely no sign that Rupert's popularity is on the wane. He has legions of adult fans as well as children and he still appears with comforting regularity. In a world going rapidly insane it is a comfort to know that Rupert remains yellow-trousered and immutable.

*   *   *

Modern readers of the *Express* may never have heard of Sidney Strube, yet for many years he was the paper's star cartoonist, the inventor of the Little Man, a strange, doll-like character with a round head and long neck who was always seen in glasses, a frock coat and sporting a spotted bow tie and a brolley. For the generation of readers between the wars Strube was as much an attraction as Giles was to become later.

In the First World War he had served with the Artists' Rifles and had been blown up by a mine. From that time on he was troubled with a bad heart. However, that did not prevent him becoming the highest-paid cartoonist in Fleet Street, indeed, in the history of journalism up to that time. It was all very different from when, in 1912, he had sold his first cartoon, entitled 'The Girl in the Taxi', for a guinea.

Yet it was not only Strube's brilliance as a cartoonist which attracted attention, for he also had a considerable reputation for being an eccentric. His most talked-about idiosyncracy was to call everybody, absolutely everybody, 'George'. This soubriquet was applied with complete impartiality to his wife, his son, his editor, Lord Beaverbrook, and even Stanley Baldwin. Nobody ever seemed to mind. In fact, on one occasion, during the circulation war of the 1930s, Elias tried to lure Strube away from the *Express* to work for the *Herald*. Beaverbrook had his favourite cartoonist rushed round to see him and gave him a contract for £10,000 per annum, a fantastic sum for those days. The reply was a typical, 'Thanks George'.

Strube, the cockney ex-publican and cartoonist, was a personal favourite of the great men of his day. Churchill, Baldwin, Lloyd George and many others collected his original works avidly, even when they were themselves the victims of his wit.

He retired in 1948 but continued to do occasional work for journals such as the *Sunday Times*, the *Tatler* and *Time and Tide*. Then, on March 4 1956, the heart which had been damaged many years before finally gave out. Ironically, two days before, he had drawn a cartoon for a singer called Leslie Sarony entitled, 'Ain't it grand to be blooming well dead?'

*　　*　　*

Another long-running feature of the paper has been the William Hickey column, which dates from 1933. Though various aspects of Hickey lore are dealt with elsewhere in the book, this seems a useful place to describe the conception and early years of what some would claim has been the most popular feature ever to appear in the *Express*.

First it is necessary to shatter the illusion that there is a person called William Hickey. There is not. Journalists and knowing readers may smile at the author taking the trouble to point out such an obvious fact, but they should pause, for I have it on the authority of a reigning Hickey that there are many admirers of the column who write in, making it very clear that they believe the character to be a real person. And certainly, as will be shown in Chapter 13, they have, especially in recent years, been given considerable encouragement for such a belief.

In fact the original Hickey was a notorious 18th century gossip writer who had a considerable reputation for loving wine and women as much as peddling rumours. The idea of stealing his name to head a modern newspaper feature is said to have come from Lord Castlerosse, a talented and witty Irish peer who, when not working on his own reputation as an heroic drinker, was a valuable member of Beaverbrook's team.

The Beaver had long been an admirer of the sort of bright, barbed gossip which had its first home in America and particularly in *Time* magazine. The British equivalent was pretty dull stuff and chiefly concerned, to borrow a phrase from e.e. cummings, 'The ex-prince of whoses, diving into a whatses to rescue miss nobody's probably handbag'. Beaverbrook dismissed these sort of people contemptuously as 'social butterflies and parasites'. What was then known as 'café society' did not rank very highly in the Beaver's scale of values. As we have observed before, he was an outsider to the cosy world of inherited titles and 'old' money and he had a strong feeling that his papers should write about people who *mattered*, people who did not just sit around being somebody.

The original *Express* gossip column had been called 'The Talk of London' and, since it was exactly the sort of social chit-chat which Beaverbrook had decided was out of date, it was decided to scrap the item altogether and replace it with a new and more vigorous successor. A title was needed. The *Time* column always used the phrase, 'Names make news: last week these names made this news', thus it was decided to call the new column, 'These Names Make News'.

This title was soon replaced, as we have seen, by 'William Hickey' and the new-style gossip column was born. Percy Sewell was the paper's gossip writer at the time, but he was to be joined by a new assistant called Tom Driberg and it was he who was eventually to turn Hickey into one of the major successes of British journalism.

Driberg was a newcomer to the paper. He had been educated at Lancing and Oxford—though he had failed to show much promise at either. By the time he reached the *Express* he had acquired an interesting set of personal characteristics. He was a High Anglican, a communist and a promiscuous homosexual; so far his only connection with gossip had been as its object rather than its originator.

His lack of academic achievement, coupled with a distaste for the more boring forms of employment, had led him to take a job in a greasy café situated beneath a brothel specialising in fat girls. Whilst this form of slumming had its attractions (the main one being that the café was situated in Church Street, Soho, and was therefore convenient for what are known as 'cottages', that is to say, public lavatories used by homosexuals), it soon became obvious that the career prospects in this kind of employment were limited.

Fortunately, Driberg's life up to that point had also included a fair amount of socialising and he knew quite a number of influential people. Among them were the ubiquitous Sitwells. Edith Sitwell used to hold Saturday afternoon tea parties at her flat in Moscow Road and she usually had a string of well-known authors and young hopefuls present. Although Driberg was rubbing shoulders with the likes of T.S. Eliot and Aldous Huxley this did him no immediate good, and it was finally the intercession of Edith which gave him a chance. It seemed that Beverly Baxter was under an obligation to one of her brothers and she therefore used that to obtain an interview for Driberg. This was in spite of the fact that the Beaver had rather a down on the Sitwell family and had been heard to declare that they got far too much publicity.

After writing a trial article and submitting it to the then features editor, Reginald Pound, Driberg was given a six-week trial as a reporter. Although having no knowledge whatsoever of journalism he was at once thrown into the whirlpool of life at the *Express*. Many of the characters he met there have been described already. However, one of them, Alan Jones, who was one of the first people Driberg worked with, was an eccentric even by the standards of Fleet

Street. His trademark was a bowler hat which he wore at all times. It was widely rumoured that he was bald and was so self-conscious of the fact that the hat was his last resort to conceal it. But the main Jones characteristic was to collar any reporter who had just been at the scene of some tragedy and bellow: 'Any babies dead, man? What! No babies dead! A story's no good without dead babies!' Even after the unorthodox world in which Driberg had just been living this must all have seemed a trifle perverse.

Driberg's first contribution to the art of gossip writing was to change the cast of characters who appeared in the column. Whereas Sewell was still doing pieces on people from the upper echelons of society, Driberg was more interested in the younger generation, his contemporaries, many of whom were engaged in the arts. Looking at a list of such people now—and they included Evelyn Waugh, John Betjeman and Nancy Mitford—they appear to be exactly the sort of Establishment figures he was trying to oust. However, in the early '30s these were the bright young things who were making news.

Although much of Driberg's early writing was the sort of inconsequential tattle which usually graces the gossip pages, he did take whatever opportunities were available to write in a more serious vein on topics of social importance. Always his bias was towards the arts and, when controversies arose, particularly those involving censorship, he was prone to wade in and brandish his pen. The *Express* was not noted for a liberal attitude to sex. Beaverbrook, though frequently engaged in extra-marital affaires, felt that a high moral tone was the right thing for his readers. Permissiveness was still the preserve of the rich. An opportunity for the young columnist to show his mettle came during public debate over a harmless Lesbian novel called *The Well of Loneliness*. Whilst Driberg supported it and the *Express*, in its editorial columns, attacked it as 'flagrant and infamous', Beaverbrook read and enjoyed it discreetly.

Sewell retired and died shortly thereafter. In 1933 Beaverbrook made his decision to get rid of the social tittle-tattle of 'The Talk of London' and to launch Hickey.

The style of the new column was a further development of what Driberg had started to achieve earlier. It was not merely a matter of choosing different subjects but also of changing the whole literary style in which the thing was presented. Instead of the bumbling formal English which, even in the *Express* where style was everything, was still prevalent in journalism at the time, the new Hickey introduced a highly compressed telegraphic delivery which even went so far as to use '&' instead of 'and' and the American 'tho'' for 'though'. Even the verbs were cut down until there was a serious dearth of them. The effect was bright, punchy and new. It was exactly the style after which Beaverbrook had been hankering.

Although Hickey was given a free hand in finding and reporting stories of interest, he was not entirely independent for it was on the gossip columnist that fell the chief responsibility for enforcing the 'white list'. One of Driberg's important duties was to acquaint himself regularly with the names of those who could and could not be mentioned. In the Beaver's good books were not only friends such as Churchill, but also good advertisers such as Mr Selfridge. On the other hand people such as Nehru, Mountbatten, Belloc and G.K. Chesterton were condemned to perpetual exclusion from the *Express*.

This is the most often quoted way in which Beaverbrook manipulated the Press for his own purposes. Another example concerns Driberg in an even more personal way. One evening in the autumn of 1935, he was walking through the streets of London looking for a taxi when he was stopped by two young Scots who were looking for a place to stay. They were unemployed and had been forced to come south in an attempt to find work.

Driberg was, of course, politically much in sympathy with the unemployed and he also found himself attracted towards two good-looking young men. The upshot was that they accepted an offer to come and sleep at his place. After some time spent in conversation they decided to go to bed but where, in the limited accommodation offered by the mews house, were they to sleep? Their host was no stranger to the ways of the world and was reluctant to leave his guests alone downstairs. As a result all three ended up in his bed. He afterwards maintained that this was a purely chaste arrangement which was not intended as a prelude to seduction. Since he was totally frank in revealing even the most intimate details of his homosexual activities, we must have good reason to believe that what he said on this occasion was the truth.

However, during the night one of the men leapt out of bed and loudly accused Driberg of having tried to assault him. There was a lengthy row after which the two miners seemed mollified. But they obviously had second thoughts and went to the police to make a charge of indecent assault.

Driberg was arrested and appeared at the local magistrates court but was then remanded on bail to the Central Criminal Court. He went to see Christiansen and the Beaver to explain his difficulties and immediately the full resources of the organisation were put behind him. Beaverbrook paid for his defence, a generous gesture which cost him £600. What was also generous but less praiseworthy was the Beaver's role in silencing the Press. After he had finished fixing the matter the only mention of the case which appeared was a very bald statement in *The Times* which merely listed when the case was going to be heard but gave no indication of its nature. Apparently the Beaver even went so far as to discuss the matter with the Lord Chief Justice.

This is not the place to give a detailed account of the court case which followed (such a description appears in Tom Driberg's memoirs *Ruling Passions*). Suffice it to say that he was acquitted.

Whilst nobody could blame Beaverbrook and Christiansen for sticking by an employee and friend, the suppression of news was, and remains, a serious fault. The Press has never, at least in modern times, held itself back from exposing ruthlessly the foibles of unfortunate public figures who were unwise enough to attract attention (one only has to remember Profumo, Lambton, Thorpe and, more recently, the unlucky Commander Trestrail). It seems only fair that the conduct of those holding public office and accepting public acclaim should be open to public scrutiny. How, then, could Beaverbrook justify his act of censorship? The short answer is that he did not attempt to justify it at all—it was merely one of the perks of being a rich and powerful man. He even used a similar favour which he had done for Lady Astor as a lever to get co-operation in that quarter.

Hickey continued to appear regularly though, when war broke out, its author had various other responsibilities. In the first place he was used by the paper as a war correspondent. Also he had political ambitions to fulfill. In 1942 he became a member of the coalition wartime Parliament, though he continued for some time with his other duties as well. This was a state of affairs which could not continue for long and after some months the new MP was thinking of resigning from the *Express*. However, in June 1943 Chris saved him the trouble by sacking him. It was said that he had used information which had been given by another member of the *Express* staff to further his political aims. Chris very quickly came to regret his decision when he found that Driberg was not that easy to replace. Several new Hickeys were tried but nobody quite had the Driberg touch. An unsuccessful attempt was made to lure him back but he had decided that, after 15 years with the *Express*, it was time to make a complete break. Instead he started to write for *Reynold's News* and continued to work as a member of the Labour Party.

The rest of Tom Driberg's literary and political career does not concern us here. In 1976 he died, having suffered a heart attack eight months previously. His autobiography was published posthumously and told for the first time the inside story of a lonely man whose abilities as a journalist and politician had masked a private life which caused him considerable pain. Whatever else one may say of Tom Driberg, he will always be remembered by readers of the *Express* as the first, and arguably the greatest, William Hickey.

*   *   *

Question: what do Mr Justice Cocklecarrot, Big White Carstairs, Dr Strabismus (Whom God Preserve) of Utrecht and Captain de Courcy Foulenough have in common? No regular *Express* reader will take more than a second to realise that they are all the creations of J.B. Morton, who for many years wrote the 'By the Way' column, signing himself as Beachcomber.

Morton was born in 1893 and, having been educated at Harrow and Worcester College, Oxford, saw service in the First World War. His early ambition had been to become a poet, but he later settled for the less glamorous, but better paid, occupation of newspaper reporter. However, he had no great gift for that profession and, had it not been for the intervention of Wyndham Lewis, who had started the 'By the Way' column, he might well have moved on to some other profession. As it was, he was recommended as the new Beachcomber and, in that role, he was to become one of the great names of 20th century journalism.

Beachcomber's secret was his ability to turn the stupidities and incongruities of everyday life into material for his column. He had an eye for an amusing character and a turn of phrase so apt that it has landed him a place in the anthologies of quotations: 'Wagner is the Puccini of music', 'Enter the Icebergs, a Jewish family from the Arctic', 'That Bourne from which no Hollingsworth returns'.

His humour was wry and sophisticated and he chose his targets with great accuracy: 'Vegetarians have wicked, shifty eyes, and laugh in a cold and calculating manner. They pinch little children, steal stamps, drink water, favour beards . . . wheeze, squeak, drawl and maunder'. Or again: 'The Doctor is said to have invented an extraordinary weapon which will make war less brutal. It is described as a very powerful liquid which rots braces at a distance of a mile'. And again: 'Miss Boubou Flaring's reading of Agatha, the wronged rocking-horse maker's daughter, left nothing to be desired except death'.

For 52 years, until his retirement in November 1975, Morton kept on producing his wild, anarchic and inventive columns. He was often asked whether he ever felt that some day his well would dry up, but he always maintained that, since life was so full of 'serious nonsense', he would never go short of material.

What sort of man was Morton himself? When *Express* writer Douglas Orgill paid his retirement tribute to Beachcomber he observed that he seemed to be a man born outside his own time; he would have been more at home in an 18th century chop-house engaged in conversation with Dr Johnson. Certainly he was not one who had much time for modern living. He loathed television, except as a cure for insomnia, and always got his wife to drive the car (he had once bought a car and gone out to practise, he crashed on the first run and decided not to try again). Apart from his writing his main occupation and relaxation was walking. He and his wife would wander for miles throughout Europe and on one occasion even decided to walk up the entire Burgundy wine-list, Macon, Nuits St George, Beaune, etc.

No lesser writer than Evelyn Waugh summed up Beachcomber's genius when he said that he possessed 'the greatest comic fertility of any Englishman'. His retirement came as a great blow to his many readers. As Osbert Lancaster put it, quoting a typical Mortonism: 'No more will the Albert Hall resound to the pathetic request, "Brahms for the love of Allah!"'

*   *   *

One of the great legends of Fleet Street is undoubtedly Harry Chapman Pincher whose revelations on national security scandals have often led people to remark that he knows more than anybody about our security services except, perhaps, the KGB.

Pincher was born in Ambala, India, in 1914, the son of Major Richard Chapman Pincher of the East Surrey Regiment. However, he was educated in England and gained a BSc with Honours in Botany and Zoology. He had military interests and joined the Royal Armoured Corps in 1936 where he remained until 1940. After that he went to work for the Ministry of Supply's Rocket Division. It was in 1946 that he first went to the *Express* as the Defence, Science and Medical editor. This was to be the start of a long and distinguished career in journalism.

By 1964 he was voted Journalist of the Year and in 1966 he became Reporter of the Decade. His revelations on security matters had repeatedly shocked the nation over its breakfast table and had made the *Express* into some of the liveliest reading in the country. But how? What was it about Pincher which made him able to penetrate areas of security which were closed to all but a few? I put this question to the woman who had been his secretary for many years, Yolande Brook. 'Damned hard work! He would just keep digging and digging until he found what he wanted. If he suspected that something was going on nothing would satisfy him until, he had finally got to the bottom of it.'

His two most famous books, *Inside Story* and *Their Trade Is Treachery* became publishing sensations. Publishers of the latter carried off something of a coup. They calmly informed booksellers—not a body of men known for their daring— that the book *would* be a bestseller, they *would* be sent quantities of it to sell and, if it did not sell, they were welcome to send it back. It sold. And sold. And sold.

*   *   *

All newspapers rely heavily on photographs to give them a strong visual appeal. However, often the photographers remain unknown outside their own profession. This is definitely not the case with Victor Blackman whose contributions to *Amateur Photographer* over the last 20 years, in addition to his work on the *Express*, have made him a familiar figure to the general public.

Blackman has worked for the paper for 25 years, having originally been

The violence of modern life was shown in a farcical light as a bunch of comic opera soldiers tried to overthrow Spain's democracy in early 1981.

employed by the *Daily Sketch*. He is the first to admit that a Press photographer's life has its moments of excitement. For example, when he was sent to Aden to cover the troubles there, he was invited to go on patrol with 'Mad Mitch', one of the British Army's more colourful characters. Blackman naively assumed that a reasonable number of soldiers would be sent with them. Not so. He found himself in a Jeep with Mad Mitch, a driver and one other soldier. As he cowered under a rear seat, very sensibly trying to avoid fire from snipers in the many surrounding buildings, Mitch was standing up in the Jeep yelling to his aide: 'There's one of the buggers, shoot him!'

On another occasion Vic found that his photographic equipment had other uses, too. At the Sierra Leone independence celebrations he was repeatedly accosted by a reveller who had been enjoying himself just a little too much. Vic asked him to get out of the way so that he could get on with his job. He didn't. He asked him again. He wouldn't. Eventually our hero pacified his unwanted companion with a sharp rap over the head using a telephoto lens. Vic, a stickler for accuracy in these matters, assures me that it was a 300 mm Novomat.

Another painful memory involves a shot he was trying to take from an aircraft. The idea was to remain suspended upside-down until a satisfactory picture was obtained. In the event this took half an hour. However, the excitement was caused by his lap strap, the only thing which separated him from eternity at that juncture. The helpful soul who had bound him into the aircraft with this device left him with the words: 'Whatever you do, don't touch the strap!' And so, for the next 30 minutes Vic was obsessed with a neurotic desire to check that it was, in fact, correctly secured. Every time he delicately probed the buckle he had visions of plunging thousands of feet to a sticky and unphotogenic end.

All these trials have had their compensations. He has been voted Press Photographer of the Year and has been sent regularly to cover the Miss World Contest. Whatever else a photographer's life might be, dull it is not.

All the tabloids had been getting great mileage out of the much-predicted engagement of the Prince of Wales and Lady Diana Spencer. The actual announcement was, however, only the beginning of a Press bonanza.

The tears and the torment behind the Royal love story

By Ashley Walton

I played Cupid says big sister Sarah, an old flame

A match written in the stars

Arm-in-arm at last for all to see ... Charles and Diana yesterday in the grounds of Buckingham Palace Pictures by JOHN DOWNING

Chapter 13

Inside the Black Lubianka

The *Express* office is a black building in a grey town. In the 1930s someone obviously thought that a black, square, glass-covered box was just what old London needed to jolly it up. Then the building was controversial, even avant garde, now it is only ugly and referred to by its detractors as the Black Lubianka. The lobby, which was once an architectural feature of the place, is obscured by the glass screens from behind which security staff scrutinise visitors. The only feature of the building which still hints at its former status as an architectural talking-point is the art deco staircase which, dimly lit, winds a majestic course past Beaverbrook's sculpted head and upwards to the floors where the paper is produced.

I had arranged to spend some time at the paper, meeting the people who produce it. I arrived at 10.15 am on Wednesday, November 5, and everything seemed quiet. The fireworks had not yet started. Mornings are not usually very spectacular in a newspaper office. Nothing has had time to happen, there are no panics, just time to look over the morning papers and plan the day ahead. Jan Kreiger, the managing editor's secretary, had planned my day to the last minute: 10.30 meet Jak, 11.00 interview Jean Rook, 11.30 see the editor, after lunch Roy Ullyett and William Hickey. So far so good. My only problem at the moment was that I was just about to meet Jak and had discovered that I did not know his real name. This, it appeared was a disability I shared with most of the *Express* staff. It was almost certainly Jackson, wasn't it? But was it Raymond, Robert, Robin? Well, something like that. Anyway, I was assured, nobody would ever dream of calling him anything but Jak.

We found him at his studio in the *Standard* part of the building. Jak produces cartoons for the *Standard* on weekdays and does one in the *Express* on Saturdays. The studio is divided in two parts; in the other one sits Frank Dickens, creator of 'Bristow' and 'Albert Herbert Hawkins, the Naughtiest Boy in the World'. The Dickens area favours Radio 1 as an accompaniment to work. Jak is more of a 'Today' fan. He was busy starting the day's cartoon, a composition which demanded what seemed like a regiment of guardsmen all standing to attention. We agreed that he would go on drawing soldiers while being interviewed, otherwise he just might miss his deadline, which would make both of us unpopular.

Jak is exactly the sort of person the public expects to be a cartoonist. In his early 50s, balding and wearing black rimmed glasses, he has a permanently amused expression and, with his tie at half-mast and protected from stray ink by a marvellous Miss UK apron, he seems ideal for the part.

How did he get into cartooning? 'I did three years in the army and then went to the Willesden School of Art. After that I joined Link House and worked on some of their magazines, you know, touching out the pubic hairs in the *Naturist* pictures and that sort of thing. I joined the *Express* organisation in 1953. They gave me the opportunity to do a lot of things I never would have done otherwise. I drove across Russia, visited the USA and went to Israel during the Six-Day War.'

How, I wondered, does a cartoonist work? 'Well, I have to start at about 7.30 am and listen to the early morning news on the radio. That's the time when I'm looking for ideas. I will usually do several roughs and then get one of them approved by the editor. Normally I can begin to draw by about 9. The deadline is 3 pm but depending on the complexity of the drawing I sometimes finish at 1 or, occasionally, have to get an extension until 4.'

Does he have much trouble getting ideas past the editor? 'Oh, no. I've only had to break in about three editors in my career. They know the sort of work I do and they just let me get on and do it.'

Are his cartoons affected by his political views? 'Oh, well it's all only politics isn't it? I mean, democracy is probably the safest way to run a country but . . .'

'Hey, Jak, she's in the club!' This morsel of information came from the other side of the partition.

'Who is?'

'The Princess of Wales, of course. It was just on the radio.'

He surveyed his lines of immaculately drawn guardsmen sorrowfully.

'Now what the hell do I do? Should I stick to this one or start again?' With thanks I left Jak to his dilemma and went off to keep my appointment with Jean Rook.

When I arrived at her office she was not there. Royal baby fever was already beginning to grip the building and people dashed here and there passing each other the news as they went. The office was clean, tidy and almost completely devoid of those personal touches which might have given a clue to the personality of the famous occupant. The only exception was a large cube of wood which sat on her desk. Through it at an oblique angle was driven a very large, very sharp nail. I wondered idly whether she pulled it out with her teeth, just for practice.

I was greeted by a pretty dark-eyed secretary who asked me to sit down and wait for the formidable lady's return. What would she be like? How do you interview the 'First Bitch of Fleet Street' and survive without major blood loss?

'What's she *really* like?' I asked Brown Eyes.

'Oh, she's very nice. Not at all what people expect.' That was comforting but, if it was true, why were we both whispering?

The door opened and Jean Rook swept in. She is an instantly recognisable figure, the blonde hair, sharp, inquisitive face and hands smothered in heavy, gold rings combine to produce an effect guaranteed to stand out in any crowd.

'Find me that quote from Princess Anne. You know, the one about her not feeling maternal.' Brown Eyes rushed to the library to start burrowing.

'How do you do? Look . . . do you think we could do this later? No, never mind let's get it over with now.'

She threw herself into a chair, grabbed a cigarette and waited for my first question. Interviewing Jean Rook is a little like an amateur jockey taking Red Rum over the Grand National course. She knows every question before it is asked and has developed a set of answers which are helpful, informative and just beg to be quoted. For those who are on the inside of Fleet Street there are illuminating remarks about well-known journalists, for those who are not there are personal stories which can be used for their human interest value. First she mentioned that she has an MA in English Literature and that she wrote a thesis on T.S. Eliot. She also mentioned that she was the first woman ever to be the editor of her university magazine. After university she tried for a job with the *Sunday Times* but failed to get it. Then there followed a spell on the *Sheffield Telegraph*, and after that the *Yorkshire Post*. 'But I was drivingly, ruthlessly ambitious and just had to get to London. Eventually I became fashion editor on *Flair*, an IPC magazine. After that I worked for the *Sun*, though of course it was run by Cudlipp in those days, not Murdoch. Then I worked on both the *Sketch* and the *Mail*. By that time I was a mother and used to work with a baby in one arm and a notebook in the other. I had started to get a reputation for being ruthless and it was said at that time that I had sacked the entire staff of 'Femail' when I went there, but that was completely untrue.'

What had made her go to the *Express*? 'There is a great difference of attitude between the *Mail* and the *Express*. The *Mail* has a very tough and bitchy atmosphere. If you write a piece someone is sure to say, "Yes, I did a bit just like that a few months ago—it went on the spike". The *Express*, on the other hand will give you enormous projection. It is not just a question of money; it's an attitude. They will do everything possible to encourage you to produce your best work for them.'

How did her present job come about? 'I was asked to lunch by John Junor who asked me why I didn't apply for a job on the *Express*. It was to be the last time I ever had to apply for a job. From then on I wouldn't *need* to apply. An hour after I spoke to John the editor 'phoned and made me an offer. The salary was so high that it was reported in *Private Eye* and the *UK Press Gazette*. When it came, the *Mail* counter offer was huge. Harold Keeble arrived at my house at 4 am to try and persuade me to stay. Vere Harmsworth spent an hour and a half trying to talk me out of leaving. But there is a glamour and flair about the *Express* which no other paper has. They have a profligate largess in doing things which you do not experience elsewhere. But it is both a beautiful and a dangerous paper. If you do not succeed you will not last long. In fact, I was told that if I didn't write like the Virgin Mary in my first column I should watch out. It wasn't entirely a joke.'

How do you react to being called the First Lady of Fleet Street? 'Oh, I don't let it bother me. They call me the First Bitch of Fleet Street as well, and I don't let *that* bother me either. I'm a very ambitious person and I know my abilities. If you aren't like that you will never succeed in this business. I'm not a naturally vindictive person but I certainly don't let anyone get in my way or damage my career. You know, I'm going to come out of this sounding *awful*. It always happens with interviews. I just sound absolutely *awful*.' She grabbed another cigarette and dragged on it determinedly.

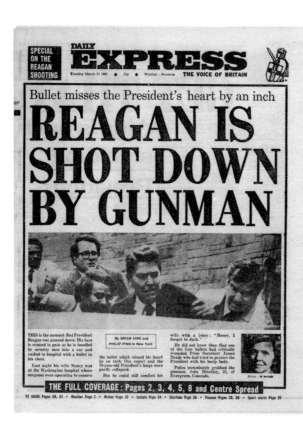

As reports of the attempt to assassinate President Reagan flowed into Fleet Street the Press responded with typically dramatic presentations. Note how the story developed from one edition to the next.

How do you go about writing your column? 'The night before I write my piece I make sure that I watch all the news programmes. Then I have two alarm clocks to make absolutely sure that I'm awake by 5 am on Tuesday morning. I usually drive to London—there's a car parking space included in my contract—and I'm ready to start by 7.30. Of course, the fear is always there that *this* time I'll sit down at the typewriter and nothing will happen. Each column has to be at least as good as the last and sometimes you wonder whether you can keep it up.'

You must have developed a rapport with your readers over the years; how do you know what they want to read? 'There are several things I have to bear in mind. Firstly, I can never deliberately provoke the readers. They can tell immediately if I am saying something merely for the sake of being controversial. On the other hand, I wouldn't want to write for a bunch of happy sheep and so I never hesitate to say what I think is true. I get an enormous post, both for and against. The one topic which is guaranteed, above all others, to get a reaction is the royal family. I once said something about Princess Margaret in a maxi skirt looking like a mushroom hammered into the ground. There were howls of protest. Also I said that the Queen needs her eyebrows plucking. The typical response to that is: "Our Queen is a wonderful lady, a good mother and an inspiration to the nation". I don't disagree—she is all those things, but she still needs her eyebrows plucking.'

Do you consciously foster the image of a 'gutsy lady'? 'No, I never think of my image in that way. I have absolute faith in my writing style and what I write is me, it is never some character I have created to amuse the readers. But I worry about the readers a lot. I am both arrogant and humble at the same time. I should like, just a couple of minutes before I die, to be able to stop and think about how good my life has been.'

That seemed an appropriate place to end. As I left, she was removing what seemed like several pounds of precious metal from her fingers and preparing to splash the story of the royal birth across the centre pages of the paper.

By this time the big news had spread throughout the building and arrangements were being made to produce appropriate features. Of course, journalists are too tough a breed to show any signs of actual panic, but there was much hunting for information and rewriting of copy. My chances of getting to see the editor, which was my next assignment, were nil. Christopher Ward had only just started as editor of the *Express* and, as a new broom, he had a lot of sweeping to do and I would have to defer my questions to another day. Lunch seemed an acceptable alternative. Journalists throughout Fleet Street were beginning to converge on El Vino's and there would be little chance of speaking to anyone now until thirsts had been thoroughly quenched.

After lunch I was looking over the afternoon schedule with mixed feelings. George Gale? William Hickey? The editor? Who could be dragged from his desk? The door opened and a face appeared round it which I did not recognise. However, the handlebar moustache attached to the face could belong to only one man. 'Mr Ullyett. I'm pleased to meet you.'

Roy Ullyett's sporting cartoons are an indispensable part of the *Express* and have been for the last 30 years. Unlike most cartoonists he does actually appear in his own work from time to time, rather like Hitchcock walking on in his own films. The tall, greying figure with pipe and moustache is normally accompanied by the Ullyett trademark—a sparrow which, according to legend, is supposed to have its nest within the dark recesses of the moustache.

Ullyett's career started during the Depression when his family intended that he should get a secure job in the iron and steel industry. He was less than enthusiastic about the prospect but spent much of his spare time drawing cartoons. In his local paper, the *Southend Times*, they were running a competition for a drawing to illustrate an advertising campaign. The slogan to be illustrated was 'Eat more fish caught by British fishermen'. Roy produced a map of England which he had managed to turn into a fisherman with a basket. The idea won him the ten shilling prize. Inspired by this early success he decided to try and combine his love of the theatre with his cartoonist's skill. He drew the entire cast of the local operatic society in their latest production and offered the sketch to the *Southend Times* for another ten shillings. Apparently the editor was so impressed by the sheer quantity of cartoon per shilling of outlay that he went ahead and bought it. The circulation shot up. At least, all the members of the cast and their relatives bought copies which, in a town the size of Southend, resulted in a massive surge in circulation. Roy was soon doing a regular cartoon for the paper and eventually he felt sure enough of his ability to ask for a pay rise. 'Don't hold a pistol to my head!' boomed the editor. 'I shall have to hold a board meeting.' He summoned the head printer and they withdrew for a few minutes. That was the entire board meeting. Roy got his rise.

His journalistic career has been a very varied one (careers in this profession always are as journalists move in and out of jobs more frequently than any other workers except, perhaps, football team managers). He started on the *Star*, went to Hugh Cudlipp's *Sunday Pictorial* and, just before the start of the Second World War, he was about to join the *Express*. However, the war years altered his plans and, when peace was finally restored, he went back to the *Star*. Then the sports editor at the *Pictorial* 'phoned and offered him a job. Not long thereafter he received another call, this time from Christiansen, and as a result of this conversation he finally joined the *Express*. That was in 1953 and Roy has been with the paper ever since. This steady employment used to worry him a little—there is a saying in Fleet Street that you are not a journalist until you have been fired from the *Express*. However, he hopes that he has found a way round that particular jinx—a couple of years ago he 'retired'. His leaving of the Fleet Street scene had all the finality of a pop star's 'farewell concert'—he left on Friday and started again on Monday (though now on a part-time basis).

In the post-war years when Roy was at the height of his career, boxing was *the* sport. He really enjoyed doing cartoons of famous fights and he used to provide illustrations for Jack Solomons to use on the front of his programmes. He learnt to draw with a brush so that the ink would dry quickly. So much of his work was done whilst in the front line that it was essential to have a technique which worked in less than ideal circumstances. If your idea of a cartoonist is of someone who dashes off witty sketches in the comfort of a studio—forget it. Roy Ullyett is here to tell you that there are few more nerve-racking experiences than drawing a big fight when the crowd starts to riot. At the famous Ali/Liston fight Roy found himself in the middle of a riot. The crowd had turned ugly after Ali's easy win and was beginning to attack the ring. Eventually Roy, sweating with nervous tension, took refuge under the canvas, a position he was forced to keep until the trouble died down.

Not all the troubles in the cartoonist's life are so dramatic. Leonard Crawley, a reporter on the *Daily Telegraph*, developed an infuriating habit of coming up to Roy as he wrestled to get a drawing done in time to reach his deadline. Crawley would peer interestedly over his shoulder and remark casually: 'You don't mind, do you?'

After so many years Ullyett has become very fond of his spot at the back of the paper. As he once said to Beaverbrook: 'If anyone starts at page one of a paper and reads all the way through he deserves a laugh if he gets to the back'. The Beaver was not visibly amused by this remark.

Ullyett arrives for work in the afternoon and, having had the morning in which to think up an idea, he produces a cartoon in an hour or two. We were now getting near to deadline so he went back to his drawing board. I had a look round the so-called 'Big Room' where journalists were putting the paper together. It was a very different place now from the calm and orderly scene of the early morning. There was an atmosphere of tension building up quite perceptibly in the air. Stories had to be written and written soon, elusive photographs had to be tracked down and brought to the office in time.

I met Jan. 'I'm supposed to see either the editor or William Hickey now. What are my chances?' She was too polite to tell me but we both knew the answer. A quick call to the editor's secretary established that he would be seeing nobody in the foreseeable future. However, William Hickey's office provided the unexpected answer that he would be right over.

Anyone who reads the *Express* regularly knows Hickey. His is the largest feature in the paper and takes up a daily page. The column has been going since the 1930s (see page 143) and has provided the readership with tantalising glimpses of a world which most of them will never enter—what used to be called café society. All the royals, aristocrats, debs, film stars and other personalities of the day make their appearance in Hickey's page. The column provides an infallible guide to the comings and goings in a world of glamour which holds the public spellbound mainly because, for most of them, it is unattainable. However, the general public are not the only readers—gossip columns are no less popular with those who appear in them. In fact people are well known for suffering the most embarrassing comments on their personal lives just for the privilege of being referred to by a gossip columnist. For newspapers this is a lucrative market and they compete fiercely for the best columnists—Dempster, Callan and Hickey. But who is Hickey? Reading his column one gets the impression of a leisured man of the world with enough money to lead an eminently civilised life without having to peddle his wares in Fleet Street. He occupies a roof garden at the *Express* building, drives an old Bristol and flies an ex-RAF Chipmunk. In between times he leads a hectic social life at smart parties and tends to end most evenings at the latest night-spot. His views are always High Tory and he exhibits an ill-concealed loathing for the French to whom he refers as 'Frenchipoos'.

Of course, as we have seen in an earlier chapter, there is no such person. Hickey is merely a caricature and he has been brought to life by a whole series of journalistic animators. Tom Driberg was, without doubt, the most famous member of this group and probably the only one who was widely known by his real name outside Fleet Street. Not all Hickeys have been so successful. Take, for example, the unfortunate Derek Tangye. He arrived at 3 pm one Sunday afternoon to begin work on the paper. He was already an experienced gossip columnist and there were high hopes that he would bring new life to this important area of the paper. But after a mere three hours of trying to create a Hickey column he admitted defeat and resigned.

One of the stars of the column was Donald Edgar (author of that most interesting book *Express '56*, which gives a fascinating glimpse of the paper during one of the most turbulent post-war years). Edgar almost went the same way as Tangye. He started badly and Chris was becoming increasingly convinced that employing him had been a mistake. However, rescue came for Edgar at the last moment. By an oversight the *Express* acquired an extra ticket for the Coronation of Elizabeth II. It was decided to send Edgar to the annexe of Westminster Abbey, a place where few other journalists would be and where he would be safely out of the way. However, instead of flopping, as had been expected, he produced a superbly candid view of the waiting VIPs, complete with a highly entertaining description of some of the foibles which they obviously did not realise they were putting on public display. From that time on Edgar was one of the great Hickeys and brought to the column a style which was entirely his own.

I was quietly rehearsing my part of the interview when a young man with a world-weary expression wandered into the room. He dragged distractedly on a cigarette and seemed to be in the throes of worrying about several major issues of international importance at the same time. 'Hello, I'm Peter Tory. I write the Hickey column. Look, I'm terribly sorry but I can't possibly see you now, my deadline's one of the earliest on the paper. I'll talk to you another time. Is that all right? Phone my secretary.' And with that he left.

Clearly a paper at deadline time is no place for an interviewer. I gave in and left. But not for long. Next morning I was back. Jan had already been at work and had managed to arrange a meeting with Michael Cummings, the paper's political cartoonist.

In a building not noted for architectural charm or imaginative decoration, Cummings' office, which he shares with Roy Ullyett, stands out as a monument to gloom. Political prisoners lose their toenails in cheerier surroundings. It is a small, very dark room with almost completely blank walls and is furnished with two drawing boards. The window looks out on to nothing more interesting than the building next door. The only decorative touch is provided by some very faded newspaper clippings pinned to a noticeboard. They are all pictures of famous political personalities and Cummings uses them for instant reference. Tony Benn stares wild-eyed into the room whilst being eyed benevolently by Mrs Thatcher— an unlikely situation.

If Jak looks like everyone's idea of a cartoonist, Cummings could pass for a senior civil servant. His lugubrious, bespectacled face is topped by white hair cut severely short, he wears glasses and favours dark suits. His manner is courteous in a way which speaks of a different age. Certainly he betrays no trace of being the sort of person who makes people laugh for a living.

I was rash enough to tax him on this point. 'Oh, don't think for a moment that cartoonists look funny! Most of them look like accountants. They're really a rather gloomy and unrelaxed group of people. In fact, when we have the Toby Club dinner and all the cartoonists get together they're all terrified of saying anything amusing. Probably they are also rather wary in case they give a funny line to a rival by accident. There is something very burdensome about trying to be funny all the time.'

How did he become a cartoonist? 'I had a newspaper background. My father was A.J. Cummings the political editor of the *News Chronicle* and my mother was an artist. I was very impressed by Low and tried my hand at drawing some cartoons. The first I sold was to Stafford Cripps' *Tribune* and I received a cheque for one guinea signed by Cripps himself.'

'At the end of the Second World War I went to the Chelsea School of Art and then managed to get a job on *Tribune*, which was being edited at that time by Michael Foot. I did drawings to illustrate reviews and then was asked to produce some political cartoons. It was during the Cold War and my work was very anti-Russian. Eventually my father told me it was time to leave *Tribune*. I was really much too right-wing for a socialist paper. The *Express* needed someone to replace Strube and I wrote to Beaverbrook to see if he would offer me the job. I got a reply which was quite typical of him, he said something like, ''Dear Mr Cummings, I have arranged for you to meet Mr Christiansen. I am just an old gentleman who wants to sit in the sun''. He always used to pretend that he had no say in the running of his papers.'

'I started in 1939 on three months' trial and at the end of it Christiansen fired me. However, Beaverbrook stepped in and told him to give me another chance. Beaverbrook was, in fact, very much in charge of the paper. He ran vendettas against certain people he disliked and, as you have probably heard, some people who incurred his particular displeasure were simply not referred to in the *Express* at all. It's said, though this may be apocryphal, that he called the list of unmentionables 'the white list', that was so that if ever he was accused of running a black list he could answer truthfully that it was not so!

'During the 1950 election I thought up a spoof Labour MP called Zilliboy Shinbag. Churchill saw the cartoons and liked them and asked for copies.'

Do you often get requests for the originals of your work? 'Yes, all the time. Nowadays I have a fixed rate which I can quote. Tony Benn asked for three cartoons but wasn't prepared to pay me for them so he didn't get them. I thought it very odd that a man who is supposedly in favour of fair treatment for the

Not all the news was bad. As well as the royal engagement the Beatles got together again.

workers does not feel that a working artist deserves to be paid. I have occasionally given work away. I gave two cartoons to Margaret Thatcher because I admire her greatly. Also I was once asked to send a cartoon to President Kaunda because he had mentioned to Mrs Thatcher at the Commonwealth Conference in Lusaka that he liked it. Well, I duly sent the cartoon but never received a word of thanks. What can you expect?'

How much freedom were you given under Beaverbrook to draw what you wanted. 'Beaverbrook was a great advocate of cartoons, he believed very strongly that they were far more effective than words in getting across a political point. In fact a reader survey once showed that the cartoons were the most popular part of the paper. *Express* cartoons have always had greater impact because they were given the necessary prominence. In fact, I can recall occasions when a cartoon has been drawn to accompany a leading article and, in the end, the leader has been scrapped and the cartoon retained on its own. From time to time I used to be invited to dine with Beaverbrook and it was usually a sign that he wanted to disagree with one of my drawings. For example, when Krushchev had Pasternak's relatives arrested on trumped up charges to do with alleged currency offences, Beaverbrook took the opportunity to tease me during dinner about a critical cartoon I had drawn. He always rather liked Krushchev and felt that it was possible to negotiate with him. I was too right-wing for Beaverbrook's taste.

'The same thing happened in the mid-'50s when Krushchev and Bulganin visited Britain. I had drawn a rather sardonic cartoon and Christiansen didn't like it. The *Express* was supporting the visit as a hopeful sign for peaceful coexistence. However, I was proved right, the visit blew up when George Brown criticised the Russians and Krushchev said that if he lived here he would vote Conservative.'

'I was never prevented from drawing a cartoon which I felt to be right. Beaverbrook and Christiansen would disagree with my views and would tell me so, but they would never attempt to censor my work. I even got into trouble with de Gaulle. He had had Pierre Laval tried and shot as a traitor and I produced a fiercely critical cartoon. De Gaulle actually approached the British Government and demanded that the drawing should be suppressed. He would not believe them when they told him that censorship of that sort was not possible in this country. In France, of course, the Government can still control the Press when it chooses to do so, and that was especially true under de Gaulle.'

Time was running out and I prepared to leave. What impressed me most about Cummings was his absolute commitment to his political views and his very personal attitude towards political figures. Many people who are involved in journalism and politics develop a sophisticated attitude which leads to purely theatrical struggles with their opponents—there is much sound and fury but very little blood. Michael Cummings is not at all like this. Some may accuse him of being over-serious but no one can deny that his views are deeply felt. He obviously reveres Mrs Thatcher, intensely dislikes Tony Benn (and takes credit for being the first cartoonist to note his wild stare), has no time at all for Ted Heath, and so on. The Right can have fewer more convinced and devoted advocates.

*   *   *

The Hickey office is quite unlike most of the others in the *Express* building. It is large, light, has a few potted plants and the walls are smothered with the photographs of the rich, successful and merely famous. The ghost of Beaverbrook has been well exorcised in this department. Even so, it is far from being the roof garden which regular readers are led to expect. But then Hickey is not what one expects either. At the time I was there the post was held by Peter Tory (he has since been replaced by Michael Leapman who used to write the 'Times Diary'). Tory, in his early 40s and an ex-actor with the Royal Shakespeare Company, has done much to create the Hickey image. It was he who decided that there should be an elegant roof garden with shrubbery and sun dial and that Hickey should drive an old Bristol. It was also he who invested the character with his large repertoire of outrageous prejudices. A lot of this character building has caught the imagination of the readers. Hickey gets plenty of letters from people who are anxious to believe in his glamorous life style.

What made him give up acting in order to enter journalism? 'Frankly, I was not a very successful actor. My rivals in Fleet Street, people like Dempster and Callan, refer to me as an ex-spear carrier. That is not inaccurate. I used to do a bit of writing now and then and eventually John Junor saw something I had written and I was given a job with the paper in 1967. But I've only edited Hickey for the last three years, and you may have heard that I resigned yesterday—I'm going to the *Mirror*.

How does one go about producing a column like Hickey? Where does all the information come from? 'There is a network of correspondents all over the place. Anyone who thinks he's got something to interest us will 'phone up during the morning and pass his information on.'

Is that why people are so free in talking about themselves? Do they not realise that they are about to be quoted in Hickey's page? 'It wouldn't make a scrap of difference if they did. The people we write about are nearly always successful, well-known and up-market, they thrive on publicity and would be dreadfully disappointed if we didn't write about them.'

Isn't there a distinct danger that, because you deal with the people who occupy the forefront of public attention, the same names will keep appearing in your column? 'Yes, that has been a problem and we have done something about it. We now have a list of people who should not be included unless there is some really pressing reason to write about them.'

He showed me the list. I didn't have time to take note of all the names on it but the names of Larry Adler, Roddy and Dai Llewellyn and Anouska Hempel caught my eye.

How do you know who will make a good story? 'There are certain people who are almost always good material. Denis Thatcher, for example. Also we have to decide whether a strong story has a good photograph to back it up.'

Gossip columnists are often accused of being needlessly cruel to their subjects. Would you say that this is a fair criticism? 'No. I'm not a cruel person, though remarks about well-known personalities are often barbed. You may have seen that we described Britt Ekland as a 'female boa-constrictor'. You have to take that sort of comment in its context. These are people who make their living from being in the public eye; if they don't get written about they cease to exist.'

Just then the 'phone went and he dashed off for a quick conference elsewhere. He returned a few minutes later with the, to me, cryptic remark, 'It's Leapman'. His staff seemed to know what that meant. 'They have chosen Michael Leapman from the 'Times Diary' as my successor,' he explained.

'How do you manage to put a column together each day?'

'Oh, its just sheer brilliance,' murmured his secretary with a trace of irony.

'Thank you. No its more a matter of waiting for things to happen. As you see, at the moment it's all very quiet, but later this morning the 'phone will start to ring and we will begin to look at photographs and try out a few ideas. The hectic time comes after lunch. Usually the whole column is put together in about an hour and a half.'

What about legal problems? Surely this is an area where there is always a risk of libel? 'Yes, we have to bear that in mind constantly and the paper has a string of lawyers whose job it is to check for libel before anything gets printed. But the problem is that they do their job by trying to play safe and keep things out of the paper whilst, as a journalist, my job is to include as much as possible. We argue over this all the time.'

'Does it bother you that, since Hickey always hides behind his *nom de plume*, you only get credit for your work from other journalists?'

No one is safe. The Pope is gunned down and the world begins to wonder whether it really is going mad.

DAILY EXPRESS
THE VOICE OF BRITAIN

The words the Pope whispered to a nurse after he fell to three bullets fired into him by a crazed gunman

How could they do it?

THE FULL STORY: See Pages 2, 3, 4, 5, 8 and Centre Pages

'Well, that will no longer be true, on the *Mirror* my column will be called "Peter Tory".'

The 'phones started to ring. A Hickey aid, who had been swigging pints of orange juice, started to make notes. As the gossip flowed in yet another column started to come to life. I left, heading in the direction of Chelsea.

*   *   *

During my research I came across the following lines in Donald Edgar's book *Express '56*:

'When I was beginning to type my column in the afternoon, I was beguiled by the appearance at the desk opposite me of Osbert (now Sir Osbert) Lancaster who came in to create one of his pocket cartoons which graced and enlivened the front page of the paper. He arrived between 3.30 and 4 pm redolent of good food, wine and talk from the now defunct St James's Club and gave a temporary air of distinction to the drab office. He was a shortish man with an impressive head, impeccably dressed, moved slowly and with dignity and when he spoke (which was rarely) his voice was deep, loud, but agreeable and the exquisitely enunciated words generally expressed a carefully composed *bon mot*. It was an impressive performance which owed something to the trained artist and something to the Foreign Office where he had spent some years.

'He sat down on one of the wretched little seats with the gravity of a Victorian Ambassador and drew some paper towards him as if he was about to write a despatch to the foreign office on certain ominous developments in the Balkans.

He shot the cuffs of his beautiful shirt, perhaps stroked his moustache for a minute and then began to draw. It seemed but a few minutes before all was done including one of those brilliant captions that so often summed up the mood of sophisticated London with wit and humour. He got up, took his work to the editor (I cannot imagine Chris or Pick doing anything but admiring the offering), returned, exchanged a few words with one of the women writers or George Malcolm Thomson, the senior leader writer, and left the office with easy non-chalance, perching his trilby hat a little—just a little—to one side.'

After having read that description of Sir Osbert I was anxious to meet him. As one of the oldest and most distinguished members of the *Express* staff who was closely acquainted with many of the most important figures in the paper's history he would be a great source of useful information. However, many years have passed since the period about which Edgar was writing. Nowadays Sir Osbert is not in good health and hardly ever visits Fleet Street. Much to the regret of his admirers he has not produced a cartoon for some considerable time. But I was in luck, a message sent to his flat brought the instant reply that he would be willing to be interviewed as long as I did not mind seeing him at his home in Chelsea.

'Did you know,' said his secretary, apropos of nothing, 'that in the old days some of the young journalists used to come back from El Vino's a bit the worse for wear and have races on secretarial chairs all round the office?'

'No, I didn't know. But what has that to do with Sir Osbert?'

'Oh, he was the winning post.'

Clearly a man of many talents.

Chelsea is normally one of London's brighter spots but, on a cold November morning, the description 'World's End' seemed apt. Sir Osbert occupies a flat in the fashionable area just a few yards from the Thames. The door was opened by his wife, better known as journalist Anne Scott-James, who showed me in to a large and comfortably furnished drawing room, where Sir Osbert sat chortling over his copy of *Private Eye*.

'How do you do? Can't get up, you know—not very well. Have you seen this?' The *Eye* contained a neat pastiche of a Lancaster cartoon. A newsvendor's bill board was announcing the news of Jocelyn Stevens' departure (see page 129) and Maudie Littlehampton commented, 'If Stevens goes can Wintour be far behind?'

'How do you feel about someone imitating your style?'

'What? You'll have to shout, I'm quite deaf these days.'

'How do you feel about being copied?'

'Oh, I don't mind. It's quite a compliment really, isn't it? Anyway, I admire Ingrams, he comes from the same village as us in the country, you know. Very capable chap.'

Sir Osbert has the bristling white moustache and imperious glare which one associates with army officers from the days of the Raj. Now he turned the glare up to force ten and surveyed the room imperiously.

'Have you seen my cigarettes? No? Well, they were here a minute ago. Be a good chap, see if you can find them for me.'

My best efforts produced no cigarettes.

'Never mind,' he murmured regretfully, 'they're bad for me anyway. Now, what do you want to know?'

Much of journalism involves asking mundane questions. Normally it does not matter very much, but when you ask them in the voice you normally use for hailing taxis they seem not only mundane but also a trifle ridiculous.

How did he start to work for the *Express*? 'I was introduced to the paper by Betjeman. He used to do a regular piece for them and suggested me as a replacement when he went on holiday. The idea for a cartoon which covered just one column in width came originally from France. I suggested that we might try the same sort of thing in the *Express* and they let me go ahead.'

'You have had a very varied career because, apart from your cartoons, I believe you have also designed a large number of theatre decors and written many books; how did you find time for it all?'

'Well, you see the cartoons only used to take about five minutes . . . no, maybe we better say fifteen—don't want to make it sound too easy! I used to get in to the office some time after lunch, do the cartoon and then hang around until about seven when it was time to go out for the evening. There was certainly plenty of time for other activities which interested me.'

'You must remember Arthur Christiansen very well; what sort of person was he?'

'Definitely one of the Great and Good. He was always absolutely 100 per cent trustworthy. He was also an awful bully—he knew precisely what he wanted for the paper and nobody got any rest until he got it.'

'There is a legend that everyone had to stand up when he entered the room, is that true?'

'Oh no, that was just a bit of Tom Driberg's fun. He always liked to play the school prefect and so whenever Christiansen came in he'd say, "Don't you stand up when the Editor enters the room?". Occasionally someone would be green enough to take him seriously.'

'I gather that Driberg was a particular friend of yours . . . .'

'He was an excellent chap and a very fine journalist. He was also an absolutely *roaring* queer who made not the *slightest* attempt to disguise the fact. He was very popular and successful because he had great ability. He even became the chief war correspondent but he never got into any trouble over security matters even though he was queer and a communist. There was always a lot of fuss about that sort of thing but it was greatly exaggerated. Ninety per cent of security is absolute balls anyway.'

'A homosexual communist seems an unlikely choice for a Beaverbrook newspaper columnist. How did Beaverbrook himself react to Driberg?'

'Well, Driberg was also a High Anglican and they used to have long arguments about God—a subject on which they disagreed! Anyway, Beaverbrook was always curious about people. He liked to have interesting people around him and he seemed to enjoy the company of left-wingers. Also, you must not neglect the fact that he was no fool—he knew what was popular in the paper and what was

It is hard to avoid sensationalism when all the news is sensational. The attack on the Queen, though made with a blank-firing gun, reminded the population of the vulnerability of public figures.

drawing the readers. He would never have got rid of a good journalist just because he didn't like his personal habits.'

'Was Beaverbrook a good boss to work for?'

'I never really had that much to do with him. I met him of course, but as long as I came in and did my cartoon every day that was all they wanted. He gave his editors hell, as you probably know. He'd 'phone them at any time of the day or night. Didn't matter even if they were on honeymoon, as soon as he wanted them they had to jump.'

'You have been with the *Express* solidly since 1939, apart from wartime. You must have had many offers from other papers so what was it that made you stay?'

'A case of "the devil you know", I suppose. They always paid me well enough, I liked the people and I had so many outside interests that I never had any chance to get bored. You haven't come across those cigarettes yet have you?'

Sir Osbert's secretary, Liz Gregory, arrived at that point and produced cigarettes. We started to talk about the news of Jocelyn Stevens' sacking. What did Sir Osbert think?

'Oh, I don't even know the chap. I believe he was no fool but I don't know much about him.'

'But he's virtually your next door neighbour, have you never met him?'

'Is he? I didn't know. There you are—I'm a bit out of touch. Anyway, newspapers are different now. They run them like giant business corporations and there's not much feeling of personal involvement any more. Very few of them seem able to make a profit even so. Well, is that all you want to know? Good, let's have a drink.'

Chapter 14

A man's best friend is his grandma

'Sunday without the *Sunday Express*? Colourless.' So says a recent advertisement. But the *Express* without Giles? Unthinkable! In the years since the Second World War Carl Giles has become, for many, the very epitome of the *Express*. His cast of characters, the formidable grandma, the sickly Aunt Vera, Chalkie the skeletal school-master and the herds of appalling children, are all closer to the hearts of the readers than any other feature the paper has ever carried. The Giles annual is a regular best-seller (currently the print run is about ¾ million copies) and is avidly collected even by those who never read the newspaper.

However, anyone who imagines that Giles is some kind of Fleet Street superstar could not be more wrong. In the first place he does not operate from London and only visits the place in order to appear at occasional official engagements. Younger members of the newspaper's staff have often never seen him at all and even old friends, such as Osbert Lancaster, always preface remarks about their colleague with, 'Haven't seen him for *ages* . . .'.

The elusive Giles long ago took refuge in East Anglia where he owns a farm in the village of Witnesham, just outside Ipswich. His cartoons arrive in London by train or, if necessary, despatch rider. He dislikes publicity intensely, avoids the attention of TV reporters and newspaper journalists alike and has brushed off with some derision suggestions that he should write his autobiography.

However, he is no lonely recluse. He certainly does not live a Howard Hughes existence of neurotic isolation. He is a naturally sociable person with plenty of interests outside newspapers and, although he can talk about Fleet Street informatively and interestingly for hours, on the whole he would really rather not. After some persuasion he did agree to be interviewed. I had tried to convince him that the story of the *Express* without Giles would be incomplete; a suggestion he politely dismissed.

Nonetheless, a roaring hot June day found me trundling through the Suffolk countryside on one of those two-car trains which stop frequently at sleepy towns and villages scarcely large enough to show up on most maps. Giles was waiting at Ipswich station to take me out to his farm. White-haired, glasses, wearing a startling red and white striped shirt, he lounged at the wheel of his Range Rover smoking one of those long, thin brown cigarettes which masquerades as a cheroot. ('I've given up smoking—these things don't count.') As we drove through the town it became clear that this Londoner had adopted Suffolk as his real home, even his accent had, over many years, become infused with some of the warm East

Anglian tones. He pointed out the town's docks and the little back streets of terrace houses with affection. It was all a very far cry from the Fleet Street jungle. It was also a long way from his origins.

Giles comes from a long line of jockeys, a profession which he never had much inclination to follow. He knew from a very early age that he wanted to draw, it was not a conscious decision, merely something which he was good at and wanted to continue doing. As a child he went to a large variety of schools but one he remembers with particular satisfaction was run by the Roman Catholic church. Not being a Catholic himself he had plenty of spare time. 'They were always jumping up to go and pray,' he remembers.

His professional training started at 14 and he thereafter graduated through many great backroom studios in Wardour Street's and Charing Cross Road's film land. At 18 he was working for Alexander Korda. 'That was the best training I could have had. They were *marvellous* places. I'd have worked there for nothing. All those people, some really great artists. You had the chance to see all the various styles—it was absolutely marvellous.' In addition to getting experience in animation, working in London's Charing Cross Road had initiated him into the realities of life. It was not very long before he was well used to the ways of the city, and the broad experience of life which it gave him was to become part of his stock-in-trade as a cartoonist.

He eventually went to work drawing cartoons for the left-wing *Reynold's News*, a paper run by the Co-op. It was there that he really came to sympathise with socialism. Today he is still a left-winger, or 'dirty red' as he calls himself, and believes firmly that trade unions have done more for the working class than organised religion ever achieved. Even so, he is not blind to the foibles of the Left and the excesses of some modern union representatives. It was a bit of trade unionism on behalf of himself and his fellow workers which caused him to leave *Reynold's News* and go to the *Express*. For at the beginning of the war most of the capitalist papers were making up the wages of men who had been called away to fight. However, *Reynold's News*, which was supposedly defending the rights of the working class, made no move to follow suit. Giles and some other members of staff went to see Alf Barnes (later knighted under a Labour Government) and put it to him that if he went into any pub in Fleet Street he would hear journalists deriding *Reynold's* for its mean attitude to the staff which contrasted so badly with the treatment which was being handed out by the Press Barons on their Tory papers.

Although their plea was successful, for Giles the victory came just too late—he had been approached by the *Sunday Express* in the person of John Gordon. It was the fact that the *Express* organisation had approached Giles which made all the difference. It forced them to offer him greater freedom than he could possibly have imagined to draw just as he pleased.

'I'd never thought of working for the *Express*. But, even though I didn't share its political opinions, that paper was like the Palladium to me and Christiansen was the great ringmaster. Also the freedom they gave me was something I couldn't have got anywhere else. And they've stuck to it right through to today. I never submit roughs. I can't work that way—I just sit down and draw the thing.'

We arrived at the farm and were met by his wife, Joan. 'My escalator' as he cryptically calls her. 'She organises me. If it wasn't for her I'd never find anything. You know, you can ask her to find a letter or a Press cutting from years back and she goes straight to it. Amazing woman.'

The house is large, modern and very comfortable. In the living room the walls are decorated with signed photographs of friends, mainly from the world of show-business—Dave Allen and Frank Sinatra grin cheerily across the room. And on another wall the familiar features of Jean Rook gaze down—she has always been a great fan of Giles' work. Entertainers seem to hold a particular fascination for him; Johnny Speight is a regular visitor and Tommy Cooper and his wife are particular friends. 'The thing about Tommy is that he never really tells jokes—he doesn't need to. You just look at this great giant standing there and you begin to laugh. I only have to see him and I'm laughing.'

One of his great delights is his workshop which is large and equipped with a huge variety of tools, many of which seem to have been collected purely for the delight he takes in them as objects which do a job well. Above all Giles gives the impression of being a very practical person who can turn his hand to most things. Certainly there is no air of 'artiness' about him. You imagine that he could build a piece of furniture, strip down an engine or draw a cartoon with equal skill. He likes cars and tends to accumulate them (we had to make a short foray to rescue a Mini which had somehow been separated from the herd and was safely returned to the company of the Lotus and the Range Rover).

The only work which he leaves to others is the running of the farm. That is carried out by tenants. But the benefit of owning your own farm, apart from financial considerations, is that the house is surrounded by some superb country-side and although Ipswich is only a matter of minutes away by car, it might as well be a hundred miles.

We decided to adjourn to the local for lunch. He mentioned that the pub was situated by the water where his boat is moored. 'I have this disease, you see. It's called sailing.' Indeed sailing is the delight of his life, as I was very soon to discover. The pub was inhabited by people whose main aim in life was messing about in boats. Like Giles many of them were compelled to do other things in order to live, but it was soon obvious that in this community boats came first and all other considerations were a poor second.

Although the locals were naturally pleased and proud to have a celebrity amongst them, they obviously regarded him first as a fellow sailor and boat-owner and only secondly as a cartoonist. I remarked on this. 'Oh, yes. We don't get any of that "Giles" nonsense down here. I know their lives and I've known all their families for years.' The sun beat down on gently splashing water and bobbing boats. In the bar men stood around discussing important issues, like sailing and boats and whether the weather would hold and whether another pint would go down well. It all seemed a very long way from Giles' other life.

We returned to discussing the *Express*. Giles had arrived just as Tom Driberg was leaving for *Reynold's News*. Thus the papers did a complete swap and, though

Driberg was undoubtedly a very talented writer, it is impossible to avoid the conclusion that the *Express* got the better end of the deal. However, Giles deeply regrets the passing of his old paper and remembers its idealism with great affection. He points out that many of the men who worked on it could, and at times did, make much more money working for the Tory papers but that they chose to stay at *Reynold*'s because they believed in what it stood for.

What about his career as a war correspondent? 'You know I spent years with WC printed on my hat. Isn't that absurd? And you know what happened then? We got near the end of the war and some bright spark in Whitehall or somewhere thought, ''WC? That's a bad joke, let's change it''. So they altered it to C. I ask you, who in the Army would walk around with C stuck on his hat? They all knew what *that* stood for!'

How did he continue to draw funny cartoons when he was in the middle of a war? Surely there could not have been much to laugh at a lot of the time? 'You do laugh, you know. And you get hardened to things. There's a great tradition of war cartoonists going way back—people like Gillray, Rowlandson and Goya. But the thing which has really stayed with me was Belsen. It was really beautiful weather when we entered that place, just like today. And it's a lovely village, you know, it looks like the stockbroker belt. All these lovely houses and well kept gardens and then three-quarters of a mile down the road was the concentration camp. We couldn't believe it when we first saw it. Then they found Joseph Kramer, you know he was the one who had the lampshades made out of human skin. Well our troops soon laid into him. No one tried to stop them. But even that turned into a farce. They had to keep him somewhere and the only secure place they could find was a refrigeration plant which had broken down, so they stuck him in there. Then during the night the Royal Engineers managed to get the power going again and nobody thought of bloody Kramer sitting in his fridge! At least, everyone said it was an accident, though I've often wondered. He was still alive in the morning though. Cold and stiff mind you, but alive. He was a great bull of a man, tough as anything.

'Anyway, that was the worst thing we saw. Even real toughies like Alan Moorehead were upset by that. And some of them couldn't control themselves with the Germans. Until then the war had just been war. People got killed, and some had their homes bombed, but the hate was controlled. But when the news of Belsen got out that really set people off. There was this little Australian reporter with us called Ronnie Monson—a real tough little back alley brawler but a great war correspondent who was in the thick of everything. We were in some bar one night when he got well plastered. Then he saw a German sitting there looking like every cartoonist's image of the typical Nazi and he really let him have it. There he was laying into this bloke as hard as he could go and the rest of us were all sitting around just watching. Well, eventually someone pulled him off but then a bit later he went back and started to have another go. I certainly didn't try to stop him. These people all maintained that they had no idea what was going on but no one swallowed that. But then Low did his cartoon of a great pile of bodies in a concentration camp with an arm hanging down limply and the caption ''Don't forget we too are Germans''. That's what a lot of people were inclined to forget.

'The thing which bothered me most was my own reaction. The first day you thought. ''My God, I've never seen anything so terrible'' and then after a few days you were stepping in things without a second thought. You didn't really notice whether it was the remains of a person or just a lump of straw. It's frightening when you start to become hardened to something like that.'

What about after the war; how did the Giles' cartoon family come about? 'When the war finished everyone was fed up with the whole thing. After six years of it they all wanted something different and so I started the family. They were all well recognised types. There was Vera, the aunt who lives out of a bottle of Aspirin. Every family has a Vera somewhere. And then, of course, there was Grandma. Well, they like Grandma because she swears and doesn't care what she says to anyone. From my point of view she's the perfect instrument for getting away with murder. I can say what I like and, as long as I put the words in her mouth, the chances are I'll get away with it. Several times I've thought she was past it and I've tried to kill her off but I always find that after a few days when she doesn't appear I start to get letters complaining and asking for her to come back. The most surprising thing is that the letters don't come from people of my generation or even from yours, they come from kids. I mean, kids these days don't have grandmas like that—their idea of a grandmother is Brigitte Bardot.'

The sailors felt that Carl had been nattering about journalism long enough—to the neglect of the important things in life. We were summoned to the bar where the talk was all of winds, sheets, rudders and cleats. It turned out that I knew the landlady. The landlady knew my publisher. We did our 'isn't it a small world?' conversation whilst the sailing talk continued. Suddenly Marje remarked, 'Do you know where Grandma comes from?' I'd read somewhere that she was based on his own grandmother but I hadn't got round to asking yet. She pointed out a small self-portrait of Giles which hangs behind the bar. 'There,' she said, 'you can see the likeness in that, can't you? Look at the line of the mouth.' And there it was, immediate and unmistakable; Giles is his own Grandma!

We started to drive back to Ipswich to take a look at the studio. I asked him about a Giles anecdote I had been told in the *Express* offices. Rumour had it that on one occasion he threatened to conceal a drawing of a surprising object (which shall remain nameless) in one of his cartoons. The upshot of this was that all his work had to be inspected to see whether the threat had been carried out.

'No, that's all bullshit. The truth is much better. I used to do it all the time. There are all sorts of things in some of those drawings—hanging from washing lines and God knows what else. I used to do it to tease the legal boy. Do you know him? Well, he's still there. He looks like a barrister even without his wig. It's his job to check everything for libel and so on. I used to make his life a misery. But sometimes I got caught out. There was some film starlet, visiting Berlin—maybe Loren or someone like that—and the RAF gave her a guard of honour. Every man in the line had this little bump in the front of his trousers. Well, that one came straight back on the train and I had to paint out the bumps—standing in the

"If you wish to remain a permanent member of this family—no politics or religion!"

station parcels office—and still get it to London in time for the deadline. It was all in their mind of course, it was just the way the shadows fell on the uniforms!'

We arrived at the studio in the centre of Ipswich. It was early evening by now and the place was deserted. In the outer office a secretary usually sits. One of her functions is to fend off enquiries on deadline days. Tuesday and Thursday are non-deadline days and the work can then·be more relaxed but if there is a cartoon to be put on a train then nothing can be allowed to stand in the way.

One of the walls of the outer room is painted entirely a greyish blue. Descending dramatically like lightning flashes from the top left-hand corner are three enormous splashes of vivid colour. As the eye follows them down it meets a couple of mop-headed Giles children who, sitting on a piece of wood suspended from the top of the wall, are busily signing 'Picasso'. 'It needed something to break that wall up. *I* couldn't get away with doing that but *they* can do what they like.'

The studio itself is large, light and airy. It looks out on to a busy street (though the East Anglian idea of 'busy' is more leisurely and attractive than, say, Fleet Street). Giles has obviously adapted the studio himself.

'This is where the workshop comes in. It's much easier if you can just make what you need. This room was just a great square box of a place when I moved in.'

I mentioned the offices at the *Express* and the fact that he seemed much more comfortable working here.

'Oh, those offices always were dreadful. Just look where they've put Jean Rook. Have you seen it?'

We took a look at some of the work in progress. A Christmas card, next year's annual cover and so on. Giles also gets very involved in doing work for all sorts of good causes which approach him. One of his favourites is the RNLI. In 1973 they gave him an award of which he is especially proud and now, down where he keeps the boat, he has often taken the helm of the local lifeboat when the RNLI has its annual celebration. It is an honour which he delights in and takes very seriously.

However, the volume of work means that he is at the office from early in the morning until about nine o'clock at night. As with all the cartoonists and journalists I spoke to, Giles has to go through the ritual of reading the papers and listening to the news bulletins to try to brief himself before he draws his cartoons. The thing he tries to bear in mind is 'What will they be talking about at the bus stops tomorrow'. His other self-imposed rule is that he never draws a cartoon which is primarily political, although many of his comments are concerned with political events. He has never believed that politics on its own makes good journalism. He points out that if politics alone sold papers, then the *Morning Star*, which has yet to discover jokes, would be the best-selling paper in the country.

The interview was just about over, and I thanked him for his help with the book. But why had he never written his autobiography?

'I could never be bothered with all that. Same as TV interviews. Everyone thinks they can go on television and be a success but then they sit there saying "Well, you know . . .". I'll tell you what; they soon think of something to say about you when you're dead. They won't need any help from me. Living in a small place like this I get to hear all the talk and it amazes me all the things I'm supposed to have said and done. It's got to the stage now where if four or five weeks go by and I don't hear anything really rotten about myself I make something up and send it round!'

We went outside. A hot day had turned into a hot evening. The train for Cambridge didn't leave for another hour. 'Ah well,' said Giles, 'just time to look in at a couple of pubs.'

Chapter 15

A chat with the Voice of Britain

In late 1981 the *Express* was at a very exciting stage—it had just acquired a new editor, Christopher Ward, who had come from the *Mirror*. Of course, these days there is nothing too unusual about new editors at the *Express*, but that does not lessen the feeling that the latest arrival may prove to be just what the paper has been looking for—a new Blumenfeld or Christiansen who will put the paper firmly in touch with its readers, provide a new sense of direction and usher in a golden age of stability and increasing circulation.

I had been trying for months to snatch a few words with the man who, without doubt, must have been the busiest in Fleet Street at that time. Taking over a paper involves the editor in an enormous amount of work; formulating policy, scouting for new talent and, at the same time, getting used to a system quite different from the one to which he is accustomed. All in all it is not a time for interviews. But behind the scenes the secretarial Mafia had been at work. Jan 'phoned Claire, the editor's secretary. Claire 'phoned Jan. Appointments were made, postponed, re-made, re-postponed. The railways went on strike, Christmas came and went, winter changed to spring. But at last the hustle and bustle quietened enough for me to meet the editor.

When I was introduced to Christopher Ward he appeared young, tall, dark and bespectacled with a relaxed and affable manner. He still had about him the air of the 'new boy' who is not yet fully a part of the organisation. Even his office utterly lacked the air of Beaverbrookian utility which characterised the rest of the building. It had all the hallmarks of the workplace of a powerful and highly-paid executive in one of Fleet Street's top jobs. There were large, comfortable chairs, a huge television set and, in the corner, stood a handsome plant glistening with sleek, dark foliage. On the walls, carefully protected by non-reflecting glass, were reproductions of famous front pages from past issues of the *Express*. I commented on the change from the rest of the building.

'Well, the desk's not new. That belonged to Baxter and when Christiansen took over he tried to get rid of it and asked for a new one, but Beaverbrook wouldn't give it to him. I'm rather glad, it's a very fine desk except that you need an enormous bunch of keys to get into all the drawers. But I agree that the rest of the building looks pretty dreary. When I arrived, the editor's office only had a bit of that embossed plastic tape saying 'EDITOR' stuck to the door. Well, I ordered the mahogany door you see now and I'm having a brass plate made. It's interesting how many customs still survive from the Beaverbrook days. People still send

The scenes that the world—and especially the world's Press—had been waiting for. Amid the tension which had permeated the early '80s the royal wedding was, in spite of media overkill, a welcome change from the previous diet of gloom and blood.

correspondence to each other in tatty old used envelopes. Look at this!' He fished a worn and much written on envelope from his wastepaper basket. 'An important letter arrived in that this morning, it's amazing that things don't get thrown away.'

We turned to business. Why, I wondered, would a man take on such a dangerous job? 'I think that the vanity of journalists is such that, whatever the dangers, the editorship of the *Express* is irresistible. Even if I knew that it was only going to last six months it would be worth it. I think that, with the possible exception of the editorship of *The Times*, this is the most important and influential job in Fleet Street. The fact that the paper has lost its direction at the moment only makes my job more appealing. And the staff have been quite remarkable. They have had to endure something like five changes of leadership in six years and yet their loyalty remains unshaken and their willingness to adapt is unsurpassable.'

I mentioned that staff loyalty had always been a feature of the paper. I had been told by older members of staff that, in Christiansen's day, a word of praise from the editor was considered to be worth more than a ten-shilling raise. 'That may well have been true—though nowadays the money would be considered pretty important too!'

What is it like being the boss of a team of highly articulate and creative people, many of whom are wealthy and famous in their own right? 'It's always a very lonely job because, even though during a 12-hour day I may only get three minutes alone, whatever decisions have to be made I will make them independently and every decision will upset somebody. Of course, journalists are naturally opinionated and strong-willed so there is always bound to be a great deal of conflict over what is the right thing to do next. On any newspaper at any time at least half the staff will tell you that the editor is making a complete cock-up of the whole thing. But although it's very difficult to run a team like this, I think the most important thing is not to compromise your own convictions. You must trust your own instinct and not let yourself be talked out of it. When you disregard that gut reaction, you start making mistakes.'
what I believed to be the right course.'

The morning conference was about to start, so we postponed the rest of the interview for 45 minutes. Outside in the anteroom Michael Cummings was busy discussing possible cartoons to accompany the result of the Hillhead by-election. There would be no time to draw one after the result was announced so obviously he had to draw two in advance covering every possible contingency. I sat down to study a copy of the new policy statement which the editor had prepared for the advertising trade.

He had started by commissioning a survey to find out how many readers watch television every evening. 93 per cent! The obvious conclusion is that the *Express* must offer its readers much more than a mere account of the previous day's news. The answer was thought to be to go for 'a more interpretive, feature-ish presentation, especially on page one'. As an example he cited the incident in which Mark Thatcher was lost in the desert and believed by many to be dead.

The *Express* asked his sister, Carol, to write a feature on the anxious hours waiting with her mother at No 10. Similarly, when the miners were about to go on strike, Joe Gormley was asked to write an article on what he thought his members should do. That article changed the whole course of the dispute and averted the threatened strike.

Another intention of the new editor is to entertain his readers, which is why he had obtained 'a dazzling array of well-known people' to write for the paper. They included Esther Rantzen, Joanna Lumley, Miriam Stoppard, Victoria Wood and Kingsley Amis—even David Bailey had been signed up to take some photographs.

Perhaps one of the most interesting intentions mentioned in this document was that of scaling-down the size of headlines. The tendency of all the tabloids to scream everything from the roof-tops—even quite run-of-the-mill news—had resulted in a situation where, if something *really* exciting were to happen, there would be no technique left which would sufficiently emphasise its importance.

One of the paper's most difficult tasks is living up to its grandiose soubriquet 'The Voice of Britain'. Under Ward it has been decided to try and keep the interest of older working-class readers whilst at the same time gathering a new young, intelligent readership. The intention now is, without trivialising the serious side of the news, to show that life also has its happy and interesting sides. It is hoped to get more women readers to read the sports pages, male readers to find interesting articles in Express Woman, and readers with no financial interests to find the City pages compulsive reading. If that could be done then the millenium would certainly have arrived. But is it possible? And, if so, is Christopher Ward the editor to do it? Morning conference was just ending, so I went back in to find out.

I pointed out that, in Beaverbrook's day the *Express* had cultivated a young image and had employed bright young staff, but that in recent years the paper had become closely identified with an outlook popularly associated with 'disgusted of Neasden'. 'Yes, I feel very strongly that we should be trying to appeal to a younger readership and, in order to do that, we will have to adopt less extreme political views, though without abandoning traditional values.'

What will the paper's political stance be? 'It must be made quite clear that I do not believe Mrs Thatcher has any God-given right to support from the *Express*. However, at the moment I feel that the Tories' policies are beginning to work and that the economy is turning the corner. Even if they lose at Hillhead tomorrow I don't think that will affect matters in the long run. On the other hand, now that the paper has got a younger and more modern editor it will become more compassionate and liberal. We will not, for example, be supporting the current agitation for the return of capital punishment. I was always too right-wing for the *Mirror* and I may be rather left-wing for the *Express* but I believe that my politics are those of the majority and that is one of the things which qualifies me to be the editor of this paper.'

What, I asked, about public support for capital punishment? There seemed to be a considerable majority in favour of it at the moment. 'People would certainly support the return of hanging and they would quite probably, given the chance, support the return of public hanging. In fact there was no shortage of people who

DAILY EXPRESS

THE VOICE OF BRITAIN

FALKLANDS
"We're back!"

By MICHAEL EVANS, Defence Correspondent
and ROSS BENSON in Buenos Aires

BRITISH Forces were "firmly established" on the Falklands last night after a day of fierce fighting.

Our troops triumphantly ran up the Union Jack under a silvery moon after dramatically gaining a beachhead at Port San Carlos on the East island.

But the Task Force suffered losses under heavy air attack by the Argentines.

Defence Secretary John Nott said the British ships were damaged, two of them seriously. Two small helicopters — probably Gazelles — were shot down and a Harrier is missing.

In reply, one Mirage and nine other enemy aircraft were shot down over the Argentine Mirages, six Skyhawks, three Pucaras and two helicopters — a Chinook and a Puma. Another Mirage was damaged.

There was sharp casualties during the air raid and an action although Mr Nott was unable to give any details. Argentine prisoners were taken.

CHILDREN SAFE

The Union Jack flies again on the Falkland Islands...hoisted by three Royal Marines at the bridgehead established at Port San Carlos

Page 2, Column 3

Enemy lose 17 planes, 5 British ships hit

DAILY EXPRESS

THE VOICE OF BRITAIN

The Falklands are once more under the Government desired by their inhabitants
GOD SAVE THE QUEEN

GENERAL MOORE'S DRAMATIC SIGNAL FROM PORT STANLEY

V F DAY

THE FALKLANDS VICTORY, SPECIAL EDITION: PLEASE SEE INSIDE

The Falklands war did much to revitalise Fleet Street. Whilst at least one newspaper indulged itself in an orgy of xenophobic rubbish, the Express was satisfied with a bit of stirring patriotic stuff which would have gladdened the heart of Beaverbrook had he been alive to see it.

thought that the Ripper should have been hanged in public. I feel that a responsible paper should lead public opinion and not follow it slavishly.'

I wondered what the *Express'* attitude to the royal family was going to be. Traditionally the paper had been extravagantly pro-royalist even though Beaverbrook's own relations with the palace had never been good. What would the future attitude be? 'When Charles and Diana went on holiday to the West Indies we ran an affectionate but slightly mischievous piece suggesting that, after the rigours of the honeymoon and the long Christmas holiday at Balmoral, a break in the sunshine was just what they needed. We had more adverse comment from readers about that piece than anything I have seen for a long time. People are tremendously protective of the royal family and are highly sensitive to any hint of criticism. We will continue to support the monarchy as we have always done and, in particular, I think that Prince Charles—whom I have met several times—is good news for the country. But that will not stop us from criticising the Royal Family when we feel they deserve it.'

Would he have published the infamous pictures of the pregnant Princess of Wales in a bikini? 'No, certainly not. Our readers would not have stood for that for a moment. However, having said that, I would not criticise the editor of the *Daily Star* for his decision to go ahead and publish. He is in direct competition with the *Sun* and in those papers it is possible to publish successfully things which we could not use in the *Express.'*

Traditionally the paper has been a straight-laced one. Beaverbrook, although no puritan in his private life, was very much against anything which smacked of pornography in his papers. Would that continue to be the paper's outlook? For example, I noticed that after Erica Roe's famous streak at Twickenham, the *Express* was almost the only paper which showed a picture of her after, rather than during, the event. 'Well they weren't particularly pretty boobs, were they? If they had been we might have shown them but I don't think our readers would have wanted to see them and it was quite unnecessary to run that picture in order to tell the story.'

When he was on the *Mirror* a decision was made not to have a regular feature showing topless girls. Did he think there was a general move away from that sort of journalism? 'Yes, I do. I was one of the people who was responsible for that decision on the *Mirror* and I think it was the correct one. I would still show a picture of a naked girl but I wouldn't do it just for the sake of titillation. People can see that sort of thing in other papers which specialise in it.'

Another attempt to gain circulation has been the recent spate of bingo competitions which have now resulted in a 'bingo war' between some papers. Did he consider this was the right way to gain readers? 'No. Personally I hate the bingo war and would very much like to stop it. I think we could do that without much loss of readership. The recent price increase from 15p to 17p has been attributed—wrongly—by some readers to the need to rake in prize money to distribute to bingo winners. I think that the short-term gains to be made from this sort of competition are not worth the annoyance to loyal, long-term readers.'

'Perhaps we could turn now to your relations with the Chairman, Lord Matthews. He is widely represented as a "builder who made good" but is there more to him than that?' 'Lord Matthews is a man who has never lost sight of his roots. Although he has accumulated considerable wealth he lives a very ordinary life at home and although he came to Fleet Street only five years ago, he has good journalistic insights. From my point of view his most valuable attribute is that he reacts as a long and loyal reader of the paper. Journalism is all about interpreting the readers' wishes and he has a very astute sense of what is right for the paper.'

How much of a free hand was he given? 'When I first started he said to me, "If you don't hear from me don't worry, that will mean I'm happy. I will only be in touch when I don't like something". And he has kept to that. He leaves me to edit the paper.'

Why should a rich man buy a newspaper? In these days it must be a loss-making enterprise. 'I keep telling him the same thing but he believes very strongly that it should be possible, even today, to have a newspaper empire which pays.'

It is constantly rumoured, and constantly denied, that the *Express* will merge with the *Mail*. Surely, since both papers appeal to the same Conservative, middle class readership, a merger would make a great deal of sense. 'As you know, Fleet Street is constantly alive with rumours and gossip, most of it quite untrue. In fact,

No escape from the royal family! By now even the fanatically loyalist Express *readers must have felt in danger of an overdose.*

in recent times the two most important events—Murdoch's purchase of the *Sun* and Matthews' buying of the *Express*—have not been predicted by the rumour-mongers. There are 2 million reasons why we should not want to combine with the *Mail*. Our readership is much larger and much more widely based than theirs. Although they like to advertise themselves as our rivals you must remember that their circulation is under 2 million whilst ours is well over. Also it is wrong to dismiss the *Express* as a purely middle class paper like the *Mail*. We traditionally enjoy a very loyal working class following in the north of England. [This is a legacy of Christiansen's campaign to build up circulation figures in that area during the 1930s—see Chapter 5.] However, the present situation could easily change in any number of ways. For example, were Vere Harmsworth to drop dead tomorrow night it might well be that the *Express* would be interested in acquiring the *Mail*. But my short-term forecast is that things are going to remain unchanged.'

The sacking of Jocelyn Stevens shortly after you took over the editorship was widely reported. What do you feel about the events which led up to his leaving? 'These dramas are rather like divorces—they are never about the things they appear to be about. Jocelyn and the Chairman had disagreed over business policy and there came a point when the Chairman felt that some of Jocelyn's remarks to other people constituted disloyalty.'

Pity the poor editor. Christopher Ward found himself with a problem which editors of previous decades would have envied. Suddenly there was more news than the public could handle. Would it never stop?

The popular image of Jocelyn Stevens is one of a mercurial figure much given to tantrums and throwing furniture. Is this how you see him? 'No, not at all. I think that this is a legend left over from his younger days. I have certainly never seen him being anything but polite. He is certainly a very hard-working man and he had a great tendency to take on more than was reasonable. He would want to oversee every aspect of the newspaper and to control even the smallest details. As an example, when I moved in to this office the TV didn't work. I asked for an estimate to have it mended and found that it would cost £80, but I was then told that this could only be sanctioned by Jocelyn—any expenditure over £50 had to be endorsed by him personally. So I took the chit to his office and said "Sign this", he said "What is it?" and I told him it was nothing to do with him.'

Just then the familiar cheerful face of columnist Peter McKay peered round the door. There were legal problems with the *Mail*'s Nigel Dempster, could Christopher discuss them over lunch? I thanked him and left the *Express* offices for the last time.

A sudden change of tempo. The atmosphere had been one of national pride and rejoicing. Suddenly we were dragged back to the sickening realities of guerilla warfare.

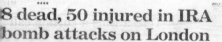

8 dead, 50 injured in IRA bomb attacks on London

BLITZ ON THE QUEEN'S ARMY

DAILY EXPRESS

THE VOICE OF BRITAIN

Don't buy a Hearing Aid

until you see this tiny non-functioning model of a remarkable invention for hearing

The day Britain bled again

● The bomb toll — Back page
● Bandstand blitz — Pages 2, 3
● Hyde Park blast — Pages 4, 5
● Queen's anguish — Page 6
● Terror campaign — Page 7

Index

Overleaf, top row left to right

Black borders, huge type and a litter of exclamation marks—all the traditional ingredients of tabloid newspapers were now present.

The shooting of John Lennon was widely characterised in the Press as 'the end of an era'. Certainly it did much to highlight the disturbing strain of lunacy which is increasingly evident in modern life. The other interesting facet of the affair was the way in which, in the newspapers, it is possible to graduate from pop idol to revered figure in just a few years.

The war with the IRA, though prolonged and dreadful, has never chilled the hearts of the nation half as much as this man. Peter Sutcliffe's career as the Yorkshire Ripper earned him a grisly record as a mass-murderer.

Two obsessions of British life—Northern Ireland and the royal family—come together in an odd alliance on the front page.

Mrs Thatcher as Cummings saw her.

Overleaf, bottom row left to right

All the tabloids obtained great mileage from the much-predicted engagement of the Prince of Wales and Lady Diana Spencer.

The riots which hit Brixton in the spring of '81 were all part of a widespread pattern of international violence that year.

Margaret Thatcher was riding high after the Falklands. The Express *was pleased to be able to support her to the hilt.*

By October 1981 the only man to have emerged from the Middle East crisis with any semblance of dignity or honour was dead, killed by fanatics.

DAILY EXPRESS

THE VOICE OF BRITAIN

No. 24,281   Wednesday July 26 1978   Weather: Rising at first   8p   ★★★★

EXPRESS
BABY
OF THE
CENTURY

Born safe—the world's first test-tube baby weighs in at 5lb 12oz and mother's delighted

By Harry Pugh

IT'S A GIRL! THE WORLD'S FIRST TEST-TUBE BABY WAS BORN LATE LAST NIGHT. SHE CAME INTO THE WORLD NEAR MIDNIGHT. BOTH MOTHER AND BABY ARE WELL.

There were no hitches, the mother, 32-year-old Mrs Lesley Brown, is "doing well" and the baby is perfectly formed. A living miracle weighing in at 5lb 12oz.

The birth will bring world acclaim for Britain's medical profession, after 12 years of research.

The two men who have created life in a test tube, gynaecologist Mr Patrick Steptoe and scientist Dr Robert Edwards, were said to be "enthralled."

They had taken no egg from donor's with Mrs Brown, fertilised it with her husband's sperm, then replanted the foetus in her womb.

Mrs Brown, William struts now even if marriage induces a stint in her hospital bed, but Mr Steptoe says "We have we would raise the

MAGIC MOMENT

There was taken to egg a riddle—at her iridical hour of a dreamt plan, then a through daughter to his first marriage, without a son.

EXTENSIVE CHECKS

IT'S A GIRL

glare, but he does care for women. He made to solve their problems. He wants the way to cover every woman can have a baby.

World-class

A fellow scientist at delicate General Hospital overseas another side of Steptoe "You may think him to do "decision" he worked with Dr. Robert Edwards, a physiology expert at Cambridge University who is well known in the field of genetic research.

A former colleague of Mr Steptoe says "We have we would raise the

Steptoe's obsession

Mrs Lesley Brown ... doing well   John Brown watched as Laura

DAILY EXPRESS

Wednesday December 10 1980   12p   Weather: Windy   **THE VOICE OF BRITAIN**

Beatle killer stalked him for three days

THE MAN WHO SHOT LENNON

THE blank-faced youth with a Beatle-style haircut stares into the camera. Today Mark David Chapman, Beatle fan turned killer, is in jail charged with a murder that has stunned and mystified the world.

JOHN LENNON was stalked by his killer for three days, it was revealed last night.

The man, charged with Lennon's murder, 25-year-old Mark David Chapman, had been carrying a revolver—and in hours of taped Beatle music.

Chapman was lurking around the Dakota apartment home in New York's West Side. He even asked Lennon for his autograph.

Lennon, 40, end

One of the last pictures ... John and Yoko a few days ago

The drama, the tributes Pages 2, 3 & 4; The man and his music Pages 17, 18 & 19

By PHILIP FINN and BRIAN VINE in New York

COURT

Daily Express Pages 20, 23 • Weather Page 2 • Bailey Page 13 • Playtime Page 22 • Stars Page 24 • Letters Page 26 • Finance Pages 28, 29 • Sport starts Page 26

DAILY EXPRESS

Wednesday February 25 1981   12p   Weather: Dry, cold   **THE VOICE OF BRITAIN**

We're in love, and it's no secret any more...

HER head rests on his shoulder ... and six months of agonising secrecy are over.

For Prince Charles and Lady Diana Spencer have had to keep their love from the world.

Yesterday it was different. Together they laughed, held hands and talked of their engagement.

They've been "serious" since September and got engaged three weeks ago. But this was the first time they felt able to let the world in on the secret.

Charles, 32, and his 19-year-old fiancée will marry at Westminster Abbey in July.

Gone forever are the days of discreet meetings. Now they both look to the future ... as King and Queen one day.

Picture by Expressman JOHN DOWNING

DAILY EXPRESS

Monday April 13 1981   12p   Weather: Mostly dry   **THE VOICE OF BRITAIN**

Walking the streets of Brixton yesterday. Whitelaw and McNee (right)

Police vow: We won't be moved, then burning and looting mobs storm back on to the streets

MORE RIOTS HIT BRIXTON

THE battle of Brixton raged again last night.

By midnight there were 80 arrests and 26 police and 24 civilians injured.

Shop windows were smashed, looting broke out again, bricks and bottles were hurled at police and a post office was set ablaze.

Wednesday nights of violence flared and whole areas in chaos were on the streets.

By DANNY McGRORY and ROBERT McGOWAN

The new riots broke out in full force. Chanting, jeering mobs of black youths were hurling bricks and set fire to buildings. They lit fires and set shops ablaze.

CONFRONT

And as blaze by area with 200 officers to confront the mob.

Another officer said: "We are rediscovering the problems that have been here before. We are trying to form 'em back"

Firemen were unable to let

Detectives probe: Who lit the fuse?

SPECIAL BRANCH detectives were trying to discover last night who may be behind the disturbances.

Police last night said plan

By OWEN SUMMERS and JOHN WENDON

A pale-faced man with a black patch — said that riots erupting across London's dockland from Saturday to Sunday. They were looting and set buildings ablaze.

Fire of fury ... car blazes in Brixton last night

The Battle of Brixton: Pages 2, 3, 4, 5, 8 & 9